SCOTTISH FIDDLERS
AND THEIR MUSIC

SCOTTISH FIDDLERS
AND THEIR MUSIC

by

MARY ANNE ALBURGER

LONDON
VICTOR GOLLANCZ LTD
1983

British Library Cataloguing in Publication Data
Alburger, Mary Anne
  Scottish fiddlers and their music.
  1. Fiddle tunes – History
  2. Music – Scotland – History
  I. Title
  787.1'09411   ML3655

ISBN 0-575-03174-3

Printed in Great Britain at
The Camelot Press Ltd, Southampton

CONTENTS

LIST OF ILLUSTRATIONS

Following page 96

David Rizzio; non-contemporary seventeenth-century representation, attrib. George Jameson (*Crown copyright: reproduction by permission of the Scottish Development Department*)

Patie Birnie; engraving after William Aikman (*Scottish National Portrait Gallery*)

A dancing lesson at Hopetoun House; engraving after Frederick Taylor (*in a private collection*)

"Macpherson's fiddle"; photograph M.A.A. (*courtesy of the Clan Macpherson Museum, Newtonmore, Inverness-shire*)

William Marshall; engraving by E. Turner after Moir (*Scottish National Portrait Gallery*)

Niel Gow; Sir Henry Raeburn, 1787 (*Scottish National Portrait Gallery*)

The Highland Dance; David Allan (*in a private collection*)

The Penny Wedding; David Allan, 1795 (*National Galleries of Scotland*)

Nathaniel Gow; *Glen Collection*, 1891 (*National Library of Scotland*)

John Hall's Kit (*Glasgow Museums and Art Galleries*, reg. no. '45–47f.)

Following page 160

Jimmy Dyer, the Cumberland Bard; postcard, 1904

A Highland Wedding; David Allen (*National Galleries of Scotland*)

Mr Owen's Institution, New Lanark

James Scott Skinner; frontispiece, *Logie Collection*, 1888

James Scott Skinner; frontispiece, *Harp and Claymore*, 1904

Francis "Markis" Jameson (*courtesy of J. F. Dickie*)

Captain Simon Fraser; *Glen Collection*, 1891 (*National Library of Scotland*)

Tom Anderson and Aly Bain, pen and ink, Tash MacLeod, 1981

James F. Dickie (*courtesy of J. F. Dickie*)

A century of fiddlers (*Aberdeen Press and Journal*)

INTRODUCTION

SCOTTISH FIDDLE MUSIC is unique and satisfying, a positive contribution to Scotland's culture here and throughout the world. I hope this book will interest those who know little about the subject while still providing new information and ideas for those deeply involved in it.

The times I have spent playing and listening to Scottish fiddle music have been among the happiest of any of my musical experiences. I have written this book as a result of my own curiosity about the background to the music, and I hope the many fiddlers who share my love of the music will have as much pleasure from reading it as I have had from their playing.

This book is by no means definitive; indeed, the study of Scottish fiddle music is only in its infancy; it is, without question, a lifetime's work, and more. In consequence, I have restricted the scope, investigating fewer people more thoroughly, rather than providing a survey with little depth. Not all composers and fiddlers will be found in this book, nor is this a compendium of Scottish melodies. Rather, I hope this work will serve some useful purpose by providing a continuation, in some small way, of the research begun by John Glen into the origins of fiddle music and the lives of the men who composed it.

Much remains to be discovered and studied: manuscripts, lost or as yet unknown, which could widen our knowledge of tune sources and transmissions; documentary evidence of the way fiddlers lived, played, and composed. Music from a certain geographic area or of a particular type could be studied in depth, as could, say, the relationship between fiddle and bagpipe music or between Scottish and Irish fiddling. Modern technological advances such as tape and video recorders could allow style to be studied in detail for the first time. If present-day interest encourages research into these or other aspects of fiddle music, the future could bring exciting insights into this delightfully Scottish gift to the musical world.

While researching this book I received generous assistance from many individuals and institutions. I would especially like to thank

David Johnson for his accurate, diplomatic criticism and scholarly help. Bill Hardie, Tom Anderson and many other fiddlers also gave up their time to share their knowledge with me. The music examples, which I have taken and edited from the original texts, are by Barry Peter Ould, whose skilful setting is much appreciated.

The National Library of Scotland offered unsurpassed help and politeness. Many other libraries, too, dealt patiently and courteously with my many enquiries: Aberdeen Public Library; Sandeman Library, Perth; King's College, Aberdeen; Edinburgh Public Library; Dundee Public Library; the School of Scottish Studies, University of Edinburgh; Edinburgh University Library; Glasgow University Library; Manchester Public Libraries; the British Library, and a number of others. The Duke of Atholl kindly put his music collection and Charter Room at my disposal, while the Earl of Ancaster allowed me access to the Duke of Perth MS. Both men generously allowed quotations and musical examples to be included here.

I would also like to thank those who supplied much useful information, and who permitted it to be quoted: Tom Anderson; the late Arthur Argo; Alan Bruford; James F. Dickie; James and Ivory Duncan; Mrs Joan Flett (*Traditional Dancing in Scotland*); Angus Grant; Alastair J. Hardie (*The Caledonian Companion*); Bill Hardie; Esther, Jeannie and Mary Henderson (*The Flowers of Scottish Melody, The Scottish Music Maker*); Mrs Sheila Hughes (*A History of Music in Scotland*); James Hunter (*The Fiddle Music of Scotland*); David Johnson (*Music and Society in Lowland Scotland in the Eighteenth Century*); Mrs Ethel Key; the late Hector MacAndrew; Jake McNaughton (McNaughton MS); Kay Matheson (Fraser's Gaelic titles and translations); and the many musicians who helped point my work in the right direction. Others who provided material and allowed quotation are *Box and Fiddle*, The Edinburgh Strathspey and Reel Society, The Elgin Strathspey and Reel Society, The Folio Society, Lismore Records, Oxford University Press, Topic Records and the Toronto University Press.

The illustrations reproduced here appear from the collections of, and with the help of: The National Galleries of Scotland; the Scottish National Portrait Gallery; the National Library of Scotland; the Scottish Development Department; Mr James F. Dickie; *Aberdeen Press and Journal*; Tash MacLeod; Glasgow Museums and Art Galleries; Dundee Art Galleries; others come from private collections.

M. A. A.

CHAPTER ONE

The Beginnings

The rote, and the recordour, the rivupe, the rist,
. . .
The lilt pype, and the lute, the fydill in Fist . . .[1]
Richard Holland, *c.* 1450

THE MUSIC OF the fiddle has been played in Scotland for more than half a millennium. The origin of the name is obscure, but possibly came from the early Romanic *vidula*, through old English *fithele* into the modern language as fiddle and into Gaelic as *fidhel* (pronounced fi'ull).

The Scottish fiddle today is the same instrument as the modern violin. Centuries ago it was much less sophisticated, having an oval or guitar-shaped body with a flat back and front, joined by ribs, and played with a bow. Gradually lutes, viols and finally violins became the popular upper-class instruments of the day; the fiddle was rejected as old-fashioned and out-of-date. In the end the fiddle itself disappeared, but the name stayed on through its associations with Scottish dance music.

Primitive as they were, the old fiddles, with their limited range and thin, scratchy sound, were once good enough for royalty: "April 19, 1497 – Item, to the tua fithelaris that sang Greysteil to ye King . . . iv s."[2] King James IV's payroll also included three other fiddlers, the first whose names have survived, Adam Boyd, Bennet, and Jame Widderspune.[3]

A "fidlar"[4] called Cabroch was employed by James V, but he may have soon been out of a job unless he was versatile, for James began ordering viols, the new favourite, from an English maker, Richard Hume. The viols had a more pleasant sound than the fiddles, and would have been easier to play in tune since they had lengths of gut tied round the fingerboard which, like guitar frets, could help stop the string accurately.

By 1538 fiddlers had been completely displaced at court by continental "violers".[5] Perhaps James was yielding to the French style to which his new wife was accustomed, but other more serious forces were at work, too, like this pointed attack, a poem by James's scribe, the cleric John Bellenden:

> Show now what kinds of sounds musical
> Is most seemly to valiant cavaliers.
> As thund'ring blast of trumpet bellical   /warlike
> The spirits of men to hardy courage stirs
> So singing, fiddling, and piping not ever is
> For men of honour or of high estate.
> Because it spouts sweet venom in their ears
> And makes their minds all effeminate.[6]

Certainly, fiddlers were not universally liked. By the time of the Reformation, any "Vagabonds, fiddlers [and] pipers"[7] not in the service of the aristocracy or a burgh who refused to leave Edinburgh were burnt on the cheek then banished. In fairness, laws of this sort were not entirely Philistine. Scotland had been plagued for years by a floating homeless population which invaded the towns trying to make some kind of frugal living. It would have been simple enough to get or make a crude instrument which might gain a beggar a penny or two more than his competitor. But holding a fiddle didn't make a man a musician, and many must have used instruments to camouflage far more criminal pursuits.

Unfortunately, the mention of fiddlers in various anti-vagrancy Acts may have contributed towards some people having negative attitudes to them:

> The poor and wandering glee-man was glad to purchase his bread by singing his ballads at the alehouse, wearing a fantastic habit, and latterly sinking into a mere crowder upon an untuned fiddle, accompanying his rude strains with a ruder ditty, the helpless associate of drunken revellers, and marvellously afraid of the constable and parish beadle.[8]

Perhaps there were some as badly off as this caricature, but with the destruction of so many Scottish records by Cromwell (who had them taken to the Tower, where they were accidentally burnt), those which remain are treasurers' accounts, records of trials and Acts of burghs or of Parliament, the bias being towards the criminal rather than the praiseworthy. The majority of people involved in music, whether in the service of families or burghs or self-employed, would have led ordinary lives, and remained relatively unknown.

The Reformation

Different and wider-reaching restrictions overwhelmed Scotland with the arrival of the Reformation, which sought to eliminate the Catholicism which had been the country's religion. Music in the church – the sung mass, the playing of the organ – vanished; the Calvinists in power went on to ban the traditional May Day games, New Year celebrations and Christmas itself, all unsanctioned by the Bible.

Gradually, men such as John Knox tried to extend their control over all amusements no matter how innocent. Dancing, however, Knox was unable to forbid even while reprimanding Mary, Queen of Scots, for enjoying it with her luters and violers. But Knox certainly made it sound a morally dangerous pastime:

> Of dancing, Madam, I said that, albeit in the scriptures I found no praise of it, and in profane writers that it is termed the gesture rather of those that are mad and in frenzy than of sober men; yet I do not utterly condemn it, providing that two vices be avoided: [Firstly] that the principal vocation of those that use that exercise must not be neglected for the pleasure of dancing; secondly, that they dance not, as did the Philistines their fathers, for the pleasure that they take in the displeasure of God's people. If they do either, they shall receive the reward of dancers, and that will be to drink in hell, unless they speedily repent, and so shall God turn their mirth into sudden sorrow.[9]

The only musical part of Mary's brief reign which Knox found pleasure in was her reception when she first arrived in Edinburgh: "Fires of joy were set forth all night, and a company of the most honest, with instruments of music, and with musicians, gave their salutations at her chalmer window. The melody, (as she alleged) liked her weel; and she willed the same to be continued some nights after."[10]

What kind of music could have drawn praise from Knox? The psalms, naturally, although Brantôme, Mary's French historian, was much less elevated by the experience: "An open air concert of nasty violins [*méchans violons*] and little rebecs, which are as bad as they can be in that country, and accompanied them with singing psalms, but so wretchedly out of tune and concord that nothing could be worse."[11] (Brantôme's use of the word *violons* suggests that violins had already appeared in Scotland, but he was writing after the event, when such instruments would have become more common.)

Not all Scots immediately gave up their old lives to settle down and meekly sing psalms. Indeed, in the 1580s the Kirk felt its moral housekeeping had accomplished little: "Scotland", it complained, had "ugly heaps of all kinds of sin lying in every nook and part . . . with abusing of the blessed name of God, with swearing, perjury, and lies, with profaning of the Sabbath-day with mercats, gluttony, drunkenness, fighting, playing, dancing &c, with rebelling against magistrates and the laws of the country."[12]

The De'il and the Reel

But there were far greater evils facing the Kirk. Scotland, under the kingship of Mary's son, James VI, and with the whole-hearted support of his book *Demonology*, suddenly discovered witches in its midst. Many psychological reasons for this kind of behaviour are given today – the judges might be called sadists, the witches hysterical or masochistic personalities, or simply those with the misfortune of having unpleasant habits which did not endear them to their neighbours. Whatever the explanation, the phenomenon seems inextricably tied up with the very repressions and resultant guilt and frustration which the Kirk helped create.

It is no surprise to find that music and dance played a part in these dangerous goings-on, since one of the underlying purposes of the witches' meetings must have been to do, or claim to do, those things which the Kirk was most strongly against. The witch hunters' and reformers' fires would have been well fuelled by reports like this, an extract from *Newes from Scotland* (1591):

> Agnes Thompson . . . confessed that upon the night of All-hallow even last, she was accompanied [by] a great many witches to the number of two hundredth and that they all went together . . . to the kirke of North Barrick in Lowthian, and that after they had landed [they] took hands on the land, and daunced this reill or short dance [accompanied by "a small trump, called a Jewe's trump",] untill they entered into the kerke of North Barrick.[13]

Ironically, since Agnes was strangled, then burnt, for her role, this is the first record of a reel as a type of dance being performed in Scotland. The names of the tunes they used are known, if not the music, "Silly bit chicken", and "Cummer, go ye before; Cummer, go ye before; Gif ye will not go before, Cummer, let me", which they all sang while dancing the reel.

Another trial for witchcraft, in 1659, of John Douglas and eight women belonging to Tranent, mentions two more melodies. The group confessed to having had "certain meetings with the devil, at which they were entertained with music, Douglas being their piper".[14] (Fiddlers were apparently not involved, at least musically, in these get-togethers. Practically, their fiddles wouldn't function as well out-of-doors as the pipes or jew's [jaws'] harps, which could better cope with the weather.) They danced to "Come this way with me" and "Kilt thy coat, Maggie". An early manuscript, the Skene MS, *c.* 1620, contains a tune with the same title, "Kilt [lift up] thy [petti] coat, Maggie" (ex. 1),[15] likely to be the same tune that the unfortunate John Douglas played on his pipes.

Ex. 1 KILT THY COAT, MAGGIE

The First Scottish Instrumental Collections
Collections such as the Skene MS first appeared early in the seventeenth century, after the Union of the Crowns. James VI's departure to London and his continued lack of interest (he revisited Scotland only once, in 1617) threw musical Scots at home back on their own resources. Deprived of the focus the presence of the court in Edinburgh had given to music-making, they looked around for other

stimuli. What they found in part was the music around them, the previously unwritten melodies in current use, which until then had only been transmitted aurally.

None of these MSS are for fiddle; lutes and viols had swept the country, and the remaining fiddlers presumably played by ear and had no need or inclination to write down what they performed. The educated compilers of the MSS naturally wrote down the music in sets for their own instruments. It is reasonably safe to assume, however, that these MSS continue the fiddling tradition, giving a picture of the general instrumental repertoire freely circulating and known to most musicians whatever their instruments. This sharing of tunes never stopped. For instance, some of the music from the Skene MS appears in later printed collections of fiddle music, although often considerably changed: "Dumbarton Drums" and "Stir her up and hold her ganging" appear in the seventeeth century in Playford's collections; "Blue Ribbon Scotch Measure" and "Goodnight and joy be with you all" in Gow publications in the eighteenth century; and "Jenny drinks nae water" and "Jenny Nettles" in *The Athole Collection* (1884).

Another tune still popular today could well have been played at a dance in 1634, on a bizarre occasion when Lady Rothiemay entertained the Highlanders who had just robbed and burnt down her neighbour Frendraught's house. She "dancit with the licht horsemen in the place of Rothiemay, the cushion dance . . ."[16] If this seems callous, she had good reason, since Frendraught had been responsible for the death of her husband and son. The tune still associated with the cushion dance, an old kissing dance, is called in the Skene "Who learned you to dance and a towdle" (ex. 2).[17] It was later collected from tradition, "as sung by girls playing on the streets in Glasgow", and printed with words beginning "Who learned you to dance, Babbity Bowster [bolster], Babbity Bowster".[18]

Ex. 2   WHO LEARNED YOU TO DANCE AND A TOWDLE

A tune which does not seem to have survived to the present day has the intriguing title "Pitt on your shirt on Monday" (ex. 3):[19]

Ex. 3 PITT ON YOUR SHIRT ON MONDAY

Some melodies in the Skene MS are also found in print in Scotland's earliest collection of secular music, usually referred to as "Forbes's Cantus" (1662). The full title of the work is *Cantus, Songs and Fancies. To Thre, Foure, or Five Parts, both apt for Voices and Viols. With a briefe Introduction of Musick, As is taught in the Musick-Schools of Aberdene by T[homas] D[avidson] M[aste]r of Musick*. Although two other editions[20] were brought out, it is sad to record there was no other music published in Scotland, except the Psalters, until 1726.

It is fortunate that, lacking printed sources, other MSS have survived to give some idea of what was being played almost three hundred years ago. Among them are the Rowallan MS (lute, *c.* 1620), Straloch (lute, 1627–9), Guthrie (viola da braccio, *c.* 1680) Blaikie (lyra-viol, 1685, 1692), Leyden (lyra-viol, *c.* 1695) and Atkinson (? violin, 1694–5). Of these, the Straloch can be found only in a partial transcript made in 1847, and the Blaikie as a partial copy made in 1854 of another copy of the 1692 MS. Some thought and some detective work may still rediscover the originals, and perhaps unearth others which have been misplaced and forgotten.

From the Rowallan lute MS, which belonged to Sir William Mure of Rowallan, an accomplished musician and poet, comes "Ouir the Dek, Davie" (ex. 4)[21] which even in this setting is clearly in the Scottish idiom:

Ex. 4   OUIR THE DEK DAVIE

But even those MSS available have not always easily yielded their secrets. The Guthrie MS was thought for some time to have belonged to James Guthrie of Stirling, a Covenanting minister beheaded in 1661 for writing a seditious pamphlet. Interesting though it would be to think that Guthrie, at odds with his conscience, secretly noted down popular music for his viola da braccio, the work is now dated after his death. It must have been someone with a sense of humour who later sewed it into a book of Guthrie's sermon notes.

The MS remained tantalizingly undeciphered until 1945, when Harry M. Willsher, in his Doctoral thesis for St Andrew's University, transcribed the tablature. Until then it had been thought that the MS contained only accompaniments to tunes which were actually there in full, such as "Ketrin Ogie", "Clout the Caldron", "Skip yon water wantonlie", "Once I loved another man's wife" and "If the Kirk would let me be".

One melody from the Blaikie MS (1692) is at least seventy years older than that MS, for it is a version of "Put up thy dagger, Jamie" (Fitzwilliam Virginal Book, *c.* 1620) called "Put up thy dagor Jennie" (ex. 5).[22] Words which fit the melody come from a satire called *Vox Borealis, or the Northern Discoverie* (1641). A fiddler and a fool, supposedly employed by the governor of Edinburgh Castle,

> goe to singing at Scots jigges in a jearing manner at the *Covenanters,* for surrendering up their Castles as followeth, The fiddler hee flings out his heeles And dances and sings: Put up thy dagor, Jamie, the parliament is ended. . . . Then the Foole hee flirts out his folie, And whilst the Fidler playes hee sings:

Ex. 5 PUT UP THY DAGOR JENNIE

Put up thy dag—ger Ja-mie, and all things shall be men———ded: Bi—shops shall fall, no not at all, when the par—li-a-ment is end—ed. Which ne—ver was in——ten—ed but on-ly for to flam thee, we have gotten the game, we'll keep the same, put up thy dag-ger, Jam—ie.

Scottish Music in England

The Scottish MSS, as well as being pleasant to devise and useful to make, would have been circulated among the compilers' friends to help make up for the lack of available printed music. But by 1650 (1651, new style), the same year Cromwell captured Edinburgh, John Playford (1623–86), a London publisher, produced *The English Dancing Master*, a volume of dance tunes complete with "plaine and easie rules" for the dances. The times were not propitious; soon Cromwell's Parliament enacted a law which would have gladdened the hearts of the Scottish reformers:

> If any person or persons, commonly called fiddlers or minstrels, shall at any time after the 1st of July be taken playing, fiddling, and making music, in any inn, alehouse, or tavern . . . or intreating any person or persons to hear them play or make music in any of the places aforesaid, they shall be adjudged rogues, vagabonds, and sturdy beggars, and be proceeded against and punished accordingly.[23]

Despite the unlikelihood that the musical diversions offered by Playford would be welcome under such conditions, *The Dancing Master*, as it was subsequently called, went into eighteen editions over the years, encompassing over 900 tunes.

Playford, with all these instrumental pieces to produce, could not have simply plucked them out of the air. He would have had to use whatever manuscript sources were available, make use of his many musical contacts, and record what he could from the playing of any fiddlers who came to his door. Although it is impossible to know just who these men were, some were either Scots or had Scottish connections themselves, for in his books, among much other music, Playford published several tunes previously known only in the Skene MS, if its dating is correct.

John Aubrey gossiped about a few of his contemporaries who might have had the opportunity and the knowledge to communicate Scottish music to Playford and his son Henry. A likely candidate is

Mr John Ogilby [who] would not tell where in Scotland he was born. . . . John bound himself Apprentice to one Mr Draper, who kept a dancing-schoole in Grayes-Inne-Lane, and in a short time arrived to so great excellence in that small art, that he found means to purchase his time of his master and sett up for himself.[24]

This suggests that Ogilby must at least have had previous training in music or dance, and a knowledge of current Scottish music.

Dr Witherborne, "A Scotchman, Physition to the King", the Duke of Lauderdale, Sir George Danvers, and Robert Murray, "inventor of the penny post, his father a Scotchman" were all in London then, along with the outside choice, Jean Baptiste Colbert, "of Scottish extraction, and that obscure enough, his grandfather being a Scottish bag-piper to the Scotch Regiment [in France]".

Playford's music shop "in the Inner Temple, neere the Church Door"[25] was also near that of John Carr, whose son Robert Carr, violist with the King's Music, later took over Playford's business with his son Henry. It is probably too much to hope that the Carrs were expatriate Scots who, like James VI's favourite, Robert Carr, had altered their name from Kerr and were a source of Scottish music for Playford.

One particular gentleman who patronized Playford had a certain acquaintance with Scottish music; but Samuel Pepys, from his own account, would have been little help:

28 July, 1666: With my Lord Brunckner went to my Lord Lauderdale's house to speake with him. We find [him] and his lady and some Scotch people at supper. Pretty odd company. But at supper there played one of their servants upon the viallin some Scotch tunes only; several, and the best of their country, as they seemed to esteem them by their praising and admiring them, but Lord! the strangest ayre that I ever heard in my life, and all of the one cast.[26]

By this time the violin was becoming established, aided by Playford's *Apollo's Banquet* (1663), containing "Instructions, and Variety of New Tunes, Ayres, Jiggs, and several New Scotch Tunes for the Treble-Violin". "The Northern Lass", now known in Scotland as "Muirland Willie', is in this book; so is "A Scotish Jigg" (ex 6a),[27] which gives evidence of some of the problems faced by pioneers like Playford:

Ex. 6a   A SCOTISH JIGG

The immediate reaction to this, the first section, might be to think, like Pepys, that it is a strange air; but clearly something has gone wrong with the tenuous connections between source and publication. The music has probably been incorrectly noted down from someone's playing or wrongly transcribed from tablature. However, if the notes are lowered a semi-tone, after the first bar, they make better musical sense, and the whole section gains a key feeling (ex. 6b):[28]

Ex. 6b

As they stand now, these six bars reveal close affinities to "Binny's Jigg" (ex. 6c)[29] from the Blaikie MS 1692, and to "Dusty Miller" (ex. 6d)[30] from *Dances, Marches* (1730), suggesting a common source for all three:

Ex. 6c   BINNY'S JIGG

Ex. 6d   DUSTY MILLER

The English thought of the jig as being the most representative type of Scottish music. According to Thomas Morley in his *Introduction to Practicall Musicke* (1597), the jig was most difficult for an English composer to comprehend: "Enjoyn him but to make a Scottish jygge, he will grossely erre in the true nature and qualitie of it." Scottish jigs are usually in 6/8 time rather than the compound 9/8 and 12/8 times favoured by the English; although a few have always been composed and played, their popularity faded as that of the reels and strathspeys rose; but the jig continued to be a mainstay of dancing in Ireland.

Edinburgh at the Restoration
The scene at Edinburgh's Mercat Cross in August 1660 was festive:

> There were . . . six viols, three of them base viols, playing there continually. There were also some musicians placed there, wha were resolved to act their parts, and were willing and ready, but by reason of the frequent acclamations and cries of the people universally through the haill town, their purpose was interrupted. Bacchus also, being set upon ane puncheon of wine upon the front of the Cross . . . was not idle.[31]

Despite the presence of violers, music in Scotland was beating with only a feeble pulse; the change in attitudes implied by the Restoration could revitalize it only gradually. The teaching of music had never died out completely; it had been ticking over in the "Sang-scules", "burgh music schools with special responsibilities for providing music in the main church of the town in which they were situated."[32]

Earlier in the century there had been such schools in, for example, Aberdeen, Ayr, Dumbarton, Dundee, Elgin, Inverness, Irvine, Lanark, St Andrews, Tain and Wigton. But low wages for the music masters invited increasingly lower standards and poor instruction; the new generation was no longer capable of learning the old Psalter tunes: "By the end of the century to sing in harmony had become unthinkable. No tunes at all were printed with the Psalter of 1650; the 1666 Psalter contained only twelve tunes. Twelve were canonized as embodying the accepted and inexpansible musical tradition of the Church of Scotland."[33]

Nevertheless, private enterprise and the relaxation of restrictive attitudes together soon provided official, if secular, music tuition. Edinburgh acquiesced first; in 1662 a Mrs Clelland was permitted to teach reading, writing, singing, playing, dancing and French in her own school which, according to the custom of the times, would have been for young gentlewomen only.

The following year James Gib offered both vocal and instrumental teaching in the capital. It is possible that Gib taught the violin, for the first known Scottish MS specifically for the violin, "Lessones for ye violin",[34] from Newbattle Abbey, Midlothian, appears not too long after, around 1680. The MS is not a tutor in modern terms, but a selection of tunes with some Scots airs alongside "bourrées, marches, galliards and minuets".[35] Dancing seems to have become more acceptable than it had been for years, for in 1679 the Edinburgh authorities had so mellowed that one Andrew Devoe was allowed to practise as a dancing master.

Nor was he alone. The local Masters of the Revels complained about those who held "public balls, dances, masks, and other entertainments in their schools, upon mercenary designs, without any licence or authority from the petitioners".[36] (The licence fees were the Masters' personal incomes.)

Devoe, who had been particularly attacked, was forbidden to have a dance at his school, that is, at the premises where he held his dancing classes. But he defended his right to make a living "teaching the children of noblemen and gentlemen to dance",[36] and fought back. It was unheard of in Europe, in his opinion, that such a ball should be an infringement of their monopoly. He won his case, setting a precedent.

However, this ruling only meant that Devoe could teach children – which, after all, was what he wanted to do. For adults the situation was very different; as far as records show, dancing in public was not tolerated at all, and indeed would face violent opposition for the next fifty years.

The First Printed Collection of Scottish Music
While Scotland was still struggling to her feet, in musical terms, England marched on, with the publication of *A Collection of Original Scotch-Tunes, (Full of the Highland Humours)*, "for the violin: Being the First of this Kind yet Printed; Most of them being in the Compass of the Flute, printed . . . for Henry Playford [in London] . . . 1700".

It would be fascinating to know why Playford decided to publish Scottish melodies. It is usually accepted that the novelty of the music would have appealed to an English audience, and that there was then a vogue for things Scottish, but there were also no doubt enough Scots in the South both to provide the contents and to buy the work for nostalgic reasons (and perhaps send copies to their friends at home).

In any case, the work seems to have been a great success, since there are now only two known copies; the rest were probably played and consulted so frequently that they finally fell to shreds. A second edition, of which only one copy survives, was advertised in 1701. Of the pieces included in 1700, some are immediately familiar, some now have different names, while others have vanished from the repertoire:

Mr McLaines Scotch-Measure
Mr McClauklaines Scotch-Measure
I love my Love in Seacreit
Madam Mc.Keenys Scotch-Measure
Cronstoune
Keele Cranke
The Berkes of Plunketty
Good night and God be with you
The Lord of Cockpens Scotch-Measure
My Lord Seforth's Scotch-Measure
Ginleing Georde
The Colliers Lass
Sir William Hope's Scotch-Measure
Stir her up and hold her ganging
Oreck's Scotch-Measure
My Lady Hope's Scotch-Measure
Peggy was the Pretiest Lass in aw the Town
Bride next
The comers of Largo Areell

Bess Bell
Dick a Dollis
A New Scotch-Measure
Wappat the Widow my Lady
If love is the cause of my mourning
The Berks of Abergelde
For old long Gine my Joe
Allen Water
Madam Sefoth's Scotch-Measure
Walli's Humour in Tapping the Ale
The Laird of Cockpen's Scotch-Measure
A New Scotch-Measure
Widow gin thou be waking
Aways my heart that we mun sunder
The Lass of Leving-Stone
I fix my fancy on her, a Round O
Quoth the Master to the Man
Cosen Cole's Delight
Holy Even, a Scotch-Measure
The deal stick the Minster

This last tune is still as well-known as it was in 1683 when a Stirling man was "tried for reviling a parson, 'in causing the piper play "The Deil [Devil] Stick the Minister"' [ex. 7].[37] Sundry pipers were there present as witnesses, to declare it was the name of ane spring."[38]

Ex. 7 THE DEAL STICK THE MINSTER

At least one third of Playford's titles are still known as songs, while another third are "Scotch-measures". Although the English spoke of "treading a measure", it is not known precisely what the dances were; since the eighteenth century the Scottish practice has been to use them for country dances. They are usually in common time, four beats to the bar; the use of crotchets or dotted crotchets is common to all, as in "Madam Mc.Keenys Scotch-Measure" (ex 8):[39]

Ex. 8   MADAM MC.KEENYS SCOTCH-MEASURE

"The comers of Largo Areell" (ex. 9),[40] the first use in print of the word reel for a tune title, is unfortunately incomplete, perhaps inaccurately recorded from someone's playing. Nor, being originally in 9/4, triple time, would it be thought of as a reel today, since reels are now in 4/4, common time, or ₵, cut time.

Ex. 9   THE COMERS OF LARGO AREELL

"Bride next" (ex. 10),[41] however, is easily recognizable as the jig known today as "My wife's a wanton wee thing":

Ex. 10   BRIDE NEXT

In Henry Playford's work can be found many of the roots of Scottish fiddle music. His collection already shows, in miniature, many of the sources: the unknown men who provided the music by singing it, playing it, or writing it down; the Scotch measures, often named after the dancing masters who performed to them and may have written them; and the reel, the lowland contribution to Scottish music and dance.

Only two elements are missing – the strathspey, which had not yet appeared, and the names of the individuals who created the music. When these are added, fiddle music reaches its zenith, and the final connections are made between the creators of the music, the players who interpret it and the individuals who dance to it or appreciate it from the audience.

CHAPTER TWO

The Eighteenth Century, I

Musick they have, but not the harmony of the spheres, but loud terrene noises, like the bellowing of beasts; the loud bagpipe is their chief delight, stringed instruments are too soft to penetrate the organs of their ears, that are only pleased with sounds of substance.[1]

Thomas Kirk (1679)

HAD HE VISITED Scotland a generation later, that English gentleman could have heard a "grand concert of music"[2] given by nineteen well-to-do amateurs and eleven professionals including Adam Craig, violin; Malcolm McGibbon, oboe; Henry Crumbden, harpsichord; Daniel Thomson, one of the King's trumpeters; and his son William, a young singer. This celebration of St Cecilia's day took place in Edinburgh in 1695.

These men, together with others like Sir John Clerk of Penicuik (1676–1755), a pupil of Corelli, could have immeasurably advanced music in Scotland even before the turn of the century. But 1696 brought the first of the "hungry years" ("King William's years", as the Jacobites called them), disastrous famines which starved the country until 1703 and again in 1709, hardly conducive to musical development.

In 1705, when there seemed to be a respite, the Earl of Selkirk, then the leader of Edinburgh society, started a fashionable club, the Order of the Horn – supposedly named after a commonplace horn spoon – which provided the focus for various entertainments, including a masked ball. But "the fanaticism of the times could not bear such ungodly innovations. The masquerade was stiled *promiscuous dancing, in which all sorts of people met together in disguise.*"[3]

Such dances, and concerts (of which there were a few others after 1695, at Pate Steil's tavern) had little chance to prosper under the pressures of continuing religious mania, physical deprivations and political upheavals. In 1707, with the Union of the Parliaments, Scotland finally bound herself to England, retaining only her separate legal, educational and monetary systems. One reason for the Union was economic, arising out of the ill-fated Darien experiment, when the Scots had tried to establish a trading company on the inhospitable isthmus of Panama. With the "Equivalent" (about £400,000 – but less than was originally agreed) the English offered to repay some of the vast losses, giving rise to the famous line "We're bought and sold for English gold – such a parcel of rogues in a nation."

Patie Birnie

Although many Scots soon went South to look after their interests, for the majority life went on as usual. From that prolific poet Allan Ramsey comes a portrait of one man who stayed very much at home, Patie Birnie, "the famous fiddler of Kinghorn" in Fife, then the northern harbour for travellers going across the Firth of Forth.

It is not known precisely when Birnie lived, although he is supposed to have had the chance – which he declined – of being in the battle of Bothwell Bridge in 1679. He appears in Ramsay's humorous "Elegie to Patie Birnie" (1721) as a musical confidence man (no doubt one of many of the type) who made his living by forcing his fiddling intentions on unwary passengers off the ferry. He would select his patrons, then

> . . . he wad gang,
> And crave their pardon that sae lang
>   He'd been a-coming;
> Syne his bread-winner out he'd bang,
>   And fa' to buming . . .[4]   /playing without
>   taste or skill

Ramsay mentions two of Patie's supposed compositions, "Willtu, willtu, do it again", for which the music has never been found, and "The Auld Man's Mare's Dead", unpublished until 1782. But there is no proof that Patie wrote this tune; indeed, Ramsay could easily have mentioned ancient tunes which Patie could never have written, just to poke fun. Still, "The auld man's mare's dead" (ex. 11)[5] in its strathspey set from Johnson's *Scots Musical Museum* is a good tune, whatever its provenance.

According to Ramsay, Patie had a low opinion of Scots who went to Italy to study music, where they were influenced by the *castrati*, the most popular type of singers in their day; one of the best, Tenducci, visited Edinburgh several times, doing much to popularize Scottish songs.

Ex. 11   THE AULD MAN'S MARE'S DEAD

. . . the corky cowp	/corps
That to the Papists' country scowp,	/Italy
To lear' ha, ha's,	/learn
Frae chiels that sang hap, stap, and lowp,	/hop, step,
Wantin the b---s.	and leap

To add interest to Patie's performances, his friend Johnny Stocks, "a man of low stature, but very broad", would dance on a table as Patie played. His presentation was varied, to say the least: "He plays, sings, and breaks in with some queer tale twice or thrice o'er he get through the tune. His beard is no small addition to the diversion," wrote Ramsay. Patie got into no more serious trouble with the Kirk than reneging on a pledge, made when ill, to give up drink, and is said to have amassed a reasonable amount of money before he died, presumably after Ramsay's "Elegie", which, despite its title, ends: "lest your grief o'er far extend/ . . . to a' Britain be it ken'd,/ He is not dead."

The Edinburgh Assemblies

Edinburgh successfully staved off public dancing assemblies until 1723, almost twenty years after their precursors, the brain-child of Beau Nash, had begun at Bath.

They have got an assembley [wrote a young Morayshire lady]

where every Thursday they meet and dance from four o'clock to eleven at night; it is half a crown a ticket, and whatever tea, coffee, chocolate, biscuit, etc, they call for, they must pay as the managers direct; and they are the Countess of Panmure, Lady Newhall, the President's Lady [Lady North Berwick], and the Lady Drum melier. The ministers are preaching against it, and say it will be another horn order: it is an assembley for dancing only.[6]

Even the possibility of such an entertainment aroused passionate protests:

It will . . . tend to vitiate and deprave the Minds and Inclinations of the younger Sort . . . a Machine of Luxury, to soften and effeminate the Minds of our young Nobility and Gentry. . . . They, instead of employing themselves in the useful Arts and Sciences . . . now made it their greatest care who should be best equipp'd and dress'd for an Assembly Night, and to strain their Fancies to invent some agreeable Love Tattle to tell the Belle Creature[s] whom they shall happen to most admire in the Meeting.[7]

The prime purpose of the Assembly, the anonymous writer continued, was "to afford some Ladies an Opportunity to alter the Station that they had been long fretfully continued in, and set off others, as they should prove ripe for Market."

Of course the Kirk was interested; a diatribe from Patrick Walker, a Covenanting minister, drew directly on his own experiences of religious persecution: "Some years ago we had a profane obscene meeting called 'The Horn Order'; and now we have got a new Assembly and publick meeting called 'Love for Love'." He was scandalized that anyone who had ever bowed his knee in prayer dared to

crook a hough to fyke and fling at a piper's and fiddler's springs. I bless the Lord that so ordered my lot in my dancing-days, that made the fear of the bloody rope and bullets to my neck and head, the pain of boots [an instrument of torture], thumbikens, and irons, cold and hunger, wetness and weariness, to stop the lightness of my head and the wantonness of my feet.[8]

Strong words, indeed, for something now regarded as one of the most innocent of amusements. But ministers held great sway over their congregations; so did their spies, described by Ramsay:

He kend the Bawds and Louns fou well,
And where they us'd to rant and reell,
He paukily on them cou'd steal,
   And spoil their sport;
Aft did they wish the muckle Deell
   Might tak him for't.[9]

The spies were encouraged to report infringements of the Sabbath (or other) restrictions, and illicit relationships. Those caught indulging in the last were condemned from the pulpit, then placed in sackcloth on the stool of repentance to be further humiliated in front of the congregation.

An early version of the jig the "Stool of Repentance" (ex. 12)[10] can be found in the William Dixon MS (1734). His MS gives what has become the second section, with variations; I have taken the first section, added later, from a set printed in Gow:

Ex. 12   STOOL OF REPENTANCE

Although Ramsay did not risk the stool, he could have been censured from the pulpit not only for attacking Kirk spies, but for defending public dancing in his poem "The Fair Assembly" (1723), where he berates the clergy for their attitudes:

Ye sourocks, hafflines fool, haf knave   /sour-faced; half
    Wha hate a dance or sang.
To see this stately maid behave,
    'Twad gie your hearts a twang!

Your hearts, said I? – Troth I'm to blame;
    I had amaist forgotten,
That ye to nae sic organ claim –
    Or if ye do, 't is rotten![11]

Even after 250 years, there is no doubting the sincerity of the poet or the ministers; the battle was more than a trivial squabble over dancing, but one between freedom and repression, far larger issues. John Jackson recorded in his *History of the Stage* (1776) that it was also more than a question of words, for "So violent were the enthusiasts . . . that about the beginning of this century, even at an assembly for dancing only, the company were assaulted and the doors of the building perforated with red-hot spits."

Captain Burt, associated with the Highland road-building projects of General Wade, wrote down his impressions of the affair, and its denouement:

> I do not, indeed, remember there was much Disturbance at the Institution of the Ball or Assembly . . . because that Meeting is Chiefly composed of People of Distinction. . . . But some of the Ministers published their Warnings and Admonitions against promiscuous Dancing. . . . Asmodeus was pitched upon as the most dangerous of all [devils] in exciting to carnality. . . . The Ministers lost ground to their great Mortification; for the most Part of the Ladies turned Rebels to their remonstrances, notwithstanding their frightful Danger.[12]

The Assembly's altruistic aims may have finally pacified the protesters. For the profits from the festivities were used to set up a charitable fund for the poor of the city which over the years helped build the Royal Infirmary and the Charity Workhouse, also a home for foundlings.[13]

Indeed, the badges worn by the Lady Directresses in the 1740s featured a pelican with "Charity" inscribed beneath, a reference to St Augustine's legend of the pelican feeding her young with her own blood, and a figurative reminder of salvation through Christ. One wonders whether the Kirk would really have thought the emblem appropriate.

The Music and the Dances

What music was played at these assemblies has to be divined from supporting material; no one thought the dances, music or musicians important enough to mention. The assemblies at Bath, however, were danced to country dances (longways dances, with men in one line, women in the other, facing towards one's partner, down the room) and minuets. Manuscripts suggest that Scotland followed Bath's lead, although Scottish sources seem to contain more instructions and music for country dances than minuets.

The Agnes Hume MS (1704) gives the earliest Scottish descriptions of a country dance with the music, which in the original is written out completely four times. The tune is "John Anderson my jo" (ex. 13).[14]

Ex. 13   JOHN ANDERSON MY JO

The first man and 2 ly turn right hands round and into their place and the second man and the first ly the same. Then d back all four and turn s. Then all hands round till the 2 couple come in the first place.

The tune is to be played over through once over every time so the first couple has time to take their drinks. To be danced with as many pairs [as] you please.

More country dance directions were recovered from the Holmain MS from Dumfries-shire: "Green Sleeves", "Cald Kale", "Hunt the Squiril", "The Dusty Millar", "This is not my own house", "Argile's Bowling Green", "The Birks of Abergeldie", "Lennon's Love to Blantyre", "The Old Way of Killiecrankie", "Bathget Bogs or Pease Straw", "Miss Hayden" and "Reel a Down a Mereken".[15]

Although no music accompanies this MS (variously dated between 1710 and 1750), it provides the first evidence of a reel being used as music for a country dance, the "Reel a Down a Mereken" (from the Gaelic *Daoine na Marachan*, the Menzies men). Two of the tunes above can be found in the Margaret Sinkler MS (1710), "Lennox Love to Blanter", unfortunately incomplete, and "Green Slievs and pudding pys" (ex. 14):[16]

Ex. 14   GREEN SLIEVS AND PUDDING PYS

This perennial favourite, here a jig, was registered with the Stationer's Company in 1580 (an early method of trying to secure a publication so that no one could copy it) as "A new Northern Dittye". To Shakespeare, as well as to Margaret Sinkler, it was a sprightly tune, not at all like the slow version popularized in the twentieth century by Vaughan Williams in *Sir John in Love*. "They do no more keep pace together," said Mrs

Ford, in the *Merry Wives of Windsor*, "than the Hundredth Psalm to the tune of Green Sleeves."

David Young

Perhaps the major collector of fiddle music from traditional and other sources was David Young, who, as a Writing Master, was probably paid to do it. Aberdeen-born and educated (Marischal College, 1722–6),[17] he provided "A Collection of Countrey Dances written for the use of his Grace the Duke of Perth by Dav. Young, 1734", presumably to bring his Grace up to date on Scottish music, since the Duke had been brought up at the exiled Stewart court in France.

The work is divided into two sections, country dances with music and instructions, and reels, music only. It contains no mention of strathspeys or use of the "Scots snap" rhythm (♪♩.), and very few dotted rhythms.

Also known as The Duke of Perth MS[18] or the Drummond Castle MS, this fascinating document is the earliest record of tunes (not necessarily under the same titles) such as "You're Welcome, Charlie Stewart", "Hey to Coupar", "This is not my ain House", "Reel o' Tulloch", "Gillie Callum", "Caber Feidh", "Sleepy Maggie", "Stumpie" and probably the best known of all, "Tullochgorum" (ex. 15):[19]

Ex. 15　TULLOCHGORUM

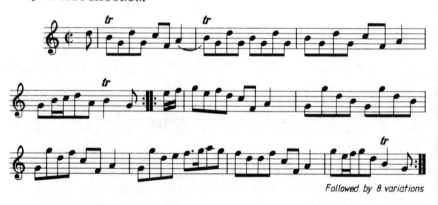

Followed by 8 variations

"Tullochgorum" shows perfectly three of what Francis Collinson, in *The Traditional and National Music of Scotland* (1966) called Scottish musical thumbprints, characteristic of much music played on the fiddle (and the bagpipe):

1. The scale used is modal, here the Mixolydian mode, basically the

same (ignoring the variations between bagpipe intonation and concert pitch) as the bagpipe scale.

2. It has the same range as the pipes, nine notes only (excepting the a″).

3. It uses the misnamed but appropriate "double tonic" – two consecutive triads, here G major and F major. On the fiddle the upper triad can be major or minor, but the lower is always major. In the pipe scale, two major triads on A and G occur naturally and so are often used in compositions.

It is outside the scope of this book to discuss in any detail the inter-relationship of bagpipe and fiddle music, but it is obvious from the list above that fiddle music has been greatly influenced by the musical characteristics of the bagpipe and, no doubt, by its repertoire.

Young also compiled "A Collection of the Newest Countrey Dances Perform'd in Scotland written at Edinburgh by D. A. Young W[riting] M[aster] 1740", also known as the Young MS[20] or the Bodleian MS, having been discovered there in 1957. About the same time, Young wrote down the music for the M'Farlane MS,[21] three volumes (the first now lost) of Scottish tunes with variations by Walter M'Farlane, Forbes of Disblair, and Young himself. The practice of composing variations for known tunes flourished during most of the eighteenth century, serving to display the skill of the composer, to make the music more interesting, and to increase the length of the tune either to suit dances or concert performances.

Other Sources of Dance Music

The Scottish MSS made in the first half of the century, amongst them the Hume, Sinkler, and those written by David Young, give only a partial picture of the music available for fiddlers at the early assemblies or for those playing at home. There were also the printed collections emanating from London, some of which surely reached Scotland.

Playford's *Dancing Master* had music and instructions for more than 900 dances in all by its last edition (John Young, around 1728), certainly more than enough to see any band of musicians through the twenty-five or twenty-six assemblies it is estimated Edinburgh held in a year. (Not, admittedly, that the musicians played from the music – they probably played from memory, as many do today – but that the printed music was available.) Other publishers, such as Walsh, produced annual batches with titles like *Twenty-Four New Country Dances*, where newly choreographed dances were set to well-known tunes.

The enterprising John Young, in his collection "full of Highland humour" (*c.* 1721), had begun to pay attention in a practical way to the needs of the musicians playing for dances. For Young arranged the tunes so that most fell into the same key or one closely related (C,C,C,C; F,F,B♭,F) in groups of three or four, easy for a musician to pick up and play for a dance, with no problems about key changes or turning over odd pages in the middle of a set. In other cases a single tune would have several variations which, with repeats, would have made up a dance set. The last piece in one set, and in the book, is the very Scottish-sounding "Hilland Tune" (ex. 16):[22]

Ex. 16   HILLAND TUNE

An anonymous publisher around 1730 seems to have had a good source of Scottish tunes, publishing, amongst others, "Sulters [souters=shoemakers] of Selkerke", "MacFossett's [MacPherson's] Farewell", "Lady Terfichen's Rant", "Andrew Kerr" and "Athol Brays", (ex. 17),[23] in the Duke of Perth MS as "Braes of Atholl":

Ex. 17   ATHOL BRAYS

followed by 2 variations

A publishing landmark (although most Scots would have known the music already) was the first printed collection of Scottish songs, *Orpheus Caledonius* (London, 1725). The compiler was William Thomson, who was undeniably Scottish. He had sung as a boy in the 1695 Edinburgh concert, and he made his reputation at court in London as a singer. Although many of the lyrics had appeared several years previously in Allan Ramsay's *Tea-Table Miscellany*,[24] this was their debut in full dress with music, arranged by Thomson, usually in a decorated style which very likely reflects just how he performed them himself.

He published another, two-volume, edition in 1733; of these hundred songs, more than twenty per cent still live on in fiddle collections in some form, as strathspey, reel, slow ("solo") strathspey, country dance, jig or quadrille. Here are two quite different sets of "Jenny Dang the Weaver" which show how much a tune can alter, Thomson's version (ex. 18)[25] and the same as a "solo strathspey" from *The Skye Collection* (1897) (ex. 19):[26]

Ex. 18   JENNY BEGUIL'D THE WEBSTER

Ex. 19   JENNY DANG THE WEAVER

Ex. 19, cont.

Music Publishing in Scotland

1726 saw, at long last, the real beginnings of music publishing in Scotland, with two and possibly three works being printed in Edinburgh. Taken as a whole, they present not only the expanding interests of the era, but foreshadow the directions music would take in the country for the remainder of the century.

Despite having had Patie Birnie despise the Italian influence, Allan Ramsay not only jumped on but drove the band-wagon which soon would fill up with foreign musicians. He asked Lorenzo Bocchi, a cellist who had arrived in Edinburgh in 1720, to set to music his cantata "Blate Johnny". Published either in Dublin or Edinburgh, it was a Scots text set for two violins, voice and continuo, a brave attempt to enter the mainstream of European music.

Thomas Bruce edited the second work, *The Common Tunes, or Scotland's Church Music made plain.*

> It contains seven practice-verses, and some quite useful explanatory notes on music by way of introduction. All the twelve tunes are given, with the single exception of COMMON TUNE; eleven others are taken from the 1635 Psalter. . . . But, greatest novelty of all is the appearance of four leaves of songs at the end of the book. . . . Three songs are given in full: "Coridon, arise", "Gather ye rosebuds while you may", and "Oh the bonny Christ Church bells".[27]

Clearly, people in and around the church were changing drastically; the inclusion of secular songs in a Psalter, which earlier would have been considered hell-bent heresy, may have even contributed to the popularity of the book, which had to be reprinted twice to fill the demand.

The third publication, which superficially might seem the most likely to have succeeded, was Volume One of *Musick for Allan Ramsay's Collection of Scots Songs*, set for violin and continuo by Alexander Stuart. But no other volumes materialized. Presumably Scottish musicians already knew the tunes, which would have been in common aural circulation, or already had copies of the Thomson music, which had come out the previous year and was a superior production to Stuart's, both in its music settings and in the engraving.

Other professional musicians – like Stuart, members of the Musical Society – also felt encouraged to try their hands at arrangements and, sometimes, composition. Adam Craig, an old hand from the 1695 concert, brought out *A Collection of the Choicest Scots Tunes* in 1730. By then Craig was second violin to William McGibbon (probably the son of Malcolm McGibbon, also in the 1695 event), a fine violinist who composed and published sonatas and Scots tunes, some with his own variations.

Although Craig's collection specifies that it is set for harpsichord, his version of "Corn Riggs is Bonny" (ex. 20)[28] is likely to give a fair idea of how he would have performed it himself on the violin:

Ex. 20   CORN RIGGS IS BONNY

(There is, by the way, no firm proof that this tune is Scottish, although Craig obviously believed it to be. As "Sawney was tall and of noble race", it is supposed to have been sung in D'Urfey's play *The Virtuous Wife* in London in 1680, and was printed in Playford's *Choice Ayres* (1681) as "A Northern Song". However, the same melody appears in the Newbattle MS "Lessones for ye violin", *c.* 1680, as "New Corn Riggs".)

James Oswald

By far the most successful and influential Scottish musician of the time was James Oswald, probably born in Dunfermline about 1711. In 1734 he advertised the publication of some minutes (as yet undiscovered), and by 1736 had settled in Edinburgh as a "violinist, organist, composer, and teacher of dancing".[29]

Early examples of his compositions can be found in his *Collection of Musick by several hands* (*c.* 1740),[30] where one composer is supposed to be the mysterious Fabbroni (a *fabbro* is a smith in Italian), responsible for "An imitation of a Highland Pibrack" and a copy of Corelli. Even if Fabbroni wasn't his alias, Oswald did admit to writing arrangements of Scots tunes and several Masonic anthems in this book.

In 1741 he issued his *Collection of Curious Scots Tunes*, amongst them "The low lands of Holand" (ex. 21)[31] "by David Rizo", a composer found surprisingly often in collections Oswald had anything to do with, and probably another of his pseudonyms.

Ex. 21   THE LOW LANDS OF HOLAND

Due to some confusions, the title of this tune later provoked great controversy as being the possible source of William Marshall's famous strathspey, "Miss Admiral Gordon" (ex. 64, page 104–5), to which it bears no resemblance. Moreover, the attribution to Rizzio (spelled various ways), a man who at that time had been dead the best part of two hundred years, reinforced the belief that he had composed fiddle music, a mistaken impression which continued well into the nineteenth century.

The Rizzio Legend

The original culprit was Thomson, of *Orpheus Caledonius* fame, who assigned seven of the songs in his first collection to Rizzio. His story, set in the court of Mary, Queen of Scots, shrouded in suitably Gothic horror and known to everyone, would have given a romantic background, if not historical accuracy, to Thomson's work. Sir James Melville, Mary's Ambassador to Queen Elizabeth, wrote of Rizzio:

> Now there came here [to Scotland] in company with the ambassa-
> dor of Savoy, one David Riccio of the country of Piedmont, who
> was a merry fellow, and a good musician. Her Majesty had three
> varlets of her chamber who sung three parts, and wanted a bass to
> sing the fourth part. Therefore they told Her Majesty of this
> man . . . [as one fit to make the fourth in concert.] Thus he was
> drawn in to sing sometimes with the rest . . . and afterwards, when
> her French secretary retired himself to France, this David obtained
> the said office . . .[32]

His position as secretary, with its attendant influence on the Queen, provoked jealousy, particularly from Darnley, who in 1565, at the age of nineteen, had become husband to the Queen. Darnley succumbed to his anger; in March 1566, he, the Earl of Morton and other conspirators viciously murdered Rizzio in a small room off Mary's bedchamber at Holyrood, dispatching him, according to one report, with no less than fifty-six wounds. Rizzio's death made him famous. The blood-stained floor (repainted from time to time) became a lasting tourist attraction while his relationship with Mary was thought, even by the crowned heads of Europe, to have put the paternity of James VI in question; Henry of Navarre is reputed to have said that he hoped King James was not the son of David the fiddler.

Rizzio is usually thought of as a lutanist as well as a fiddler or violer. There is only the slightest possibility that during his few years in Scotland his musical interests led him to collect a few local tunes and that these – beyond any reasonable expectations – were cherished and preserved until they reached Thomson, who used them in his collections.

There is as yet no evidence that Rizzio either collected or composed music. Yet, following Thomson's collection, the legend of Rizzio's involvement in Scottish music lived on, tunes "by Rizzio" or "as set by Rizzio" appearing not only in Thomson and Oswald but in Watt's *Musical Miscellany* (1729–31), Sadler's *Muses Delight* (*c.* 1760), Peacock's *Fifty Favourite Scotch Airs* (1762), Clark's *Flores Musicae* (1773) and James Davie's *Caledonian Repository* (*c.* 1829–30).

Thomson, perhaps because too many people realized Rizzio had not been a composer, omitted all references to him in his next, larger, collection in 1733. It appears that no one – at least in Edinburgh – was fooled by Oswald's claims either, since it seems to have been common knowledge that "Rizo" was just an alias of Oswald's. [33] As Allan Ramsay wrote:

> When wilt thou teach our soft Aedian fair   /Edinburgh lady
> To languish at a false Sicilian air;
> Or when some tender tune compose again,
> And cheat the town wi' David Rizo's name?[34]

Oswald in London

Ramsay's poem bade farewell to Oswald, who left to seek his fortune in London about 1741. He was aided when he arrived by the Scots already there, by the patronage of the Earl of Bute, and through his membership in the Temple of Apollo.[35] This was a Scots-dominated musical society to which belonged Thomas Erskine, 6th Earl of Kelly, Stamitz-trained composer of the Mannheim school; Captain (later General) Reid, amateur flautist and composer, donor of the Reid Chair of Music at Edinburgh University; and Dr Charles Burney, music historian of Scottish descent, his name having been changed from MacBurney in his infancy.[36]

In 1742 Oswald published two collections of *Curious Scots Tunes,* which included some music with Gaelic titles such as "More N'Ighean Ghiberlain" (The Gaberlunzie's Daughter) and "Failte na Miosg" (The Musket Salute), along with those in English, among them "She's

sweetest when she's naked" and "The Bottom of the Punch Bowl"
(ex. 22):[37]

Ex. 22 THE BOTTOM OF THE PUNCH BOWL

The majority of these gave only the melodic lines, a practice praised by
Benjamin Franklin when writing to Lord Kames that old Scottish airs
needed no harmony:

> Whoever has heard James Oswald play them on his violoncello, will
> be less inclined to dispute this with me. I have more than once seen
> tears of pleasure in the eyes of his auditors, and, yes, I think, even his
> playing those tunes would please more, if he gave them less modern
> ornamentation.[38]

In 1743 Oswald embarked on his great series *The Caledonian Pocket
Companion*, which by 1759 (the dates of Oswald's publications are
only given as a general guide, since no two authorities agree on them)
had reached its twelfth volume and contained more than 550 tunes
overall. In Book III (*c.* 1745) are two tunes, both called "A new
Strathspey reel", of which ex. 23[39] is one.

Oswald, for a change, proudly admits these are his own work; they
are the only tunes called Strathspeys or reels which appear in the entire

Ex. 23   A NEW STRATHSPEY REEL

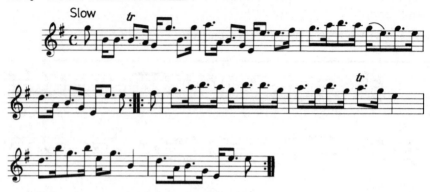

Caledonian Pocket Companion, although there are rants, Scots measures and even a "Strathspey wriggle", wherever that might have come from. The only possible earlier reference to the strathspey seems to be in the title "Strath spray's Rant" (ex. 24)[40] in Walsh's *Caledonian Country Dances* Book II, 1743–4 (the style of the melody is similar to some in David Young's Duke of Perth MS; there, this tune is called "Sir Alex MacDonald's Reel"):

Ex. 24   STRATH SPRAY'S RANT

Aside from composing the first titled strathspey in print, Oswald wrote other pieces in the Scottish style such as "The Lass of Inverness" and "A Scot's Lament", but their melodies wander rather too much to be completely satisfactory musically. A more pleasing tune which he may have written appeared in 1740 as "My Love's bonny when She Smiles on me" (ex. 25).[41]

The title had changed to "The Flowers of Edinburgh" by the time it reached the *Caledonian Pocket Companion*; in Sadler's *Muses Delight*[42] it is "The Flower of Edinburgh, set by Sigr. D. Rizzio", perhaps a hint that it was really by Oswald. In subsequent versions the rough edges of the original have been smoothed out to bring it to its present shape:

Ex. 25   MY LOVE'S BONNY WHEN SHE SMILES ON ME

Another tune from Oswald's works which is still widely played is "She griped at the greatest on't" (ex. 26);[43] somewhat tidied up, it is known today as "The East Neuk of Fife":

Ex. 26   SHE GRIPED AT THE GREATEST ON'T

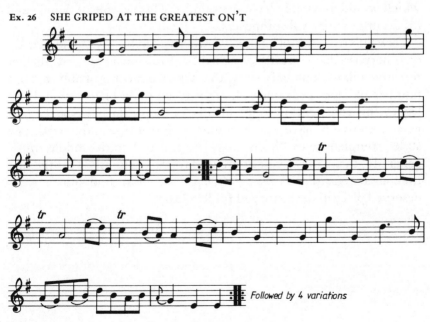

Followed by 4 variations

By 1747 Oswald had obtained a licence[44] from the King to print the music of the Society of the Temple of Apollo, "That he had composed and employed others to compose". It is likely that he had a hand in writing the music for the Society's pantomime *Queen Mab*, produced at Drury Lane in December, 1750; "The Last Dance" (ex. 27),[45] especially, has the shape and feeling of many Scottish dance tunes:

Ex. 27   THE LAST DANCE

Last section omitted

Oswald's family claimed after his death (thought to have taken place at Knebworth in 1769) that he was the composer of many melodies he had published without attributions. Presumably some of these could not have been acknowledged earlier because of the politics which would inevitably have surrounded The Temple of Apollo and his dealings with rival composers.

Oswald's own compositions, whether said to be "by David Rizzio" or otherwise, have greatly enriched Scottish music; indeed, further research will undoubtedly show that Oswald most probably wrote a number of tunes previously thought to be traditional. Beyond this legacy, his contribution to the history of the strathspey – as the first person known to have written a tune with that title in the strathspey style, complete with "Scots snaps" – and to Scottish fiddle music generally, through the vast number of tunes he published for the first time in the *Caledonian Pocket Companion*, must find him a well-deserved place in the history of fiddle music.

CHAPTER THREE

The Eighteenth Century, II

He left Blair and went to the house of Lude, where he was very cheerful and took his share in several dances, such as minuets, highland reels (the first reel the Prince called for was "This is no mine ain house" etc) and a strathspey minuet.

2 September 1745[1]

IT IS QUITE fitting that Prince Charles, travelling through Perthshire during the '45, should be the first person quoted as mentioning a strathspey. At first glance, its association with the minuet might seem better left hidden, but the fact that the "strathspey minuet" was undoubtedly the strathspey proper can be shown by a similar description from another foreign-educated gentleman, Captain Topham, a visting English officer. Writing in the 1770s, Topham compared the strathspey, which he didn't know, with the minuet, which he did:

> Another of the national Dances is a kind of quick minuet, or what the Scotch call a *Straspae*. We in England are said to *walk* a minuet: this is galloping a minuet . . . nothing of the minuet is preserved except the figure; the step and time most resemble an hornpipe.[2]

The reel the Prince requested, "This is not my ain house" (ex. 28),[3] had been included as a country dance in David Young's Duke of Perth MS in 1734, and was first published in Scotland fifty years later in the same syncopated rhythm. Today it is played as a strathspey.

Ex. 28   THIS IS NOT MY AIN HOUSE

Allan Ramsay described a reel, the threesome, in his poem "Second Canto to Christ's Kirk on the Green" (1716):

> When a' cry'd out he did sae weel,
> He Meg and Bess did call up;
> The lasses babb'd about the reel,   /bobbed
> Gar'd a' their hurdies wallop,   /made their buttocks shake
> And swat like pownies when they speel   /sweated; climb
> Up braes, or when they gallop,   /hillsides
> But a thrawn knublock hit his heel,   /thrown clod
> And wives had him to haul up,
> Haff fell'd that day. . . .[4]

Here Ramsay's reel is danced by one man and two women, although in practice any combination would have been acceptable; in its first illustration, a caricature by Rowlandson, Dr Johnson, Boswell and a kilted Highlander dance it on "Dun-can in Rasay". The reel for three or four could have been performed outside, if the conditions were favourable, or inside, behind closed doors, to avoid the prying eyes of the Kirk. The reel was possible even in the crowded tenements of Edinburgh's old town, where Mrs Cockburn lived in the second half of the century:

> On Wednesday I gave a ball. How do ye think I contrived to stretch out this house to hold twenty-two people, and had nine couples always dancing? Yet this is true . . . Mrs Mure and Violy Pringle came and danced a reel and went off. . . . Our fiddler sat where the cupboard is, and they danced in both rooms; the table was stuffed into the window, and we had plenty of room. It made the bairns all vastly happy.[5]

The Edinburgh Assemblies

After the furore of the '45 the capital settled back into its old ways, re-forming the Assemblies "for polishing the youth and providing for the poor". The treasurer of the Edinburgh Assembly reported in August 1746 "that he had conversed with several musicians and after some Difficulties had hired seven":

Thomas Robertson	} Haut boys	John Reoch	
Charles Calder		James Cameron	} Fiddles
		John Willson	
		Robt Hutton	
John Thomson	} Bass	[Bass fiddle, i.e. Cello]	

Their pay was calculated according to the number of people present at the Assembly: "Not exceeding 100 persons, 6 s[hillings]; not exceeding 150, 7s 6d; above 150, 10s; allowance for drink for the whole musicians 1s 9d", with the warning that "if they appear there in drink or fail in giving punctual attendance that they shall be dismist the Service".[6]

The Assembly Minutes refer to one of the musicians again, in 1750:

> The treasurer reported that Robert Hutton one of the Assembly musick had been applying to him to have his salary ogmented and be put on the same fooling [hopefully he meant footing] with the rest of his brethren, as he was now considerably improved in his playing having studied under Mr [William] McGibbon for severall years. The treasurer also reported that he had made tryall of his performance on the violin and found him suficiently qualified for playing in the Assembly.
>
> The directors considering that the said Robert Hutton was blind and had no way of living and that their funds was designed for charity agreed to give him the same allowance with the rest of the music.[6]

However charitable, the employment of a blind fiddler can only mean that the musicians' repertoire was limited. Probably all of them played from memory, some or all learning by ear; uncomplicated music, both technically and harmonically, would have been the staple fare.

The writer Oliver Goldsmith, then a student in Edinburgh, left a bored account of a typical evening at the Assembly:

When the stranger enters the dancing-room he sees one end of the room taken up by ladies, who sit dismally in a group by themselves, and at the other end stand their pensive partners that are to be. The ladies may ogle and the gentlemen may sigh, but an embargo is laid upon any close converse. At length the lady directress pitches upon a gentleman and lady to minuet, which they perform with a formality approaching to despondency. After five or six couples have thus walked the gauntlet, all stand for a country dance, each gentleman furnished with a partner from the aforesaid lady directress. So they dance much and say nothing, and this concludes an assembly.[7]

The Lady Directresses[8] then were Lady Leven, Lady Minto, Mrs Grant and Lady Jean Ferguson. Their dress, and that of the other ladies present, was dominated by the hooped skirt, which could be up to four yards in circumference, a lethal weapon at a dance, where it could wreak havoc on the shins of an ardent suitor or a poor dancer. Nevertheless, they were popular for the best part of fifty years, despite their inconvenience:

> What a fine thing I have seen to-day: O Mother, a hoop!
> I must have one, you cannot say nay; O Mother, a hoop!
> For husbands are gotten this way to be sure,
> Men's eyes and men's hearts they so neatly allure;
> O Mother, a hoop, a hoop! O Mother, a hoop![9]

Individualists who didn't follow the prevailing fashions were barred from the Assembly. The rules were matter-of-fact:

> No lady to be admitted in a night-gown [an informal dress] and no gentleman in boots. The dancing to begin precisely at five o'clock afternoon in winter, and at six in summer. Each sett not to exceed ten couples and to dance but one country-dance at a time. The couples to dance their minuets in the order they stand in their severall setts. No dancing to be begun after 11 o'clock at night.[10]

Even if a person were correctly dressed, he might still be denied the pleasure of the Assembly's company, at the word of the Lady Directress:

Upon one occasion, seeing a man at the assembly who was born in a low situation and raised to wealth in some humble trade, she went up to him, and without the least deference to his fine-lace coat, taxed him with presumption in coming there, and turned him out of the room.[11]

The imperious lady active here was one of the best-remembered Directresses, Miss Nicky Murray, who gave *ton* to the event and didn't hesitate to bring her knowledge of the social pecking order into play: "On hearing a young lady's name pronounced for the first time she would say: 'Miss —— of what?' If no territorial addition could be made, she manifestly cooled." In Miss Murray's "Miss —— of what?", the polite social query of the age (asking the name of one's property or estate, by which the family was known), lies the background and explanation of so many fiddle tune titles which have immortalized the landed gentry and their families, the dedicatees of so many splendid melodies composed by Scottish musicians.

Robert Bremner (c. 1713–89)
Much of the music for these social gatherings would have been supplied by Robert Bremner. Although details of his background are as yet scarce (he may have been from Aberdeen or the Northeast, where many Bremners still live), he had set up in business by 1754:

Robert Bremner at the Sign of the Golden Harp opposite to the Head of Blackfriars Wynd Edinburgh sells all sorts of Musical Instruments viz. Bass violins, violins, &c. N.B. As the undertaker intends to serve Gentlemen and Ladies with everything in his way at the London price it is therefore hoped they will encourage him and whatever music is wanted that he has not shall be immediately sent for.[12]

London publications such as Oswald's, Rutherford's and Walsh's works were already available, but soon Bremner did not have to depend entirely on the South, since he had begun publishing on his own. His *Collection of Scots Reels or Country Dances* "With a Bass for the Violoncello or Harpsichord" was brought out in fourteen eight-page sections between 1757 and 1761. It is the earliest Scottish publication of dance music specifically, and contains the next strathspeys after Oswald's. Against his first strathspey, "The Fir Tree",

Bremner wrote "N.B. The Strathspey Reels are played much slower
than the others." (The anonymous one-time owner of a Bremner
collection I have seen added to the index page "Strath:spey signify
very slow", so there would be no mistake about it.)

Amongst Bremner's other strathspeys are "Ruffian's Rant"
(known today by its song title, "Roy's Wife of Aldivalloch"),
"Rothemurches Rant" (ex. 29)[13] and "The Miller's Wedding"
(ex. 30),[14] which later served Burns as his music for "Comin' through
the Rye"; Burns used strains one and four; these are strains one and
two.

Ex. 29   ROTHEMURCHES RANT

Ex. 30   THE MILLER'S WEDDING

Scordatura
The fiddler's immediate difficulty, if he simply takes up his fiddle and
tries to play "The Miller's Wedding", is that it sounds like musical
gibberish. The secret lies in the notes written before the music marked
"scordatura", literally, "mis-tuning". Here it indicates that the fiddle

must be retuned to the notes indicated; in this case, only the G string is changed, raised to A. After that is done, the first two bars would sound like this:[15]

Ex. 31

etc.

The player does not need to transpose pieces written in scordatura, since he reads the notes and fingers them as if the strings remained at their usual pitch. Quite a number of composers and collectors of Scottish fiddle music notated pieces using this device, probably developed from lute and viol tunings, which were altered according to the key being played so as to make use of open strings. On the fiddle, scordatura tuning produces a rich, ringing sound when the open strings are played along with fingered notes.

Oswald used some scordatura settings in the twelfth book of his *Caledonian Pocket Companion*, all tuned a e' a' c"#. Here are the first two sections of "McIntosh's Lament" (ex. 32)[16] in that tuning:

Ex. 32   MCINTOSH'S LAMENT

This piece, in eight sections, is obviously based on bagpipe material, in particular the *pìobaireachd* (pibroch), although this, piper's *ceòl mór* (great music), has had almost no influence on present-day fiddling.

Arrangements

It must be emphasized that almost all of the dance music collections from the eighteenth century, excepting Oswald's *Caledonian Pocket Companion*, provide more than the unaccompanied melodies fiddlers are accustomed to seeing today. Early compilers or composers included a bass line suitable for cello or harpsichord, although many were, admittedly, extremely basic, hardly worth printing. But Bremner, a skilled musician who probably did his own arrangements, could write a bass line which enhanced the melody. As was the practice of the time, the harpsichordist, if one were playing, would add to the given bass line such chords or embellishments as musical taste and skill permitted.

An attractive example of the kind of bass line possible is that for "The Hen's March" (ex. 33),[17] set for two violins and continuo in

Ex. 33   THE HEN'S MARCH

Bremner's *Collection of Airs and Marches* (1761); unusually, the bass line here stops so as not to clutter up the overlapping violin parts in the second section.

The musical idea for this melody may have come from a brief motif "The Hen's March, or Farmyard" (ex. 34),[18] from the pantomime *Fortunatus*, performed in London in 1753, and published by Oswald. (A Shetland version of ex. 33, called "The Hen's March o'er the Midden", has become very popular in Scotland within the last twenty years.)

Ex. 34 THE HEN'S MARCH, OR FARMYARD

Neil Stewart

Bremner followed Oswald to London in the 1760s, leaving Edinburgh open for his successor, the music publisher Neil Stewart (or Steuart), whose first volume of *The Newest and Best Reels or Country Dances* appeared about 1761. His choice of title, like Bremner's, suggests two things: reels were now being danced in public along with the country dances and minuets Goldsmith had described in the early

1750s; music for the two types of dances, reels and country dances, could be used interchangeably.

One of the reels Stewart published was "Bernard's Well", (ex. 35),[19] an Edinburgh landmark for those who took the waters to improve their health. The value was no doubt more psychological than medical, although the water was said to be "impregnated with iron and sulpher . . . and highly diuretic".[20]

Ex. 35   BERNARD'S WELL

Another reel is "The Braes of Tully met" (in Perthshire) (ex. 36),[21] also known by such titles as "D. Dick's Favourite", "Birnie-boozle", "Miss Grant of Grant" and "Knit the Pocky". Some sources give Robert Petrie (1767–1830) as the composer, but the tune had been published before he was born.

Ex. 36   THE BRAES OF TULLY MET

The "Braes of Auchtertyre" (ex. 37),[22] another tune celebrating part of the Scottish countryside, near Crieff, first printed by Stewart as a reel in C, is now better known as a strathspey in A, and was played by James Scott Skinner as a pastoral in the last century. (Although some collectors such as Skinner and James Hunter give one James Crockat as the composer, this is far from certain.)[22]

Ex. 37 BRAES OF AUCHTERTYRE

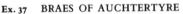

Stewart did include in his collections several tunes he called strathspeys, like "Invercalld's Reel, A strathspey" (ex. 38),[23] although he didn't mark them "Slow", as Bremner had.

Ex. 38 INVERCALLD'S REEL

It is interesting to note in passing that two of the three tunes with Highland associations and names, "The Braes of Tully met" and "Invercalld's Reel", use dotted rhythms and are strathspeys. This is hardly incontrovertible proof that the strathspey originated in the Highlands, but traditional belief has certainly always supported that theory.

Dancing Masters
Aside from publishers, Edinburgh attracted a cross-section of teachers and musicians, which in turn created a certain healthy competitiveness:

> Whereas it has been suggested that M. Froment does not dance so well as certain masters, he hereby obliges him to perform with anyone in town, and to lay down twenty guineas if the trial goes against him in the opinion of competent judges.[24]

Whatever Froment's skill, he appeared the following year, 1746, dancing "The Scotch Measure and the Highland Reel"[25] at the Haymarket Theatre in London.

One of the most successful dancing masters was Ayrshire-born David Strange; his pupils included the scientifically minded Mary Somerville, who described him in her memoirs:

> He was exactly like a figure on the stage; tall and thin, he wore a powdered wig, with cannons at the ears, and a pigtail. Ruffles at the breast and wrists, white waistcoat, black silk or velvet shorts, white silk stockings, large silver buckles and a pale blue coat completed his costume. He had a little fiddle on which he played, called a kit. . . . Every Saturday afternoon all the scholars, both boys and girls, met to practise in the public assembly rooms. . . . We used to always go in full evening dress. We learnt the *minuet de la cour*, reels and country dances.[26]

Most dancing masters would have played the violin or kit, so that they could demonstrate the steps to the dances with the music. Strange also employed others to play for him occasionally, one being Charles Stewart, who advertised himself "musician to Mr Strange" when he brought out a collection of his own minuets and other tunes.

Strange, who taught in Edinburgh from 1764 to the end of the century, had impressive qualifications; he had studied under Vestris, under Maltère, teacher to the Royal Family in Paris, and in London under Sir John Gallini. Perhaps Strange actually taught something to Gallini, too, for he was the first to describe a Scottish reel, in his *Treatise on the art of Dancing* (1765):

> It is to the Highlanders in North-Britain, that I am told we are indebted for a dance in the comic vein, called the *Scotch Reel*, executed generally, and I believe always in *trio*, or by three. When well danced, it has a very pleasing effect, and indeed nothing can be imagined more agreeable or more lively and brilliant, than the steps in many of the Scotch dances. There is a great variety of very natural and pleasing ones.[27]

Another of Gallini's pupils was a Mr Barnard (probably the dedicatee of a Gow reel, ex. 81, p. 132), while a Mr Martin, at one time Strange's assistant, taught minuet, louvre, French, English and Scots high dances (step or solo dances), country dances and cotillions.

As usual, some Scots moved to London to try to better their prospects. George Jenkins, a friend of the Gows and possibly from Perthshire himself, was a teacher of "Scotch Dancing" there; he published his first collection in 1793, containing his composition "The Marquis of Huntlys Highland Fling" (ex. 39):[28]

Ex. 39   THE MARQUIS OF HUNTLYS HIGHLAND FLING

Another expatriate dancing master was Duncan MacIntyre, who published some of his compositions in London in 1795. He too was probably acquainted with the Gow family for they published some of his works, among them "Miss Downie's Strathspey" – re-christened, presumably in his honour, "Honest Duncan" – and "Miss Coxe's Strathspey" (ex. 40):[29]

Ex. 40   MISS COXE'S STRATHSPEY

Other Musicians

The art of violin-playing as well as dancing was becoming increasingly sophisticated. The most influential publication of the era, found throughout homes in Scotland, was Geminiani's *Art of Playing the Violin*, a book which appeared a generation before Leopold Mozart's. Ahead of his time, Geminiani favoured the then revolutionary practice of placing the chin on the left of the tailpiece. His instructions on bowing, too, would be familiar to any player today, as would the last of the ornaments he describes: "The Close Shake cannot possibly be described by Notes as in the former examples. To perform it you must press the Finger strongly upon the String, and move the Wrist in and out equally, swelling the Sound by degrees, drawing the Bow nearer to the Bridge."[30] Today that is called vibrato.

Even by mid-century Edinburgh's musical base had broadened; in addition to the continuing Musical Society concerts at St Cecilia's Hall (purpose-built in 1762) and the assemblies, entertainments like Comely Bank (Edinburgh's answer to London's Vauxhall Gardens) operated alongside the theatres, no longer prohibited by the Kirk as they had been in Allan Ramsay's day. So up-to-date had the city become that one theatre band staged a very modern-sounding strike,[31] with good reason, as it turns out, since some had been unpaid for upwards of seven years. Clearly they were not full-time musicians.

Amongst the Musical Society players, who would have been well acquainted with the works of Corelli, Handel and Haydn, were Daniel (or Donald) Dow, Alexander McGlashan and Robert MacIntosh,[32] all of whom contributed to the fiddle repertoire. Dow (1732–1783) was probably from Kirkmichael, Perthshire; he taught in the capital from the 1760s, organized concerts, played the violin, and composed. He published *Thirty-Seven New Reells and Strathspeys* which he had written in about 1776. "Sir John Stewart of Grantully's Reel, a strathspey" (ex. 41),[33] with its dotted rhythms and "Scots snaps", would definitely be considered a strathspey today.

Ex. 41   SIR JOHN STEWART OF GRANTULLY'S REEL, A STRATHSPEY

But some of Dow's other pieces illustrate how vague the distinctions between strathspeys and reels still were: of the three other tunes in the book called strathspeys, one has many "Scots snaps", one has only one, and the third has none at all. Amongst his other compositions, several do have "Scots snaps" although they are not called strathspeys, for example, "Sir Arch[d] Grant of Monemusk's Reel" (ex. 42).[34] When the Gows republished this in the 1790s they altered it rhythmically (glossed above the staff)[35] by adding more "Scots snaps", smoothed out some dotted patterns for variety, and shortened and changed the title to "Monymusk, a strathspey":

Ex. 42   SIR ARCH[d] GRANT OF MONEMUSK'S REEL

Dow also produced the fascinating *Collection of Ancient Scots Music* . . . "consisting of ports, salutations, marches or pibrachs". In it he saved some of the harp compositions of Rorie Dall (O'Caithean, an Irish-born harper to several Scottish noble families, according to Francis Collinson) such as "Lude's Supper", "The Fiddler's Contempt", and "Rorie Dall's Sister's Lament". By today's standards they are structurally rather formless; that may have been the original style, or perhaps they lost something in translation from whatever was Dow's source. Although Dow probably played all the tunes in the collection himself, a better choice for today's player is the anonymous composition "The Black girl is not Cheerfull" (ex. 43):[36]

Ex. 43   THE BLACK GIRL IS NOT CHEERFULL

Like Dow, Alex McGlashan (173?–1797) was a violinist with the Musical Society and gave concerts in St Cecilia's Hall. He is said to have been an excellent composer; although his collections of fiddle music bear his name on the title page, his name never appears in the text as a composer, while William Marshall's name, for instance, does. However, this may be an example of the same modesty which kept Niel Gow and others from attaching their names to all of their compositions. McGlashan's collections contain two versions of the tune now called "The Mason's Apron"; the most similar is "The Isla Reel" (ex. 44),[37] from his second book.

Ex. 44   THE ISLA REEL

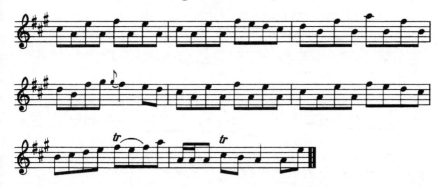

The title of his second collection, "of Strathspeys, Athole reels", is interesting, since it could be read as if the tunes then beginning to be called strathspeys were, in the Atholl district, called reels. This would tie in with the early collection titles which mention "Strathspeys or Old Highland reels", and would also imply that the strathspey came from a wider area than the valley of the Spey.

Robert MacIntosh (d. 1807), the third of the Musical Society professionals, styled himself a composer and included a derivative sonata in his first work. He was probably from Niel Gow's village, Inver, and had settled in Edinburgh at least by 1773. The Musical Society was not entirely dependent on his playing, though, since it was willing to let him go when money was short;[38] the Aberdeen Musical Society was happy with him for a while, and he was employed there as leader for several years.

MacIntosh's first collection of *Airs, Minuets, Gavottes and Reels* [1783][39] was mostly set for two violins, with a bass for cello or harpsichord, like Bremner's earlier march book. This could suggest that dance music was played with harmonies between the two violins, as a general practice, but it is more likely MacIntosh was following baroque musical convention by writing for a trio. However, his Scottish fiddle compositions such as "Lady Charlotte Campbell's New Strathspey" (ex. 45)[40] and "Lady Charlotte Campbell's Reel" (ex. 46)[41] have lasted longer than his classical attempts. (See p. 68.)

His son Abraham MacIntosh, also a musician, produced three books of dance tunes, two in Edinburgh, one in Newcastle. His tune "Miss Jessie Scales Hornpipe" (ex. 47),[42] is not as well known as "Buckingham House" (or "Athole Brose", ex. 73, page 111), probably his composition.

Ex. 45   LADY CHARLOTTE CAMPBELL'S NEW STRATHSPEY

Ex. 46   LADY CHARLOTTE CAMPBELL'S REEL

Ex. 47   MISS JESSIE SCALES HORNPIPE

By the last quarter of the eighteenth century minuets and country dances, which had been the only public dances of the '40s, had given way to the national dance, the reel, finally acceptable to those who patronized the Assemblies. Topham, whose description of the "Straspae" is found at the beginning of this chapter, also recorded his impression of a reel, in 1775:

> The general dance here is a reel, which requires that particular sort of step to dance properly, of which none but the people of the country have any idea. The perseverance which the Scotch ladies discover in these reels is not less surprising than their attachment to them in preference to all others. They will sit totally unmoved at the most sprightly airs of an English country dance, but the moment one of the tunes is played, which is liquid laudanum to my spirits, up they start, animated with new life, and you would imagine they had been bit by a tarantulla. . . .
>
> In most countries the men have a partiality for dancing with a woman; but here I have frequently seen four gentlemen perform one of these reels seemingly with the same pleasure and perseverance as they would have done, had they had the most sprightly girl for a partner. . . . Besides minuets and country dances they in general dance reels in a separate part of the room.[43]

It is difficult to decide whether the publications of Bremner and Stewart brought reels and strathspeys to the attention of those people who had previously shunned dancing them in public, or whether the publications came about because there was a sudden demand. But books of fiddle tunes like these were surely an influence which helped to bring Scottish dances and their music from the kitchen into the parlour. With new works by local musicians beginning to appear almost monthly, it must have been an exhilarating time. But better was to come, with the music of William Marshall, Niel and Nathaniel Gow and Simon Fraser who, amongst them, created or collected the greater part of the modern fiddler's repertoire.

CHAPTER FOUR

The Northeast

Farewell, ye dungeons, dark and strong,
   The wretch's destinie!
McPherson's time will not be long
   On yonder gallows-tree.

   Sae rantingly, sae wantonly,
     Sae dauntingly gaed he,
   He played a spring, and danc'd it round,
     Below the gallows tree.[1]

          Tune: "Macpherson's Rant" (or "Farewell")
          Words: Robert Burns, 1788

JAMES MACPHERSON, whose legend Burns developed in this song, lived in Banffshire from about 1675 until 1700, when he was hanged for murder. If that had been all, he would have long since been forgotten. But, as the story goes, on the cold November morning of his execution Macpherson marched on to the scaffold with his fiddle in his hand. Stepping on to the platform he took up his bow and played his last message to the world, his rant. After the music died away, he offered his violin to the assembled spectators, but no one was brave enough to take it from the hands of a condemned man. He looked around scornfully, lifted the fiddle and broke it over his knee, its notes silenced forever.

Most people who know this story believe that before he was hanged Macpherson composed and played the rant which now bears his name. However, there seems to be no contemporary evidence that he was a fiddler, much less a composer. Turning to the trial records, published in 1846, one finds this sole reference to Macpherson and anything musical: "M'Pherson . . . wes one night in the house at that tyme, and drunk with the res, and danced all night."[2] The only musician mentioned in this account is Peter Broune, who "went sometymes to Elchies, and played on the wiol" and "got money sometyms for playing on the wiol . . ." (He may have been one of the "Browns of Kincardine" referred to later in this chapter as early strathspey players and composers.)

Nor is the earliest broadside ballad helpful. "The Last Words of James Mackpherson, Murderer",[3] printed about 1705, contains nothing about the dramatic gesture with which he is thought to have ended his life, and nothing about fiddling. Apparently there is a later version, which adds to the title the words "To its own proper Tune". It is quite likely that the tune was written after the event to suit the broadside, for it fits the words perfectly. Here are the last four lines from the oldest broadside, along with the music, first found in the Margaret Sinkler MS, 1710, as "McFarsance's Tesment" (ex. 48):[4]

> Then wantonly and rantingly
>   I am resolv'd to die
> And with undaunted Courage I
>   Shall mount this Fatall Tree.

Ex. 48

It maybe that over the years traditional memory fused Macpherson's story with the musical facts about Peter Broune, who was on trial at the same time. Certainly the accepted view of Macpheron as a fiddler seems to have had no literary currency prior to the Burns verses which began this chapter. In the absence of other information, whether or not Macpherson composed the tune which carries his name, and played it on the fiddle before he died, is left to the reader to decide.

Aberdeen and Francis Peacock

Elsewhere in the Northeast, several gentlemen were busy writing down fiddle music for their own pleasure. One was George Skene of Skene, near Aberdeen, whose manuscript was written between 1717 and about 1740. It includes a number of song tunes, bagpipe-style sets and reels, some of which Skene probably wrote. His friend and neighbour William Forbes of Disblair was fond of the fiddle too; he composed variations on Scottish tunes, some of which appear in the M'Farlane MS (Edinburgh, 1740) written down by David Young.

Young was one of the founders of the Aberdeen Musical Society, modelled on that of Edinburgh, in 1748. Another was Francis Peacock, appointed to the post of dancing master the previous year; he was to serve the city faithfully for almost sixty years. He was also a violinist and cellist for the Society's concerts, where he would have met Robert MacIntosh, who led the group for several years, and the great agricultural improver Sir Alexander Grant of Monymusk, a fervent supporter of all forms of music. Grant, one-time president of the Musical Society, imported the Englishman Thomas Channon to teach the tenants on his estate to sing harmonized psalms, a most liberal attitude for the times. The laird in turn was celebrated in a practice-verse, that is, secular words set to a sacred tune to enable it to be practised outside the church: "How lovely is thy dwelling-place, / Sir Archie Grant to me;/ The home-park, and the policies,/ How pleasant, sir, they be."[5]

Musically, Aberdeen was reasonably active, as can be seen from this list of events taken from the *Aberdeen Press and General Advertiser* in 1758:

7 Feb.: An Assembly in the Mason's Lodge, last of the Winter Subscription

9 Feb.: General meeting of the Aberdeen Music Society to be held in the Concert Hall

21 Feb.: Alex. Grant of Monymusk elected President of the Music Society for the coming year

2 May: Mr Tait's Concert to be held in Mason's Hall on 12 May at 6 P. M. 2/6d. each (sold at Booksellers, Coffee House and New Inn)

15 May: A Ball at Mason's Hall

20 June: An Assembly in Mason's Hall, Gentlemen 2/6d., Ladies 1/6d.

19 Sept.: A Ball at Mason's Hall. Gentlemen are asked to be properly clothed

Nevertheless, aside from Young, Aberdeen and its musicians contributed little to the vast amount of fiddle tunes which were composed and collected during the next fifty years. Although Peacock issued his own arrangements of Scottish airs in 1762, they are of little importance compared with his major work, *Sketches Relative to the History and Theory but more especially the Practice of dancing as a necessary accomplishment for the youth of both sexes*, which appeared in 1805 near the end of his long and useful life. This book gives the first comprehensive discussion of dancing as it was taught in Scotland; in it, the names of the Highland reel steps are given in Gaelic, then translated into English:[6]

Kemshoole, or Forward Step. [*Ceum*=step + *siubhal*, to proceed, walk]

Minor Kemkossy – Setting or Footing step. [*Ceum* + *coiseachd*, walking]

Double Kemkossy – Setting or Footing step. [*Ceum* + *coiseachd*, walking]

Lematrast – Cross Springs. [*Leum*=spring + *trasd*=cross]

Seby-trast. Chasing Steps, or Cross slips. [*siabadh*=act of brushing away + *trasd*]

Aisig-thrasd. Cross-Passes. [*Aisig*=transfer + *trasd*]

Kem Badenoch, a minor step. [*Ceum* + Badenoch, a district in Strathspey]

Fosgladh. Open Step. [*Fosgladh*=an opening]

Cuartag. Turning Step. [*Cuartag*=an eddy, curl; *cuartach*=circular]

Presumably these steps originated in the Highlands instead of being English or French imports to which Gaelic names were later given.

Indeed, the Highlands were understood in the eighteenth century to be the Gaelic-speaking area which spread from Perth north and northeast over the Cairngorms to Nairn.

In Peacock's time Gaelic culture was much more in evidence than it is today, and he did not hesitate to give praise where it was due:

> I once had the pleasure of seeing, in a remote part of the country, a Reel danced by a herd boy and two young girls, who surprised me much, especially the boy, who appeared to be about twelve years of age. He had a variety of well chosen steps, and executed them with so much justness and ease, as if he meant to set criticism at defiance. . . . Our colleges draw hither, every year, a number of students from the Western Isles, as well as from the Highlands, and the greater part of them excell in this dance; some of them, indeed, in so superior a degree, that I myself have thought them worthy of imitation.[7]

Angus Cumming

To search for the music these Highlanders might have danced to, it is appropriate to investigate the first collection published by a person from Strathspey, "where this species of Scottish music is preserved in the greatest purity",[8] as Angus Cumming wrote of his *Collection of Strathspeys or Old Highland Reels* (1780). In his preface, he gives as his *bona fides* that he "follows the profession of his fore-fathers, who have been for many generations Musicians in Strathspey". Angus mentions none by name, but more background can be found in Thomas Newte's *Tour of England and Scotland in 1781*:

> According to the tradition of the country, the first who played them [strathspeys] were the Browns of Kincardine [-on-Spey], to whom are ascribed a few of the most ancient tunes. After these men the Cummings of Freuchie, now Castle Grant [Grantown-on-Spey], were in the highest estimation for their knowledge and execution in Strathspey music, and most of the tunes handed down to us are certainly of their composition. . . . The last of that name, made famous for his skill in music, was John Roy Cumming. He died about forty years ago, and there are many persons still alive who speak of his performances with the greatest delight.

If one accepts the premise that Angus Cumming thought of all the tunes he published as strathspeys, that is, in the strathspey style, then a detailed examination of his work might shed light on what the strathspey was to him in his day.

The rhythms Cumming notated provide an obvious starting point. But the "Scots snap", which players today feel has always been an integral part of the strathspey, occurs in only seventeen out of his total of sixty pieces. The figure is often misprinted as ♪♩., making analysis harder, although that may have been due to difficulties with the engraver. Most frequent is the simple dotted rhythm ♩.♪ , present in all but five of the melodies (a figure based on the first two sections of any piece, excluding any variations). If this rhythm is truly characteristic of strathspeys, then an early example would be "McFarsance's Tesment", ex. 48. The first four bars of "Glen Morisone's Reell" (ex. 49)[9] (found in the David Young 1734 Duke of Perth MS as "The Confederacy", and now called "You're Welcome Charlie Stewart") also show this pattern:

Ex. 49   GLEN MORISONE'S REELL

Another feature is series of repeated notes of the same pitch: birls, ♫♪, two semi-quavers followed by a quaver, and doodles, ♫♫♪, usually four repeated notes. In the Cumming work, birls and doodles appear in fourteen tunes each, while both are used in another five, as in "Lethen's Reell", a strathspey (ex. 51)[10] composed and published as the reel "Bonnie Annie" (ex. 50)[11] by Daniel Dow four years earlier. The notes of the two sets are identical, except for Dow's having one extra note. Rhythmically, however, Dow's piece was originally in undotted notes except for three two-note groups, two being in the first two bars:

Ex. 50   BONNIE ANNIE

etc.

In Cumming's version the rhythms are much more complex. His set is printed below with the same incorrect notations as the original, to show how difficult it can be to decide precisely what Cumming meant:

Ex. 51   LETHEN'S REELL

This is a simple demonstration of how to turn a reel into a strathspey, and *vice versa*, by simply altering the rhythms; the speed would have changed naturally to suit the dance. The differences in the time signatures are not significant, for the practice of the times was relaxed on such matters, although some publishers, such as Bremner, did try to write the reels in ₵ and strathspeys in C .

There is rhythmically such an embarrassment of riches in this collection that all that can be said about the style of playing in Strathspey is that it did not use unvarying quavers or crotchets. It is likely that the penchant for dotted rhythms came from two sources, the rhythm of Gaelic speech patterns, and the bagpipes.

As for the tunes themselves, about one-third occur here for the first time, although this figure could be lower. (Glen, in the *Glen Collection of Scottish Dance Music*, gives a higher proportion of first appearances for the Cumming Collection, but he missed several tunes, such as "Lethen's Reell", which had been published earlier; no doubt more research would further reduce the number.) The majority were either published earlier by Bremner or Stewart, or came out the same year, 1780, in McGlashan's first collection. The remainder add little to the fiddler's repertoire. "The Bishop" (ex. 52)[12] is one of the better tunes:

Ex. 52   THE BISHOP

William Marshall (1748–1833)

At the other, more creative, end of the scale is William Marshall, a successful and prolific composer, second in sheer output only to James Scott Skinner (Chapter Nine). Born in the old town of Fochabers, near the Spey in Morayshire, he was a retainer of the last Duke of Gordon, becoming head steward at Gordon Castle and later factor on the Keithmore part of the estate. From this secure, if feudal, position he pursued knowledge voraciously, becoming a mathematician, architect, astronomer, clockmaker, violinist and composer – self-taught, we are told, in each skill.

Following the line of thought which the Gaelic associations with fiddle music provide, it seems that Marshall may have come from a Gaelic-speaking background:

> Having got access to books, and being of a very studious disposition, his acquirements kept pace with his ambition. In a short time he was thoroughly conversant both in the grammar and pronounciation of the English language. Nothing he often said distressed him more than to hear a badly pronounced word.[13]

Admittedly, this may refer to the differences between the Northeast dialect and the then equivalent standard English, but at that time the area in which Marshall lived was still Gaelic-speaking.

Unlike most other fiddler-composers of the century, Marshall did not have to make a living from his music. He is not known to have played publicly for concerts or balls,[14] nor to have taught either fiddle or dancing, although several later players have been called pupils of Marshall.

He seems to have been, in the best sense, a very gifted amateur:

Music [wrote one of his acquaintances] was always his favourite amusement; although without any intention of publishing he was constantly composing. The *good old strathspey* with which he had been accustomed in his youth was his favourite measure, and he used to repeat with delight the lines of Skinner:[15]

There needsna be sae great a phrase
Wi' dringing dull Italian lays,
I wadna' gi'e our ain Strathspeys
For half a hundred score o' em;

. . .

    They're dowff and dowie at the best   /dull and dismal
Wi' a' their variorum:
    They're dowff and dowie at the best
Their allegros and a' the rest,
They canna please a Highland taste,
Compared wi' Tullochgorum.[16]

Marshall's own "Highland taste" – and skill – developed so rapidly that he was able to publish his *Collection of Strathspey Reels* (in two parts) by 1781. His talent was already evident in pieces like "Miss Admiral Gordon's Reel. A Strathspey" (ex. 64, p. 104), the "Marquis of Huntly's Reel, A Strathspey" (ex. 53),[17] and "The Marquis of Huntly's Farewell" (ex. 54).[18] (See p. 80.)

Dissemination of Music
Marshall published no more collections for over forty years, but nevertheless his music became popular and was widely known. A correspondent writing in the 1920s presents as good a picture as any of how this might have taken place, although he gives no documentary evidence:

Marshall's tunes, before publication, were evidently freely circulated in MS. The method whereby his music became so popular is interesting. A MS copy was usually obtained by the leading fiddler of the district – sometimes the dominie, occasionally the minister – who was able, as it is put, to play from the book. If the new

Ex. 53 MARQUIS OF HUNTLY'S REEL, A STRATHSPEY

Ex. 54 THE MARQUIS OF HUNTLY'S FAREWELL

strathspey or reel was a success musically, the other fiddlers in the district, who played by the ear, had to see the stampin' and the bowin', and thereby succeeded in mastering the latest.[19]

One clergyman in a position to circulate Marshall's music was the fine musician Father George Gordon, priest at Keithock, near Dufftown. It has been suggested he furnished bass lines for Marshall's second collection; perhaps Marshall's outstanding slow air "Chapel Keithack" (ex. 55)[20] was a musical offering in return for the Father's help.[21]

Ex. 55   CHAPEL KEITHACK

Others writing about Marshall have humorously described the process of aural transmission. As an example, a local fiddler passing by hears Marshall playing over a tune in his kitchen. He quietly creeps over to the window and, having a quick ear and a ready mind, memorizes the melody. Immediately he goes up to Marshall's door, as if he had only just arrived, calling out that he has a grand new tune to play to him. Marshall settles back, in anticipation, only to hear the tune he has just written himself.

There is certainly a grain of truth here, if only in that Marshall's music must have been extensively transmitted by ear and in MS. As will be discussed in Chapters Five and Six, a number of his melodies were published long before he had them printed himself. Not only the Gows, but Charles Duff, John Anderson, James Aird and Alexander McGlashan must all have had access to Marshall's music from some source before they could print it. These early sets are often almost precisely the same as Marshall printed them twenty or thirty years later, suggesting that the music was transmitted in MS, at least to the publishers, rather than by ear.

Marshall's Renaming of His Own Compositions
If anything about Marshall's music is less than pleasing, it is his habit of changing the names of tunes. He did not hesitate to alter the title if it was no longer up-to-date, and could suit a better purpose, as displayed in this letter written to the Marchioness of Huntly in 1822, the year he was preparing to publish his collection: "I must observe that I could not compose one for Huntly Lodge that pleased me, and as P——r died upwards of three years ago . . . and as the strathspey was better known, [a] great favourite never published . . . I called it Huntly Lodge."[22]

While working on his last collection, issued posthumously in 1845, Marshall wrote to his publisher: "One strathspey I have named to a lady who found herself disappointed [with the music, presumably, rather than in love; tune titles were often changed when a woman married and took a new name or a man took a new title]. If she likes the first one better, or any of the others, you can exchange."[23] His melodies were clearly written without any particular person in mind; the titles were simply words added so that individuals could be flattered, and the tunes would have some way of being recognized. He wrote to his publisher: "I have named some of the tunes which must be attended to, and as to those not named you can use your own discretion,"[24] which shows how little interest he had in the matter.

Marshall's first collection suffered the most from this renaming. Of the forty-nine pieces it contains, forty-two were republished in his later collections, thirty-one of them with different titles:

1781 Title	*1822 Title*
Gollochy's Farewel, a Strathspey	Balvenie Castle
Johnston's Reel, a Strathspey	Mr John Angus' Reel – of Calcutta
Lady Anne Gordon's Reel	The House of Letterfourie, A Reel

Lady Ann Hope's Reel

Lord George Gordon's Reel

Miss Agnes Ross's Reel

Miss Burnet's Reel

Miss Gordon of Cairnfield's Reel
Miss Grant of Knockando's Reel

Miss Halket's Reel [A major]

Miss Hopkin's Reel
Miss Jeanny Williamson's Reel
Miss McQueen's Reel, a Strathspey
Miss Ross's Reel
Miss Sally Eglison's Reel
Miss Watson's Reel [B minor]

Mrs Gordon of Bellie's Reel, a
    Strathspey
Mrs Ross's Reel

Run down the Town in haste
Strathdown, a Strathspey
The Illumination 9th Feb^r 1781
There's nae harm done Goodwife
The Road to Berwick

Miss Stewart's Strathspey –
    Pittyvaich
Mrs L. Stewart's Reel – of the Island
    of Java
Miss Ross' Strathspey [some
    rhythmic changes]
Miss Jane Stewart's Strathspey –
    Pittyvaich
Miss McPherson's Reel – Edinburgh
Mrs Anderson's Strathspey – of
    Fochabers
Cullen House, A Strathspey [A
    minor]
Miss Cruickshank's Reel – Glass
The Mortlach Reel
Miss Grant's Strathspey – of Elchies
Drumbain's Reel
Miss Young's Strathspey – Banff
Belhevie House, a Strathspey [C
    minor]
Dandaleith, a Strathspey

Mrs Colonel Gordon of
    Leitchieston's Reel
Miss Watt's Reel – Mether Cluny
Drumin's Strathspey
The Fochaber's Rant
Mrs Glennie's Reel – of Maybank
The Buck of the Cabrach

1781 Title	*1845 Title*
A Hornpipe	Lady McNeil, Reel
Dutchess of Gordon's Reel, a Strathspey	Linlithgow Loch, or Provost Dawson's Favourite, a Strathspey
George's Square	Lady Louisa Hamilton Reel
Lady Louisa Gordon's Reel, a Strathspey	Miss Farquharson of Invercauld, a Strathspey [several notes changed]
Miss Gordon of Glastirum's Reel	Miss Louisa Duff, Reel
Miss Jeanny Ross's Reel	Miss Syme Wilson, Reel
Miss Ketty Allan's Reel	Mrs H. Inglis, a Strathspey
Miss Wedderburn's Reel	Colonel W. Marshall of the 79th Reg^t of Foot

Republished in 1822, titles basically unaltered

Arthur's Seat   Lord Alexander Gordon's Reel

Glenfiddich	Marquis of Huntly's Reel, a Strathspey
Lady Charlotte Gordon's Reel	Miss Abercromby's Reel
Lady Madaline Gordon's Reel	Miss Admiral Gordon's Reel, a Strathspey
Lady Susan Gordons Reel	The Duke of Gordon's Reel, a Strathspey
	The Marquis of Huntly's Farewell

Development of Better Technique

I do not propose to consider here the 1845 collection of eighty-one tunes; although Marshall worked on it almost until his death, it was out of his hands when it finally appeared, arranged with piano more in mind than violin. This presentation, combined with various printing errors and little first-rate music, makes it less important than his other two collections, of 1781, in two parts, and 1822.

By 1822 his position as a technical innovator of fiddle music was clear, although some of the Gow compositions, particularly Nathaniel's, had already made increased demands on the player. John Glen gave the opinions some fiddlers held about the problems Marshall's music presented for them:

> Among Mr Marshall's friends there were some who found the melodies too difficult to play, either on account of wide intervals or other transitions, while others complained of their compass being more extensive than that to which they were accustomed. To them his answer was that he did not write music for bunglers, and as all his tunes could be played, he advised them to practise more, and become better players.[25]

The most obvious difference between Marshall's music and that of his predecessors and contemporaries is his wide choice of keys. He revelled in the flat keys, which require the fourth finger to be used more often than the usual fiddle keys A, E, D and G, where the open strings can be used more frequently. In 1781 he used C, G, D, A, E, F, B♭, C minor, G minor and B minor. (This is only roughly accurate; for a few tunes which are modal and use the "double tonic", or have a key signature at odds with conventional usage, I have selected the most sensible key.) In 1822 Marshall went much further with the flat keys, with 19 tunes in F, 30 in B♭, 16 in E♭, and three in F minor (four flats), almost half of the 140 tunes which were not reprints.

Nor was that all. In some pieces there are double stops, which, if

Ex. 56 MR HOY, GORDON CASTLE

played as indicated would demand moving into third position, as in "Mr Hoy, Gordon Castle" (ex. 56).[26]

Some bars of a piece such as "Chapel Keithack" (ex. 55), would be easier to play and more legato in third position, while a few, like "Sir Walter Scott Bar'", require the third position to reach d''', although Marshall used that note only once in "Sir Walter" – perhaps he wanted to bring on the "bunglers" gradually.

In bowing, aside from the expected intricacies of playing strathspeys, the greatest difficulties arise where there are leaps across three strings, as in "Miss Wharton Duff" (ex. 57).[27] The melody is made simpler to play than it could have been by the stacattos, which allow a fraction of time for the bow to be lifted over the intervening string. In the first four bars of "Miss Burnet's Reel" (ex. 58)[28] (1781 set and title)

Ex. 57　MISS WHARTON DUFF

the leap of the octave G forces the player into third position in order to manage the slur which connects the two notes. In fact, the bowing would hardly be possible unless one was in that position; then the whole first section could be played *in situ*.

Ex. 58　MISS BURNET'S REEL

By ignoring the usual limitations of key and range which had operated previously almost as if by an unspoken agreement, Marshall provided a number of excellent compositions which showed the way the music could develop, thus extending the potential for later composers.

Technique and Style

Many Scottish fiddlers still accept that Marshall was greatly influenced by the Italian violinist Stabilini, leader of the Edinburgh Musical Society orchestra for a number of years, who is said to have been a frequent visitor to Gordon Castle. Stabilini did not arrive in Edinburgh until 1783, so he would have had no influence at all on

Marshall's 1781 collection. He may have helped later, though, by giving advice about one of Marshall's technical problems – "a difficulty he sometimes experienced in executing the high shifts, from the shortness of his fingers", as a friend described it, "but a false note was never detected in consequence."[29] The writer was probably not a violinist himself, and may have misquoted Marshall, since it is actually easier for someone with small fingers (or small hands) to play in the higher positions since the distances between the intervals decrease as one moves up the finger-board.

If Marshall had short fingers this would help explain why so many of his pieces use third position, and why he so exploited the flat keys, particularly $B\flat$. There, using the fourth finger in $E\flat$ on the A-string would have been less of a stretch than using it for $E\natural$, a semi-tone higher, since in descending passages it is preferable to use the fourth finger and not the open string, for smoothness. But of course this is only conjecture.

The few comments which have come down to us about Marshall's playing are platitudinous and well-meant, but give minimal insight into his skill or individuality. Nevertheless, for the record,

> [his playing was] characterized by a fullness of intonation, and accurate brilliancy of expression. Equally removed from vulgarity on the one hand and over refinement on the other hand, so inspiring was the effect that when he played in company the lively reel or strathspey, the inclination to dance on the part of both old and young became irresistible. The slow airs and melodies afforded still more scope for the exercise of his fine taste. His style of executing them was extremely touching, and delighted all who heard him.[30]

Music was never Marshall's life, much less his greatest concern. As a contemporary wrote: "Notwithstanding his predilection for music he seems to have generally regarded it as secondary to his graver studies, and always to duty or business of importance. I have known his violin to remain encased for months together without ever being touched."[31]

Despite his relative isolation from the profession of music Marshall still managed to compose more than 250 tunes, some quite outstanding, of which many are still popular. This he accomplished writing purely for himself, without the pressures which drove more competitive composers to produce new collections and invent new airs which they felt might catch the public's fancy.

One of his finest strathspeys, "Craigellachie Bridge" (ex. 59),[32] should, as it were, play him out. He was obviously inspired by the new bridge built by Thomas Telford, and his enthusiasm can be seen in this letter to one of his sons in 1814:

> Craigellachie Bridge is now finished . . . beautiful piece of work-manship . . . it is 150 feet span, and the iron work above extends to 170, and upwards. The approaches to it are also beautiful, and will be of the greatest utility and convenience, not only to us who are immediately concerned, but the whole country in general. I hope you will soon have the pleasure of galloping across it, and the additional pleasure of seeing your sister and friends on the other side of the Spey.[33]

Ex. 59   CRAIGELLACHIE BRIDGE

Lesser Lights

Where Marshall had a gift of genius, others in the Northeast had to try to succeed through sheer hard work. Isaac Cooper (?1754–?1820) lived in the coastal town of Banff, where he advertised as a teacher of "The Harpsichord, The Violin, The Violincella, The Psaltery, The Clarionet, The Pipe and Taberer, The German Flute, The Scots Flute, The Fife in the regimental Stile, The Hautboy, The Irish Organ Pipe . . . And the Guitar, after a new method of fingering . . ."[34]

He published several collections, the first in 1783, because he felt the public were so much "imposed upon by people who have published them anew, and at the same time were only old reels, with new names, and most of them end on the wrong key, than which nothing can be more disagreeable to a delicate ear."[35] (Might he have been thinking about the Cumming collection?)

Cooper seems to have been moderately successful in his various pursuits, since according to his accounts he was able to employ a musician to play for some classes and his balls (although the pupils' would have borne the cost) which would have allowed him to devote his time to teaching the dance steps.

His best known composition is "Miss Herries Forbes Farewell to Banff", no doubt because of its association with Burn's song "The Lass o' Ballochmyle", although Burns had no part in choosing Cooper's tune, but had wanted his words set to "Ettrick Banks".

A contemporary of Cooper's was John Morrison, who worked in Peterhead, a fashionable spa in the eighteenth century. His efforts to make a living were marred by continuing financial problems. He tried his hand at almost everything: teaching dancing, copying and selling music, dealing in instruments, playing the organ for church services, organizing balls and running a ship's chandlery. His first collection appeared in 1800, his compositions competent but unremarkable.

By 1805 his fortunes were failing; the *Aberdeen Press and General Advertiser* published this notice:

> Sale at Peterhead. There will be enforced a sale by public order at the house of John Morrison, ship-chandler and musician in Peterhead on Monday 11 April next at 10 o'clock forenoon. The whole shop goods and household furnishing which belonged to the said John Morrison; likewise a very excellent keyboard organ consisting of three and a half viz. stop diaphragm flute 5th and half open diapason, and also a very fine-toned violin and violoncello.[36]

Morrison survived his bankruptcy; battling his creditors, he tuned organs, sold harpsichords, taught dancing and gave organ and fiddle lessons. But for his second collection he only managed to raise the money to print two pages, and wrote the rest out by hand for any subscribers who wanted a copy. Despite his enterprise, his name was recorded at his death in 1848 as simply "Fidler, Peterhead".[37]

Back in Aberdeen, the plum post of leading dancing master, on Peacock's death, seems to have fallen to Archibald Duff. He and his brother Charles, based in Montrose and later Dundee, for a time divided the area south of Aberdeen between them, offering various services from music publishing to piano-tuning. While still in Montrose, in 1794, Archibald had had printed his first collection of strathspey reels for the "Pianoforte, violin and violoncello". Although mentioning the piano on a title-page was not new, its existence, and that of the cottage piano in the next century, would significantly affect Scottish music.

To give some idea of the state of music in Scotland just before 1800, here is a selection from Archibald's subscribers' list; I have starred the names of those who at some time or other either published their own music, collections or sheet music, or had compositions appear in others' works:

*John Anderson, music seller, Perth
George Allan, musician, Forfar
*David Allan, musician, Forfar

James Allan, musician, Forfar
Alex Bremner, dancing-master, Elgin
John Bowick, organist, Dundee
★T. H. Butler, organist, Montrose
Peter Bowie, musician, Perth
★John Bayne, dancing-master, Perth
David Baillie, musician, Perth
★J. Clarkson, Jun., dancing-master, Stirling
★Mssrs Corri, Dussek & Co, Edinburgh
J. Cuison, musician, Edzal, nr Brechin
J. Cameron, musician, Bredalbane Fencibles
Duncan Cumming, musician, Braemar Castle
—— Day, Theatre, Montrose
★Charles Duff, musician, Dundee
James Douglas, dancing-master, Huntly
Charles Davies, music-master, Montrose
★Lawrence Ding, [dancing-master and publisher] Edinburgh
★Sampson Duncan, musician, Coupar Angus
William Gray, musician, Whitthills
John Gordon, musician, Arbroath
Andrew Grant, musician, Buckie
Mr Thomas Hill, music-seller and stationer, Perth
★Mssrs Johnson & Co, Lawnmarket, Edinburgh
★John Low[e], dancing-master, Brechin
David Low[e], musician, Brechin
John Laing, musician, Coarston
Patrick M'Lean, dancing-master, Perth
Donald M'Intyre, dancing-master, Dunkeld
J. Mitchell, musician, Theatre, Montrose
Alexander M'Hattie, musician, Cullen
★Mr Peter Moncur, musician, Dundee
Patrick Mortimer, musician, Cullen
★Mr Robert Petrie, musician [Kirkmichael]
Mr John Purdie, dancing-master, Perth
Edward Simpson, musician, Theatre, Montrose
William Shaw, musician, Stirling
Alexander Simpson, musician, Kirrymuir
John Sivewright, musician, Braemar Castle
★Mr John Watlen, music-seller, Edinburgh
A. Watson, dancing-master, Aberdeen

Edwin Wells, teacher of music, Aberdeen
William Wilkie, musician, Ballinshoe
Mr Robert Wright, musician, Montrose
J. Young, musician, Montrose

As can be seen, the Northeast had at the end of the eighteenth century an abundance of musicians, and, by inference, of music-making, a state of affairs unlikely to be equalled anywhere in the country today. Cooper, the Duffs, Morrison and Marshall were only a few of the many individuals involved in Scottish dance music when it was at its most creative and exciting. This expanding interest had developed gradually over the century, partially as a result of dramatic changes in social attitudes. Beyond that, there had to be musicians who could and would show the way. One of the most influential was Niel Gow from Perthshire, the subject of the next chapter.

CHAPTER FIVE

Niel Gow

(1727–1807)

– Breakfast with Dr Stewart – Niel Gow plays – a short, stout-built, honest Highland figure, with his greyish hair shed on his honest social brow – an interesting face, marking strong sense, kind open-heartedness, mixed with unmistrusting simplicity —[1]

Robert Burns

NIEL GOW WAS Scotland's most famous fiddler when Burns met him in 1787. Two hundred years later he still remains the archetype, the father-figure for all who have followed. His long and successful career, unique style of playing, his compositions and his character combined to make him memorable. But something more in the man, or some need, some hunger in the society in which he lived, made legends grow, embellishing his life like variations on a simple Scottish melody.

His family name is found in the records of his home county, Perthshire, as early as the seventeenth century. Indeed, one of his ancestors could have been Patrick Gow, of Pitcastle, near Ballinluig, mentioned in a complaint by the King's Advocate in 1609. This Gow was alleged to have "taken part in an attack on some of the citizens of Dunkeld along with others . . . all armed with swords, gauntlets, platesleeves, bows, dirks, targes, broad-axes, two-handed swords, hagbuts and pistolets".[2] Gow would have been a Gaelic speaker, as were the other inhabitants of that part of the Highlands, and as Niel Gow himself might well have been.

Niel was born in Strathbraan, just up the river Tay from Inver, near Dunkeld, to John Gow and Catherine M'Ewan. They were peaceful folk, weavers, who expected their son to follow the family trade. (He himself always spelled his name Niel; for consistency and clarity I have done the same.)

But Niel had the music in him; his destiny lay elsewhere. He is said to have originally taught himself how to play on a kit, his first and only teacher being John Cameron, otherwise employed by Sir George Stewart of Grandtully, not far from Inver. Little more is known of his early life, although there have been suggestions that he was "out" briefly in the '45. (As the Gow legends grew he was solemnly credited with composing the Jacobite rallying song "Wha'll be King but Charlie", an honour he never sought.) He was married twice, first to Margaret Wiseman, then to Margaret Urquhart. By his first he had all his children, William, John, Andrew, Nathaniel, and Daniel, who died in infancy. All the others became involved in music. Nathaniel, the longest-lived, had the greatest impact; his work as a publisher and composer is considered in the following chapter.

Niel's Career
Niel Gow's first real opportunity seems to have come about in a way as familiar and as useful now as it was then – he won a competition, described in the *Scots Magazine* in 1809. The author of this extensive memorial to Niel is not mentioned in the magazine; later writers concur it was by a Dr McKnight, though Nathaniel Gow wrote that it was by "Principal Baird of the College, Edinburgh".[3] It is likely that Nathaniel provided the factual information, common practice in those days, or actually wrote it himself.

> A trial of skill having been proposed amongst the best players of the country, young Niel for some time declined the contest, believing himself to be no match for such masters in the art. At last, however, he was prevailed on, to enter the lists; and one of the judges, who was kind, being made the umpire, the prize was adjudged to Niel Gow by a sentence, in the justice of which the other competitors cheerfully acquiesced. On this occasion, in giving his decision the judge said, that he could distinguish *the stroke of Niel's bow* among a hundred players. Having now attained the summit of his profession at home, the distinguished patronage, first of the Athole [Atholl] family, and afterwards of the Duchess of Gordon, soon introduced him to the notice and admiration of the fashionable world. From this period Gow's excellence was doubtless unrivalled in his department of Scotch national music.

Success is seldom so simple; there is no doubt, though, that the Dukes of Atholl did encourage and employ their local fiddler, and that they helped make him a national celebrity. The third Duke paid him a retainer of £5 a year, although what work Niel did for that sum was not mentioned. A charming contemporary watercolour at Blair

Castle shows him playing to two of the Atholl children; it would be pleasant to think his responsibilities were no more arduous.

However, the Murrays (the family name of the Dukes of Atholl) took him up to London, where he entertained them and their friends, physically and spiritually a long way from Inver, but a commonplace trip to the nobility, who spent summers at their Scottish estates and winters in the capital for the "season" and the sitting of Parliament. A relative of the Duke, the young Mary Murray, heard Niel play in London in 1779:

In the evening we had Gow, the famous Scotch player on the fiddle, who played several tunes. . . . The Maddens sung again and the Scotch fiddler played Donald and other tunes. . . . I went to General Robertson's. After tea Miss Robertson Played. Then the Scotch Fiddler appeared. I danced a reel with Miss Murray, Lord Drummond and Captain Murray.[4]

No less well-known at home in Scotland, Niel played for dances and assemblies for more than forty years, accompanied by his brother Donald, vamping on the "bass" fiddle [cello] and, after his death, by Malcolm MacDonald and, later, Patrick Murray, both Inver players. Niel could command a far higher fee than other fiddlers, fifteen shillings for an engagement compared to the usual two-and-sixpence to five shillings,[5] although for a "gig" at Creiff, say, he would have had to travel about twenty miles each way (though a shilling in those days was worth several pounds in purchasing power).

He played for Masonic Lodges, the Caledonian Hunt Balls and other public and private entertainments. But like dance bands who play the Scottish circuit today, even Niel could be unavoidably detained and miss a dance because of the weather. A sister of Lady Nairne, the poetess, tells what happened one time when Niel did not turn up to play:

Niel Gow, a famous Highland fiddler, having been appointed to be at Orchill last month, I was asked there in hopes of having a fine dance, and Niel ran in my head for several days. Well, away I went, but no Niel that day; well, tomorrow will bring him; but tomorrow came and went in the same manner; at last comes music at supper the second day; but alas it was a scraper, the only one of three or four that were sent for that were not engaged; but however, the spirit moved us, and away with tables, chairs, and carpets in a moment; we had but three beaus; one of them, not liking the music took a sprained ankle; the other bassed to the fiddler in hopes of improving him; Maggy Grahame could not dance, so that our ball was principally carried on by three, for the storm froze up the company as well as Niel Gow.[6]

Niel was always in great demand; once, when he was ill, it is said that the Caledonian Hunt postponed its yearly ball until he was well enough to play for them. His appearance guaranteed an excellent evening, his enthusiasm and skill giving something extra to the music he played, "the effect of the *sudden shout* with which he frequently accompanied his playing in the quick tunes, and which seemed instantly to *electrify* the dancers, inspiring them with new life and energy, and rousing the spirits of the most inanimate."[7]

Niel Gow's Style

However, the most striking aspect of Niel's playing to those who heard him was its individuality, particularly, it is thought, his use of what is now called the up-driven bow, a stroke unknown and untaught in the classical tradition. It is used primarily for the rhythmic figure ♪ ♪. ♪ ♪. The straight line in the example is a straight slur, used to indicate that the notes are detached although played in one bow. Alastair Hardie in *The Caledonian Companion* says the stroke "gets its name from the fact that the second note of the up bow is accented by means of increased bow travel and pressure. [To play it] Take the initial semi-quaver near the point of the bow, leaving a whole bow for the following three notes. Kick the final semi-quaver."[8]

It is of course impossible to know exactly what Niel's playing was like, although descriptions survive which point the way:

There is perhaps no species whatever of music executed on the violin, in which the characteristic expression depends more on the power of the *bow*, particularly in what is called the *upward* or returning *stroke*, than the Highland reel. Here accordingly was Gow's forte. His bow-hand, as a suitable instrument of his genius, was uncommonly powerful; and when the note produced by the up-bow was often feeble and indistinct in other hands, it was struck in his playing with a strength and certainty, which never failed to surprise and delight the skilful hearer. As an example may be

David Rizzio: David the fiddler – the
first Scottish folk-music collector?

The Effigie of PATIE BIRNIE.
The Famous Fidler of Kinghorn;
Who gart the Lieges gawff and girn ay,
Aft till the Cock proclaim'd the Morn:

Tho baith his Weeds and Mirth were pirny,
He reesd those Things were langest worn.
The brown Ale Barrel was his Kirn ay,
And faithfully he toom'd his Horn

Patie Birnie: A busker of the old school

Above: Dancing lesson at Hopetoun House: likely a caricature of David Strange, kit in hand, ruffles at throat

Below: "Macpherson's fiddle": Was this Macpherson's, or Peter Broun's?

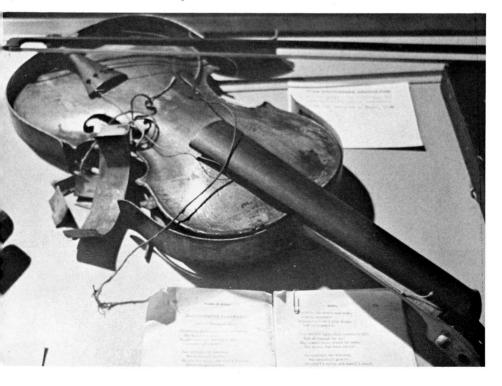

William Marshall: "the first strathspey
composer of the age" – Burns

Niel Gow: Scotland's most famous fiddler

The Highland Dance: Niel, with his brother Donald on "bass";
the figure on the left is probably James Murray of Abercairney

The Penny Wedding: An inexpensive, communal way to celebrate a bridal; the Kirk banned them as immoral

Above: Nathaniel Gow: A
worthy son, and creative
successor

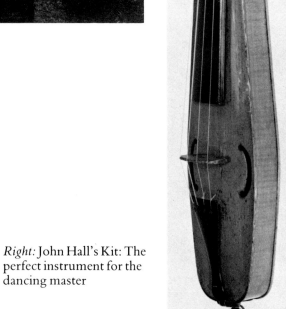

Right: John Hall's Kit: The
perfect instrument for the
dancing master

mentioned his manner of striking the tenor C in "Athol House". To this extraordinary power of the bow, in the hand of great original genius, must be ascribed the singular felicity of expression which he gave to all his music, and the native Highland *gout* of certain tunes, such as "Tullochgorum", in which his taste and style of bowing could never be exactly reached by any other performer.[9]

"Athole House", by Donald Dow, was originally published as a country dance in the *Edinburgh Magazine and Review* in 1773. In Dow's version it is totally lacking in dotted rhythms; when the Gows put it into their *First Repository* they changed the rhythm in a few places and called it a reel. Interestingly enough, the Gow alterations make it possible to see just what might have made Niel's playing so unique. For the first four notes in the last bar have been changed to the pattern suited to the up-driven bow, and using that bowing the "kick" on the final semi-quaver, the "tenor C", could very well have been just what gave Niel's playing its memorable magic and power. Here is "Athole House" (ex. 60)[10] in the Dow set, the small notes above showing the Gow rhythmic changes:

Ex. 60   ATHOLE HOUSE

Early commentators have agreed that it was the up-driven bow which gave Niel's playing such character, although no other evidence, aside from traditional belief, has been brought forward before. Alastair Hardie's definition has come from a similar traditional source, being a style of playing passed down from generation to generation. It is fitting that the two should come together to provide a possible insight into Niel's playing, thanks to one of Niel's appreciative audience mentioning a tune and describing how part of it sounded.

It is quite possible, even probable, that Niel revolutionized fiddle playing. Even if he did not create the up-driven bow stroke, he must have promoted it and made it widely known. His style, whatever it was, became synonymous with the correct way to play. How this may have come about was described by William Honeyman in 1879, writing about ballroom musicians, who often had to play "for twelve hours at a stretch". "Little wonder", he went on, "that they discovered the easiest ways of producing the desired effect, and, having found them, adhered to them most religiously – laying down as a law to all who followed, that that and no other was *the style* in which the music must be played."[11] It is difficult to think of Niel laying down the law about anything; but the style would have been followed because it was the simplest, most effective and least wearying way of playing during a long evening's work.

Of course, Niel was not confined to playing strathspeys and reels. "He excels most in the strathspeys," wrote Dr Garnett, a London clergyman who visited Niel in the eighteenth century, "which are jigs played with a peculiar life and spirit, but he executes the laments or funeral music with a great deal of pathos."[12] One of the most beautiful laments he could have played is one of his own compositions, "Niel Gow's Lament for the Death of his Second Wife" (ex. 61).[13]

Later Life

As Niel grew older, he played less, keeping close to his home in Inver. At that time not only was nearby Dunkeld a famed beauty spot ("the resort of all tourists, both foreign and domestic"[14]) but Inver the only place for miles where the Tay could be crossed in relative safety and comfort. Elizabeth Grant was undecided in her youth which of the local attractions was more appealing, the ferry or the fiddler:

> On this journey I first remember old Niel Gow being sent for to play for us at the inn at Inver – not Dunkeld – that little village we passed through, and went on to the ferry at Inver, which we crossed the following morning in a large boat. It was a beautiful ferry, the stream full and deep and dark, the banks overhung by fine timber trees, a glimpse of a newly-planted conical hill up the stream, only

Ex. 61 NIEL GOW'S LAMENT FOR THE DEATH OF HIS SECOND WIFE

Slow and pathetic

thick wooding the other way. I don't know whether this did not make more impression upon me than Niel Gow's delightful violin, though it had so over-excited me the night before that my father had had to take me a little walk by the river-side in the moonlight before I was rational enough to be left to sleep.[15]

No doubt Niel enjoyed being sought out by the passing gentry; of course, he was much more socially acceptable than Patie Birnie, who had hung on to coat-tails at the Kinghorn ferry at the turn of the century. Gow became, in fact, almost a national monument, thought of as being a characteristic "model of what national partiality conceives a Scottish highlander to be".[16]

This is not to say that he did not merit fame and attention; he did, certainly, for a number of reasons, not only musical. But he had come into his prime at a time when James MacPherson's "Ossianic translations" had sparked off a romantic interest in the Highlanders and their culture (an interesting paradox, when short years before they had been thought barbarians) culminating in the novels of Sir Walter Scott and influencing the arts throughout Europe.

He was, without question, in the right place at the right time. Many travellers, great and small, met Niel Gow. Of these, the one best-remembered today is Robert Burns. His description of Niel, which opened this chapter, is brief. But there is a reasonably reliable account which expands upon the visit. It was communicated by Patrick [Peter] Murray, Niel's cello player, to another Dunkeld man, Alexander Robertson:

> Arriving at Dunkeld, the poet, along with his Edinburgh friend, William Nicol, the identical "Willie" of "Willie brewed a peck o' Maut", put up at the principal inn in the town, once known as Culloden House . . . making the acquaintance of Dr Stewart [of Bonskeid] . . . an enthusiastic amateur violin player and well acquainted with all the tunes familiar in the north country.[17]

The Doctor took Burns and Nicol to Niel's cottage; they found him at home, and willing to oblige:

> . . . the magician of the bow gave them a selection of north-country airs mostly of his own spirited composition. In this he was aided by the worthy doctor, while Peter Murray, another native fiddler, played the bass [cello]. The first tune played was "Loch Erroch Side", which greatly delighted the poet, who long afterwards wrote for the same melody his touching lyric "Oh, stay, sweet warbling woodlark, stay!"
>
> At Burns's request, Niel next gave them his pathetic "Lament for Abercairney", and afterwards one of the best-known compositions in the Highlands, "M'Intosh's Lament" [ex. 31]. Dr Stewart volunteered an old Highland marching air, "We'll take the High-way" [*Gabhaidh sinn an Rathàd Mòr*]. "Tullochgorum", [ex. 15] and other well-known native airs were duly honoured, after which the whole party adjourned to the little old-fashioned inn at Inver, where there was a famous *deoch* or parting friendly drink.

All the tunes Niel played are traditional save "Loch Erroch Side" (ex. 66, p. 105), arguably one of his compositions, and "Niel Gow's Lamentation for Abercarney" (ex. 62),[18] definitely his own composition.

Ex. 62 NIEL GOW'S LAMENTATION FOR ABERCARNEY

One last traveller's tale is a picture of Niel seen through the eyes of Dr Garnett:

> We were favoured with a visit from Niel Gow [he was "favoured", while the Grants had simply "sent for" old Niel] a singular and well-known character and a celebrated performer on the violin. . . . His only music is that of his native country, which he has acquired chiefly by the ear, being entirely self-taught; but he plays the scotch airs with a spirit and enthusiasm peculiar to himself. He is now in his seventy-second year and has played publicly at assemblies on his instrument for more than half a century.[19]

His Compositions Debated

There is one interesting omission from Dr Garnett's sketch: he says nothing about Niel's compositions. Of course, Niel might have played them to the Doctor and left him none the wiser, if the information that the tune was by Niel was not asked for or given. But it does suggest that there was more interest in his character than his music, at least to the passing stranger, unlikely in any case to be overly familiar with Scottish music.

As it turns out, there has been doubt about which tunes are really by Niel. Even the title page of the first collection (1784), bearing the words "by Niel Gow" was criticized by John Glen because such an attribution gave "good grounds for supposing that all the tunes were claimed by Niel Gow, if not otherwise stated . . ."[20] However, the full title reads "*A Collection of Strathspey Reels with a Bass for the Violoncello or Harpsichord Most humbly Dedicated to her Grace the Dutchess of Athole by Niel Gow at Dunkeld*", as easily read as a collection simply dedicated by Niel to the Duchess (incidentally a Scottish first, this dedication, and a useful way of obtaining patronage).

Glen may have been peeved that only three composers were actually named in the work, Niel Gow ("Niel Gow's Lamentation for Abercarney"), and two gentlemen amateurs, Sir Alexander Don and William Nisbet. But surely no Scots at the time would have ever thought that Niel was claiming that he had composed "Tulloch-gorum", "Stumpie", or "This is not my ain House", for instance, which had long been current. All could be found in David Young's MSS fifty years earlier.

The Gows have been justly criticized for seldom attaching the names of composers to the music they published, and being rather arbitrary about authorship even when they did. But this is unlikely to irritate fiddlers, who do not have to know who wrote a tune in order to play it.

Indeed, Niel suffered from his tunes being anonymous as much, if not more, than most, particularly in the light of later attacks on his honesty about writing what he claimed. It was most likely the era's obligatory affectation of modesty and humility about one's skills, unknown in our modern world, which prevented Niel from claiming more of his own works at the outset. Twenty-eight tunes in the first collection were in later editions credited to him; thirteen in the second collection, later, compared with two originally; five in the third, versus two, and thirteen in the fourth, by which time it had been realized that if Niel wrote it, the book should say so.

Niel's delay in claiming his own tunes has given rise to unjust accusations of plagiarism. George S. Emmerson in *Rantin' Pipe and Tremblin' String* and James Hunter in *The Fiddle Music of Scotland* both

(Words in brackets are the correct titles; others are given by some critics)

Tune in question	Alleged original tune, possible composer and date	First Gow publication	Claimed by Niel	Comments
"Hon. George Baillie's Strathspey"	"Highland Skip," Donald Dow, 1776	1st Coll. 1784	1st Coll. 2nd Ed 1801	Not the same tune.
"Hon. Miss [Mrs] Drummond of Perth"	"Miss Grace Gordon's Strathspey", William Marshall, 1781	1st Coll. [2nd Coll.] 1788	2nd Coll. 2nd Ed. 1803	No such title in Marshall.
"Lady Grace Douglas"	"Mrs [Mr] Gray of Carse", Chas. Duff, c. 1790	3rd Coll. 1792	Never	No composer given in Duff. (The date of his collection is uncertain).
"Miss Drummond of Perth"	"Miss Sarah Drummond of Perth", Malcolm McDonald, 1789	3rd Coll. 1792	3rd Coll. 2nd Ed. 1807	No composer given in McDonald.
"Miss [Mrs] Minzies of Culdare"	"Braes of Glendochart", Robert McGlashan, 1786	1st Coll. 1784	1st Coll. 2nd Ed. 1801	No composer given in McGlashan.
"Miss Margaret Graham of Inchbrakie"	"Marquis of Huntly's Reel, A Strathspey" William Marshall, 1781, I	1st Coll. 1784	1st Coll. 2nd Ed. 1801	Second section similar, not identical.

followed John Glen's lead in accusing Niel and Nathaniel of, basically, musical theft. A look at some of the evidence for and against Niel, shown on the previous page, may go some way in clearing his name.

There are several other oft-quoted examples for which it would be fair to show the music to give a clearer idea of the validity of the criticisms against Niel. Gow's "Major Graham" [of Inchbrakie] (ex. 63)[21] (first collection; claimed in second edition) was thought by Glen to be a "plagiarism" of Marshall's "Miss Admiral Gordon's Reel. A Strathspey" (1781, I) (ex. 64):[22]

Admittedly, they use similar motifs, but so do many other

Ex. 63   MAJOR GRAHAM

Ex. 64   MISS ADMIRAL GORDON'S REEL. A STRATHSPEY

melodies, even some by Marshall himself, for instance the beginning of "Lady Georgina Gordon's Strathspey" (1822) (ex. 65):[23]

Ex. 65   LADY GEORGINA GORDON'S STRATHSPEY

Marshall has never been accused of having used "Miss Admiral Gordon" as a basis for that tune, and there seems to be no reason why Gow's reputation should continue to suffer.

Burns thought them sufficiently dissimilar to use each for writing different songs; he also thought Gow's "Loch Erroch Side" (ex. 66)[24] unlike "I'm o'er young to marry yet" (ex. 67),[25] published by Bremner in the 1750s. The two pieces are similar; it is likely that Gow was unconsciously influenced by the earlier piece, but no more than that, although this is of course a matter of personal opinion.

Ex. 66   LOCH ERROCH SIDE

Ex. 67   I'M O'ER YOUNG TO MARRY YET

The most puzzling example is "The Marquis of Huntly's Snuff Mill" (ex. 68),[26] published and claimed by Niel in his fourth collection, 1800:

Ex. 68   THE MARQUIS OF HUNTLY'S SNUFF MILL

In 1781 Marshall had included in the second part of his collection "Miss Dallas's Reel" (ex. 69),[27] here transposed from G to F to facilitate comparison:

Ex. 69   MISS DALLAS'S REEL

Common usage has divided the credit, James Hunter most recently using the Gow title, giving Marshall as the composer but publishing the Gow version. Who actually composed it is still in question. However, it should be pointed out that of all the tunes Marshall republished from his first collection, one of the very few omitted or ignored was "Miss Dallas". Nor did he ever refer to the Gows as having printed that particular piece without attaching his name to it, although in the introduction to his 1822 work he mentioned several other examples of just that omission. Perhaps Marshall, for whatever reason, tacitly agreed to let Niel Gow have the credit.

Musical Similarities

It is in the nature of tonal music to have limitations; restrict it further by limiting the range to that of a violin played only in first position (two octaves and a third), the length to a mere sixteen bars, and one has what becomes in effect an exercise in miniaturization. Confine it to several characteristic rhythmic patterns (say, strathspey, reel and jig) and it becomes almost miraculous that so much Scottish dance music of such quality and individuality exists at all.

Composers from Gow through Marshall to Skinner have been criticized for publishing, as their own, tunes which very closely resemble ones published earlier under different titles and by different or anonymous hands. Some of this criticism has been justified, some has been incorrect, drawing on incomplete knowledge; the remainder will always be in question. Trying to trace the origins of old melodies can be a rewarding and illuminating pursuit. It can also degenerate into a musically intellectual "I-spy", which must be continually guarded against.

It must be remembered how familiar the first-class fiddlers were with their repertoires. Certain musical patterns and devices would have become quite unconsciously absorbed into their playing. Many more sophisticated composers have related stories about composing their first symphony, playing the score proudly to a friend, only to be sadly deflated on being reminded that Beethoven had used the same ideas a hundred and fifty years earlier.

Bearing these thoughts in mind, one should accept the music as a grateful recipient, rather than a judge. Those readers still curious about the original composers of any piece could do no better than to ignore any written surmises without evidence, going directly to the music as originally printed before deciding for themselves.

Niel's Other Compositions

Quite a lot of Niel's tunes are written in the pipe style. Basically this means using a limited compass of nine notes, the range of the highland bagpipes, and the harmonic device called the "double tonic", which the natural pipe scale expresses with the use of two triads. In fiddle music the upper triad can be major or minor, while the lower is always major. Niel's "Miss Stewart of Grandtully's Strathspey" (ex. 70)[28] is a good example of this, the notes A, C♯ and E in the first bar outlining the upper triad, here major, the notes G, B and D in the second bar the corresponding major triad a whole tone lower. The range is from g′ to a″, nine notes:

Ex. 70   MISS STEWART OF GRANDTULLY'S STRATHSPEY

His strathspey "Strathearn" (ex. 71)[29] is another in pipe style, although it has a range of ten notes. Here a minor upper triad is implied by the B♭ in the key signature:

Ex. 71 STRATHEARN

Many of Niel's strathspeys and reels are competent but hardly earth-shaking. They rely heavily on pipe conventions, and often on simple repetition of the melodic material an octave higher in the second section (easy to remember) rather than bringing in new, but related, material. His slow airs express more of his undoubted musical abilities. "Farewell to Whisky" (ex. 72)[30] would have been a real tear-jerker, composed as it was to lament the prohibition of making whisky in 1799. "It is," explained Niel or Nathaniel, "expressive of a Highlander's sorrow on being deprived of his favourite beverage":

Ex. 72 FAREWELL TO WHISKY

His Character
    Niel Gow's Farewell to Whisky

You've surely heard of famous Niel,
The man who played the fiddle weel;
He was a heartsome, merry chiel',
    And weel he lo'ed the whisky, O!
For e'er since he wore the tartan hose
He dearly liket Athole brose!
And grieved was, you may suppose,
    To bid "Farewell to whisky", O!
. . .

[Says Niel:]
I'll tak' my fiddle in my hand,
And screw its strings whilst they can stand,
And mak' a lamentation grand
    For gude auld Highland whisky, O!
Oh! all ye powers of Music, come,
For 'deed, I think I'm mightly glum,
My fiddle-strings will hardly bum,   /play badly, sound like
    To say "Farewell to whisky, O!"[31]   a drone

This innocuous poem by Mrs Lyon, the wife of a minister at Glamis, shows Niel in the stereotyped role of a fiddler who likes his dram. So upset was Drummond, in his *Perthshire in Bygone Days*, by this caricature that he spent several pages in Niel's defence:

The publication of [the poem] has mainly led to the popular falsehood that Niel Gow was a drunken man. It were a matter of regret if the memory of a man – who for half a century was the delight and admiration of the nobles and educated people of Scotland, from the Tweed to the Tay – should, by the indiscretion of an individual who knew so little of him that she could not even spell his name [Neil, in her original], go down to future generations tainted by the unmerited blemish that he was a devout worshipper of Bacchus.

. . . To complete the foolish picture, she says "He dearly liket Athole Brose" because she found . . . a strathspey and title "Athole Brose; or Niel Gow's Favourite", thus concluding, with womanly simplicity, that the brose, and not the strathspey, was Niel's favourite!

"Athole Brose" (ex. 73)[32] is taken here from Gow's *Third Collection*:

Ex. 73 ATHOLE BROSE

(Athole Brose is, according to one recipe, a drink made from the water in which oatmeal has been soaked, mixed with honey and whisky. Stirred with a silver spoon, it is bottled and kept until needed.)

Drummond's indignant horror may have been over-reaction, but he was fighting against centuries of prejudice against fiddlers, dating back to the laws against vagabonds and itinerant musicians, which popularly presented them as drunken and, providing they were capable, no doubt immoral.

Niel Gow's career and character led away from this picture, helping to balance the centuries in which to be a musician, particularly one who made his living at it, was potentially to be outside polite society. There is only one oft-repeated story about Niel and drink amongst all those which have been printed about him; I suspect it reflects more on his abundant sense of humour than on any alcoholic inclinations. Here is a version picked up by Robert Southey, the Poet Laureate, who had little ear for dialect:

Some one was praising it [the "good road" from Dunkeld to Perth] to the Duke of Atholl at whose expense it was made, in the presence of Niel Gow, a performer on the violin of some reknown in these parts; Niel, who was a person privileged to say anything, replied, "They may praise your braid roads that gains by 'em; for my part, when I'se gat a wee droppy at Perth, I'se just as lang again in getting hame by the new road as by the auld one." On such occasions he could manage to keep the road, but it was a zig-zag course, tacking always from one side of it to the other.[33]

Those who knew Niel said he drank little, only water at home, unless there were guests. He was not a teetotaller, though, and knew quality – or the lack of it – when he saw it:

His son Nathaniel frequently sent him presents of shrub and ale. In acknowledging one of them he wrote, "I received the box and twenty bottles of ale, which is not good – more *hop* than faith – too strong o' the water &c. My compliments to Meg [Nathaniel's wife] and give her a guinea, and ask her which of the two she would accept of first."[34]

Anachronisms and Confusions

Many of the stories about Niel, although they may have been based on actual events, contain so many inaccuracies and impossibilities that no credence can be given them, as John Glen pointed out in the last century. One concerns a violin which is supposed to have been given to Niel by a London dealer, when Niel was up with the Duke of Atholl. After some discussion the dealer ("said to have been a Mr Hill") told Niel "I shall give it you if you play 'The Ewie wi' the Crooked Horn', in anything like the style in which I heard it in your own country." Niel played his best, and the dealer presented the violin, "a veritable 'Gaspar di Salo in Brescia'", to the understandably sceptical Gow, who "said to his son, 'Come awa, I'm feared he may rue and take it back'"[35]

It is unlikely this ever happened; W. E. Hill and Sons, the firm of violin dealers whose predecessor might have been involved, seem to have no record of such a transaction, or even a sale to the Duke, as a joke privately arranged between them for Niel. Although there is a violin at Blair Castle, home of the Dukes of Atholl, labelled "Niel

Gow, 1784", which Hills examined early this century, in their opinion "although an old instrument, it was made by some local self-taught maker and is of no real value."[36] Other fiddles which Niel Gow is supposed to have played are still in circulation; indeed, it would be surprising if in his long stint he had only ever played on one. But if anyone wants to look for the "Gaspar di Salo", there is one more clue – inside is supposed to be a label saying "Broken on the ice at Stairdam in 1784, and mended in Aberdeen. – N. Gow."[37]

In another anecdote Niel got a free bow, also in exchange for playing a tune. In 1793 he was supposedly in Princes Street, in Edinburgh, where he went into Penson and Robertson's music shop to look for a bow; nothing suited him. Then he noticed a copy of "Peas and Beans", which he had just published, on the counter. The shopkeeper saw him pick it up and said, "If you play that over without a pause or a mistake, I will make you a present of the bow." Niel played, and the man was astonished at his skill, saying, "You must have seen that piece before!" "To be shoore," said Niel, "I saw it fifty times when I was making it."[38]

Aside from the unlikelihood that an Edinburgh music-seller wouldn't recognize Niel Gow, there are other discrepancies, pointed out by John Glen: "There was no music-seller in Princes Street in 1793 . . . Niel Gow died in 1807 . . . 'Peas and Beans' was not a composition of Niel, but of his son Nathaniel, and was not published in his father's lifetime."[39]

What seems to have happened is that this story, and others like it, arose from a confusion between Niel and Nathaniel. Save for the date, 1793, the story could have fitted Nathaniel perfectly. While there are relatively few stories about Nathaniel, some about Niel make him active in the years after his death. For instance, Niel was described as having led the band at a ball given in the Assembly Rooms when George IV first visited Edinburgh, difficult for Niel to have done, since he had been dead fifteen years. His son, however, did lead that ball, and no doubt this and other stories credited to Niel actually happened to Nathaniel, or were about him. Since his father had such fame, the distinction between the two men was dulled; anything interesting in the fiddle line was automatically credited to Niel, and thus stories about him continued to circulate much longer than they may have in other circumstances.

Lady Nairne's poem "The County Meeting" shows this ambiguity. The lady herself, wrote her editor, "excelled in the Terpsichorean art, her skill in which won the admiration of Niel Gow, that king of Scottish fiddlers":

> See Major O'Neill has got her hand,
> An' in the dance they've ta'en their stand;
> (Impudence comes frae Paddy's land,
>   Say the lads o' our County Meeting.)
> But ne'er ye fash! Gang through the reel –
> The country dance, ye dance sae weel –
> An ne'er let waltz or dull quadrille
>   Spoil our County Meeting.
>   . . .
>
> Afore we end, strike up the spring,
> O' Thulican and Hieland-Fling.   { all four
> The Haymakers, and Bumpkin fine!   { are dances
>   At our County Meeting.
> Gow draws his bow, folk haste away
> While some are glad and some are wae,
> A' blithe to meet some ither day,
>   At our County Meeting.[40]

Lady Nairne (1766–1845) certainly was acquainted with Niel, but the Gow in the poem must be Nathaniel, because the "dull quadrille" was not introduced to Scotland until 1815–16, after Niel's death, by the dancing master Finlay Dun, who imported it from Paris.[41]

Niel and the Aristocracy

Some stories remain which are based on Niel's sense of humour and the equal footing he appeared to be on with the nobility. He was well aware that all men are brothers under the skin; titles mean nothing, unless one lets them. Rather than being chastized for his bluntness, he was applauded. This is not to say that the following stories are verbatim; rather they fall into such a pattern that the attitude they show must have been a basic part of his character.

One such story tells about the Duke of Atholl showing Niel a room in Dunkeld House. Either bragging or complaining, the Duke mer ioned that the varnishing had cost over £100. Unimpressed, Niel offered to show him a room in his own Inver cottage which had cost much more. The Duke duly arrived at Niel's, "only to be shown THE

OLD FIDDLER'S KITCHEN, black and glossy with the 'smeek' of many
hundred loads of peat which the owner calculated came to more than
the sum named."[42]

Niel saw things as they were, not as they were expected to be seen,
confusing to those unaccustomed to such direct perceptions:

> Being one day at Dunkeld House, Lady Charlotte Drummond
> [probably Murray] sat down to the pianoforte, when Niel said to
> the duchess, "That lassie o' yours, my leddy, has a gude ear." A
> gentleman present said, "I thought, Niel, you had more manners
> than to call her grace's daughter a lassie." To which our musician
> replied, "What wud I ca' her? I never heard she was a laddie", which
> while it more astonished the gentleman, highly amused the noble
> parties themselves.[43]

Cynically one could say that they could afford to be amused. One man
is seldom a threat to a settled society, particularly when that man is, in
one way or another, in the employ of that society. But they meekly
accepted what Niel said, and how he said it, despite his having no time
for obsequious fawning. On another occasion, the story runs, part of
the company at a ball in Atholl House negligently lingered on in the
ballroom after supper had been announced:

> Niel, who felt none of the fashionable indifference about supper and
> its accompaniments, soon lost patience, and addressing himself to
> the ladies, cried out, "Gang down to your suppers, ye daft limmers,
> and dinna haud me reelin' here, as if hunger and drouth were unkent
> in the land – a body can get naething dune for you."[44]

His Private Life

There is little documentation about Niel's life in general, much less his
home; but this touching letter, preserved by Joseph M'Gregor,
suggests he must have been an affectionate and sympathetic father. It
was written, presumably to Nathaniel, when his brother Andrew was
very ill in London, where he and another brother, John, had a
music-publishing business.

> If the spring were a little advanced and warmer, I would have
> Andrew come down by sea, and I will come to Edinburgh or
> Dundee to conduct him home. We will have milk which he can get

warm from the cow, or fresh butter, or whey, or chickens. He shall
not want for anything.[45]

Andrew did come home; he died in 1793 under his father's roof.

It is necessary to quote extensively from the *Scots Magazine* article to
see more of Gow's qualities of intelligence and humanity:

> In private life, Niel Gow was distinguished by a sound and vigorous
> understanding, by a singularly acute penetration into the character
> of those, both in the higher and lower spheres of Society, with
> whom he had intercourse; and by the conciliating and appropriate
> accommodation of his remarks and replies, to the peculiarities of
> their station and temper. In these he often shewed a high degree of
> forcible humour, strong sense and knowledge of the world, and
> proved himself to have at once a mind naturally sagacious, and a
> very attentive and discriminating habit of observation. His moral
> and religious principles were originally correct, rational, and
> heartfelt, and they were never corrupted. His duty in the domestic
> relations of life, he uniformly fulfilled with exemplary fidelity,
> generosity and kindness. . . . Though he had raised himself to
> independent and affluent circumstances in his old age, he continued
> free of every appearance of vanity or ostentation. He retained to the
> last, the same plain and unassuming simplicity in his carriage, his
> dress and his manners, which he had observed in his early and more
> obscure years.

Niel Gow's most important contribution to Scottish fiddling is in
some ways his personal integrity and his inner independence. Were it
not for these aspects of his character, I do not believe his personality
would still seem so real and human today, after almost two hundred
years. One poet saw Niel thus:

> Old "famous Niel!" Still many a story runs
> Of his great wit and worth, and jokes and puns –
> A brave and jolly dread-none sort of man –
> Great at the fiddle – glorious at a can –
> To all alike, whate'er their rank and name
> Unchained by fashion – and there rests his fame![46]

Dr Garnett, the visiting minister, captured Niel's unique quality in one sentence: "He has acquired by tuning his lyre what he considers an independence and which is therefore truly such."[47] With this independence, consistent in all accounts about him, the musical gifts which enabled him to produce some outstanding compositions, and a marathon of a career as a working fiddler whose style influenced generations of other players, it is not surprising that Niel Gow is still thought of as Scotland's greatest fiddler. Shortly after his death this anonymous epitaph appeared: "Gow and time are even now,/ Gow beat time, now time's beat Gow." But time, fortunately, has not yet caught up with Niel, who is still with us through his music and his unique example of what a fiddler can be.

Other Perthshire Fiddlers

Some Perthshire fiddlers moved away from their county, like Dow, McIntyre and MacIntosh; those who stayed, although they were understandably overshadowed by Niel, nevertheless were still able to contribute to musical life. Robert Petrie (1767–1830), from Kirkmichael, published four collections between 1790 and 1805; in his first can be found versions of melodies originally for the harp, transcribed from the fiddle-playing of General Robertson of Lude, an estate next to the Duke of Atholl's at Blair Atholl.

Another four books came from Malcolm MacDonald (*fl.* 1785–1800) who lived at Inver and played cello with Niel after his brother Donald died. His first effort contained all his own compositions, according to Glen, while the later ones drew heavily from other composers. John Bowie (1759–1815), musician and music-seller in Perth, published the first descriptions of country dances since Bremner's, although by 1789, when they came out, they would certainly have been superfluous.

Sampson Duncan (*fl.* 1790–1822) from Kinclaven in Fife also worked in Perth, and in other parts of Scotland, fiddling with Nathaniel and Niel (who, on his deathbed gave him one of his fiddles, which Duncan prized enormously). Duncan never reached the heights of having his own collection published, although one of his tunes, "Saunders Brane", appears in many others'. The title refers to Saunders Borlum, from whom he took lessons; Duncan's father was a miller, and Saunders' payment was in "brane", bran or oatmeal.

Two other fiddlers Niel would have know quite well worked on the Atholl estate. John Crerar[48] (1750–1840) was the head gamekeeper, so renowned that his portrait is found in Landseer's painting "Death of a Stag in Glen Tilt". Crerar seems to have had lessons from Niel, who may have encouraged him to compose. Four of his reels, all with Atholl associations, were included in McGlashan's second collection in 1786: "Forest Lodge", "The Duke of Atholl's Forest", "The Banks of the Garry", and "The Bridge of the Garry at Struan". The Gows published another almost certainly written by Crerar. "The Craig of Barn's. A Strathspey" (ex. 74):[49]

Ex. 74   THE CRAIG OF BARN'S. A STRATHSPEY

Peter Hardie (*c.* 1775–1863) is also said to have worked for the Duke of Atholl, although it is not known in what capacity. A story in Honeyman's *Scottish Violin Makers*[50] suggests that he worked with dogs, so he too may have been a gamekeeper, as that is one of their responsibilities. He is supposed to have been born about 1775 and died in 1863, and to have been a cousin of the great Scottish violin maker Matthew Hardie (1755–1826), who worked in Edinburgh. Although Peter's exact birth date is not known, he is considered the first (saving Matthew) in the line of the musical Hardie family, whose most recent members are fiddlers Bill Hardie (*b.* 1913) and his son Alastair (*b.* 1946), who have done a great deal to promote the Northeast style of playing.

A small number of Peter's tunes were published as sheet music in Aberdeen in the nineteenth century. More of his work can be found in his music book, a manuscript in the Atholl Collection at the Sandeman

Library in Perth. It is most likely he too studied with Niel and was influenced by him; certainly his own few compositions show similarities. Although a number of the titles of the tunes he copied are in Gaelic, supporting his nick-name "Highland Hardie", his own compositions are in English; an attractive slow air is "Peter Hardie's Lament for Sir M. Dick" (ex. 75):[51]

Ex. 75 PETER HARDIE'S LAMENT FOR SIR M. DICK

The final local fiddler mentioned here is one Niel might have known in his old age, when Duncan M'Kerracher (1796–1873) was a child. He was born in Inver and published three books of tunes, some of his own compositions, others by a Captain Daniel Menzies, who had died by the time M'Kerracher printed them (without his name attached). Although M'Kerracher was styled "The Atholl Paganini", his showmanship excelled his musicianship (thence perhaps the title?); the high point of his performances was apparently his playing while wearing a Masonic apron. For much of his life he lived in Niel's old cottage at Inver; the comparison between the two ends there, Niel having overshadowed better men than Duncan, during his own time, and up to the present.

CHAPTER SIX

Nathaniel Gow

(1763–1831)

Gow's fiddle suddenly burst forth from [where] he had established his little orchestra. All were of course silent "as through his dear strathspeys he bore with Highland rage." . . . He changed his strain to an adagio, and suffered his music to die away in the plaintive notes of Roslin Castle. . . .

"He is his father's own son," said Touchwood. . . . "It is many a long year since I listened to old Niel at Inver, and, to say the truth, spent a night with him over pancakes and Athole brose; and I never expected to hear his match again in my lifetime."[1]

Sir Walter Scott, *St. Ronan's Well*

NATHANIEL GOW WAS Niel's second youngest, born at Inver. His father is said to have taught him on the same kit he had used, a practical substitute for a half-sized fiddle. Soon he was sent to Edinburgh, perhaps to stay with his brother William, where he continued to study, violin with Robert MacIntosh and Alexander McGlashan, and cello with Joseph Reinagle. His first professional appearance was, according to Glen, with McGlashan in a band Nathaniel more or less later inherited, and led for almost forty years.

He was well-established in Edinburgh by 1782. That year he was appointed one of His Majesty's trumpeters in Scotland, and gained a place as musician to the Edinburgh Musical Society. It would have been simple indeed for him to study with the teachers he had, since all were employed by the Society, as were Daniel Dow, Robert Ross, William Napier, Pietro Urbani, Domenico Corri and J. G. C. Schetky; all contributed printed collections of Scottish music or some of their own compositions to the repertoire.

Playing with the Musical Society would have broadened Nathaniel's musical education, introducing him to Corelli, Handel, Haydn and Scotland's own Earl of Kelly, amongst others. When the Society's minute books cease in 1795, Nathaniel was still a paid member, although for a number of years his salary had been regularly docked, once two-thirds of his pay, for "being late for their rehearsals or not turning up at all",[2] an understandable problem considering the increasing demands his own pursuits made on his time.

The First Gow Collections

Nathaniel Gow was ideally placed to superintend his father's first works through the press: in the capital, he could be in daily contact with the publisher Neil Stewart; any difficulties with the harmonization or presentation of the music could have been solved easily, since he had the cream of Scottish and immigrant European musicians as his colleagues.

It was Nathaniel who in his own words "set and prepared"[3] all of the Gow works, incidentally altering the history of Scottish fiddle music, since there is probably not one piece where his editorial hand has not been felt, not one pristine Niel Gow set in existence. His involvement would at least have included providing bass lines, and no doubt making the music acceptable, in the current style, by adding whatever decorations were suitable. Nevertheless, producing the music as played by Niel would have been the most important aim.

To the first collection (1784), when he was twenty-one, Nathaniel contributed several of his own compositions, probably including some of the variations, a foretaste of things to come. By the third collection (1792) over half of the 57 tunes were his, while his father was represented by five.

In the second collection (1788) he tentatively advertised that he was prepared to sell the Gow works. He gradually consolidated his position and took the next logical step, joining William Shepherd, "a young man versant in music",[4] to form Gow and Shepherd, music publishers, in 1796.

A Band Leader

Like his father, Nathaniel was soon employed to lead the groups which played for the dancing assemblies around the country. By 1797 he had begun promoting his own balls, usually at the George Street Assembly Rooms built in the New Town in 1786. They were infinitely better appointed than the crowded quarters of the old premises off the High Street.

> The accommodation within is uncommonly elegant. The principal ball-room is 92 feet long, 42 feet wide, and 36 feet high. It is lighted by eleven large crystal lustres; it has an organ at the upper end; and in a circular recess on one side, at a convenient height, is the orchestra . . .[5]

The setting may have improved, but the amount of work required from the band was prodigious: "Dancing commenced soon after 12 o'clock and continued without intermission till two o'clock, and finished with the favourite set of quadrilles from the Scotch Airs."[6] This would have been not two, but fourteen hours' playing, with little respite. Nor was that occasion unique:

> Mr Gow's ball on Tuesday was as crowded and brilliant as usual, and was honoured by the attendance of the noblemen and gentlemen of the Caledonian Hunt. The band was excellent, and in the course of the evening many slow national airs were performed, among which "The Lament of Flora McDonald", and "The Memory of Joys that are past" were particularly admired. Dancing commenced about 1 o'clock with the favourite new Country Dance of "The Clydesdale Lasses", and was continued with great spirit till past two, when the company called for "Britannia Rules the Waves", and this whole concluded with "Good night and Joy be with you all".[7]

("The Lament of Flora MacDonald" is said in the Gow collections to have been written by Nathaniel's son, Niel Gow Jnr. James Hogg, the "Ettrick Shepherd", who provided words for it as a song, wrote later: "He said it was an ancient Skye air, but afterwards told me it was his own."[8] It is reminiscent of a number of other tunes, and there are doubts about whether it is his composition, or whether it was an old air which he improved.)

"The Memory of Joys that are past" (ex. 76)[9] is by John MacDonald, a Dundee dancing master:

Ex. 76   THE MEMORY OF JOYS THAT ARE PAST

First published in Charles Duff's collection in 1790, MacDonald's piece, as well as "The Clydesdale Lasses" and "The Lament of Flora MacDonald", was published by Nathaniel in 1822, the same year as the ball at which they were performed. It made practical sense for him to play what he published, thus publicizing the music and creating interest. It worked the other way around, too, so that one reason for the ball would have been to popularize the music to aid sales.

In 1788, his second collection featured a top nine of what the well-dressed Edinbourgeois was dancing to; from then on he produced occasional sheet music "as performed at his annual ball", which usually came out the same week, featuring such topical titles (to his own melodies) as "The Grand Duke Nicholas Welcomed to Edinburgh", "Miss Platoff's Wedding", and "The Earl of Dalhousie's Welcome from the Pyrenees" (ex. 77).[10]

The London Circuit
In England the house of Atholl sponsored the son as they had the father; they set up a benefit concert (where Gow would get the profits) when he was south for a royal wedding; it made £130. And there were always other London visits for the Murrays' private entertainments, like one described by Sir James Murray in 1816:

Platoff [the Hetman, a Russian noble] was dancing a Cossack dance which is neither more or less than a dance which is known in the Highlands of Scotland by the name of the sword dance, and which is extremely elegant. As the Duke of Richmond came [in] with Percy he took a shy fit and stopped, but when I informed the Duke of his reason, he very good humouredly danced a reel, and then Platoff exhibited again. Knowing he was fond of Music, I had Gow's band playing during dinner. . . . Platoff said that the musick was so exhilarating that he felt his spirits mounting and he fancied himself at home. . . . That which won his heart was "The Braes of

Ex. 77   THE EARL OF DALHOUSIE'S WELCOME FROM THE PYRENEES

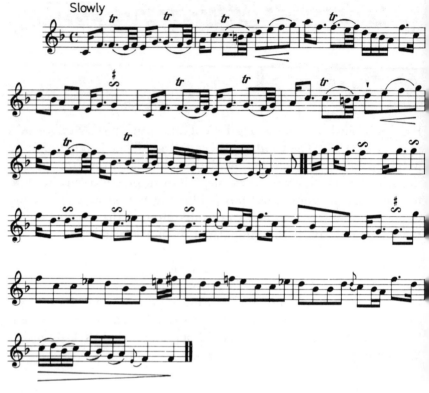

Tullimet" [ex. 35] which he begged to have frequently played. . . .
Tomorrow I have a large party; the Gow's band and a piper in full
costume are to be here.[11]

Playing during the meal has never been any musician's idea of the ideal
ambience in which to perform, but it is unlikely the host's demands,
whatever the size of the feast, would have reached to twelve hours of
continuous music, like Gow's Edinburgh balls.

     He and his band played too at Willis's (once the famous Almack's) in
London, where the best society danced. Gow's music and style of
performance would have found a welcome there if this admonition to
the ball-going public by Wilson, an influential London dancing master,
is anything to go by:

     Snapping the fingers, in Country Dancing and Reels, and the
     sudden howl or yell (introduced in some Scotch parties as partly

National with them) too frequently practised, ought particularly to be avoided, as partaking too much of the customs of barbarous nations . . .[12]

M'Gregor wrote that when in London Gow played often for and with the Prince Regent, "a respectable violoncello player",[13] who in 1822, as King George IV, visited Edinburgh for festivities stage-managed by Sir Walter Scott. At Dalkeith Palace the King paid particular attention to Gow, who was playing there, to the extent that he left the banquet table to speak to him, "ordering at the same time a goblet of generous wine to the musician, and expressing the delight he experienced not only on that, but many former occasions."[14] Nathaniel played to the King at the Peers' Ball, too, and at that of the Caledonian Hunt. He still submitted his bill, adding modestly, "my own trouble at pleasure, or nothing, as his Majesty's approbation more than recompensed me."[15]

His Versatility

Nathaniel's career flourished almost from the beginning. In 1798 the Caledonian Hunt presented "their musician, the famous Nathaniel Gow", ten guineas as a bonus; in 1807 they decided that "for performances at their balls he should receive a stated yearly salary of twenty guineas."[16] Nor was money his only reward. The Earl of Dalhousie made him a gift of a silver goblet at one ball; with it came this note: "An old friend of Gow's requests his acceptance of a cup, in which to drink the health of the thousands who would wish but cannot attend him tonight."[17] Other admirers gave him instruments they knew he would treasure, Sir Peter Murray of Auchtertyre a cello, Sir Alexander Don "a valuable Italian violin".[18]

Basically, though, despite his titled patrons, he was still a musician for hire. He played for balls organized by Corri at his Edinburgh Pantheon, for other assemblies in Perth, Dumfries, Inverness and elsewhere. Aside from his intermittent appearances with the Musical Society, he is listed as a violinist in the orchestra which played for the Edinburgh Music Festival in 1815, not a competitive event, but a series of concerts.

In order to make a living as a musician it was necessary to be able to turn one's hand to a number of related skills; neither the possibilities nor specialities open to musicians today were available to Nathaniel. Teaching was a useful adjunct. He ministered mostly to the children of the nobility, instructing them in violin and "pianoforte accompaniment". It appears from his accounts that at one time "he sent once a week to the Duke of Buccleuch's at Dalkeith Palace, a distance of only six miles, and received two guineas each lesson, besides travelling expenses."[19] Dean Ramsay wrote of Scottish music as it was studied around that time:

> It has a particular character of its own, and requires to be performed with a particular and *spicy* dexterity of hand, whether for the bow or keys. Accordingly, young ladies used to take lessons in it as a finish to their musical education. . . . I recollect at the beginning of the present century my eldest sister, who was a good musician of the school of Pleyel, Kozeluch, Clementi, etc., having such lessons from Nathaniel Gow, a celebrated reel and strathspey performer.[20]

His other interests were his compositions, his publishing and his shop, "the most extensively patronized musical establishment in Scotland".[21] Certainly he offered every possible requirement for the musician, hardly equalled in Scotland today. The advertisement in his fourth collection (1800), published by Gow and Shepherd, "Importers and Publishers of Music", reads:

Patent Piano Fortes	Clarinets by different makers
Grand Piano Fortes	English Flutes of all sizes
Harpsichords	Fifes of all sorts
Spinets	Steel Forks for Tuning Pianos
Guittars	Mutes Brass Box or Ivory
Violins at diff^{nt} prices	Bows for Violins, Kits, Tenors and
Tenor Violins	Violoncellos
Violoncellos	Bridges, Pegs, Tailpieces
Patent German Flutes	Strings, Reeds
German Flutes box tipped and Plain	
Hautboys	

Instruments let out tuned and repaired; Bugle-horns & Trumpets for the Cavalry; Gentlemens Hunting Bugles; Irish Bagpipes, Highland Bagpipes, tipped and plain; Flagaletts, Psalters, Harps. . . .

And last, but not least, music.

The Gow Attributions

Unfortunately, the music presents the greatest problem, for Nathaniel's reputation as a composer and compiler of Scottish dance music, like his father's, is shadowed by the same undeserved reputation as a plagiarist. Cromek inadvertently started it when, in his *Reliques* (1808), he included this note written by Robert Burns:

> Speaking of "MacPherson's Farewell", it is said, Gow has published a variation of this fine tune as his own composition, which he calls the "Princess Augusta". Again, in the same book, "My Tocher's the Jewel", it is said, this tune is claimed by Nathaniel Gow. It is notoriously taken from the "Muckin' of Geordie's Byre". It is also to be found, long prior to Nathaniel Gow's era, in Aird's selection of airs and marches, the first edition, under the name of "The Highway to Edinburgh".

Nathaniel replied on the title page of the fifth collection, 1809:

> To the public. Nath. Gow cannot for a moment suppose that Mr Burns meant anything injurious to him or any of his father's family. The bard evidently laboured under some mistake, which, owing to his death, cannot now be accounted for. Suffice it to say that both assertions in the Reliques are false.

He goes on to point out, justly, that he did not attach his name to either tune. Nor is "Princess Augusta" like "MacPherson's Farewell". And while "My Tocher's the Jewel" may have been taken at some time from "The Muckin' of Geordie's Byre",

> [Nathaniel] found the tune in Oswald's *Caledonian Pocket Companion*, Book III p. 28, as a quick jig; it struck him that it would be pretty if slow, and being without a name, he called it "Lord Elcho's Favourite". Oswald's book was published as long prior to Aird's era as Aird's was to that of Gow.

The disputed tune is called a "Giga" (ex. 78)[22] by Oswald. Gow's version is almost precisely the same, his only additions being the surprisingly few shown above in brackets.

But this, sadly, was just the beginning of the righteous attacks which are typified by John Glen's biographical sketches of the Gows. So full of damning assertions were they (e.g.: "Among the eighty-seven tunes [claimed by Niel] at least a fourth are constructed from old

Ex. 78   GIGA

tunes, or are plagiarised to some extent"; Nathaniel was "unscrupulous", "entirely to blame for the sins of omission and commission", and "plagiarised to some extent") that later writers have taken Nathaniel's bad character as gospel according to Glen, particularly in accusing him of having plagiarised the music of William Marshall.

What the Gows did do with Marshall's music is indeed interesting, the more so that neither Glen nor later writers seem to have noticed that the Gows published many of his compositions years before he ever had them in print; obviously this music was in general circulation by aural transmission, or, more likely, because of the similarities of their first printed appearances compared with Marshall's later versions, in manuscript.

Music by William Marshall First Published in a Gow Collection

Marshall Title	Date	Gow Date	Composer Claimed by Gow
Duke of Gordon's Birthday	1822	1799	Marshall (Gow's first Repository, 3rd ed.)
Kinrara Strathspey	1822	1800	None
Lady Georgina Gordon's Strathspey	1822	1806	None
Lady Madelina Palmer's Strathspey	1822	1791	None
Madame Frederick	1822	1791	None

Mrs Hamilton of Wishaw	1822	1791	None
Newfield Cottage	1822	1788	Included as "Marshall's Strathspey"
The Duchess of Manchester's Farewell to the Highlands	1822	1809	None
The Duchess of Richmond's Strathspey	1822	1791	None

Aside from any controversy about "Miss Dallas" (ex. 69), "Miss Admiral Gordon" (ex. 64) and "The Marquis of Huntly's Reel" (ex. 54), discussed in Chapter Five, made their second appearances in Gow collections with Marshall's name as composer, as did others: "Lord Alex Gordon"; "The Doctor" (called "Gollochy's Farewel" or "Balvenie Castle" by Marshall); "Duke of Gordon's Birthday"; "Lady Louisa Gordon's Strathspey".

There are others the Gows published only once, without Marshall's name:

Gow Title	*Marshall Title(s)*
Johnny Pringle (published by Pringle before Gow as "Miss Jane Campbell's Strathspey")	Miss Burnet's Reel/Miss Jane Stewart's Strathspey, Pittyvaich
Look Before You	Miss Agnes Ross's Reel/ Miss Ross's Strathspey
Look Behind You	Lady Anne Gordon's Reel/ The House of Letterfourie
Marquis of Huntly's Farewell	Same
Mrs Gordon of Bellies	Same/Dandaleith
The North Bridge of Edinburgh	Miss Watson's Reel/Belhelvie House

Finally, there is one tune, "The Bobers of Brechin, a Reel", which appeared in Gow's *First Repository* (3rd ed.) as being "by Mr Marshall", but is found in none of Marshall's collections. Another melody attributed to Marshall is "Jenny Latin", published by McGlashan and only found there.

Ironically, no one ever suggested that Marshall did not write the tunes he later published just because Gow had already put them into print, although that argument is continually used against the Gows' own compositions. What Marshall thought about the Gows' behaviour is clear from his introduction to his 1822 collection:

The author of the following Sheets, now humbly submitted by him to the Public, thinks it necessary to mention that several of his Strathspeys & Reels have occasionally been Published by most of the Collectors of Scottish Music, without his Permission: of this however he does not much complain, especially as he had not till now, any intention to Publish them himself: His only Complaint is their not mentioning his Name along with those Reels of his Composition they Published, which for obvious reasons, were by some neglected, but in particular, their changing the original names given by him, to other names, according to their own fancys and this being not generally known the Author has thought it necessary to apprize the Public of it, assuring them that this work is entirely his own Composition. . . .

In the musical text Marshall mentions only three tunes specifically, "Kinrara Strathspey", "Miss Jane Stewart's Strathspey, Pittyvaich", and "Forglen House". The first two appeared previously under different titles in Gow works, the third in a collection of Charles Duff's, a Dundee dancing master and music-seller.

Nathaniel is of course not excused for having altered the titles and omitted Marshall's name, for whatever reason, but for critics to call it plagiarism (to steal or purloin and pass off as one's own) is surely too strong under the circumstances.

The Gows were not alone in publishing Marshall's music; so did Pringle, Duff, John Anderson, James Aird and Alexander McGlashan, whose third collection included nineteen of Marshall's tunes, many with different names, although he did say they were Marshall's. But, as Glen said of Gow, "Did he have Marshall's permission?"[23]

Nor were the Gows' own compositions safe from being borrowed; Aird, Pringle, Urbani, Watlen and others printed works by them and from their collections with no attributions, but no one has rushed forward to defend the Gows and attack their "plagiarists".

A few tunes obviously remain in limbo until more research is done, particularly on the dating of certain collections, where at the moment it is impossible to say whose version of a tune was published first. Those interested can find more disputed pieces in the *Glen Collection of Scottish Dance Music* and in George S. Emmerson's *Rantin' Pipe and Tremblin' String* (Montreal, 1971).

Nathaniel's Own Compositions
Nathaniel and Niel wrote so many good tunes, whose authorship is

undisputed, that it is hard to understand why they are so frequently accused of resorting to piracy in order to fill up blank spaces in their published collections. One tune which should be included without question in Nathaniel's list of compositions is "The Millar of Drone". Although it was published about 1801 by John Pringle, it has no composer's name by it, while the other two tunes on the same page are clearly identified as composed by Pringle himself. Nathaniel printed it the next year as his own composition, and I have no doubt that "The Millar of Drone" (ex. 79)[24] is indeed his own work:

Ex. 79   THE MILLAR OF DRONE

Fortunately, many of Nathaniel's works remain totally unchallenged, greatly respected and enjoyed, fine contributions to the fiddler's repertoire which reflect credit on his use of his talents. He possessed a wider musical knowledge and theoretical background than his father, although he never branched out into classical types of composition beyond variations, as did some of his contemporaries.

But it must have been a strain that, from a combination of pride and necessity (as Sir Walter Scott was forced to do with his writings in his later years), he had to turn out collections of dance music every few years, as well as sheet music which, to be successful, had to capture the public's fancy. One way of accomplishing this was by dedicating collections to the nobility (a practice initiated in Scotland by the Gows), who could be counted on to buy them and give some away to their friends. Society belles, too, remained in firm favour as dedicatees of individual pieces. What must at the time have given those ladies a passing glow to their vanity is now usually their only memorial. Some of these tunes are "Miss Johnston of Hilton", "Mrs Wemyss of Cuttlehill", and "Lady Elizabeth Lindsay's Strathspey" (ex. 80):[25]

Ex. 80   LADY ELIZABETH LINDSAY'S STRATHSPEY

Nor were the gentlemen ignored; Sir George Clerk of Penicuik, Burns's friend Major Logan, himself a fiddler and composer in a small way, and Master Frances Sitwell all received their musical compliments from Nathaniel in his compositions, as did an Edinburgh dancing master in "Mr Barnard's Reel" (ex. 81):[26]

Ex. 81   MR BARNARD'S REEL

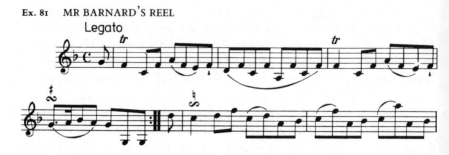

A name which appears often in the Gow Collections (indeed, the fourth is dedicated to him) is Hugh Montgomerie, or Montgomery, the Earl of Eglinton, himself an amateur composer, an anonymous collection of whose works Nathaniel published, on his instructions, as "by a Gentleman" [1795]. For him Nathaniel wrote "Coilsfield House" (ex. 82),[27] named after the Earl's Ayrshire home:

Ex. 82   COILSFIELD HOUSE

For the Fife Hunt, by whom he was employed to play for their balls, Nathaniel wrote the perennial favourite "Largo's Fairy Dance" (ex. 83),[28] here in C, its original key:

Ex. 83   LARGO'S FAIRY DANCE

Naturally, he wrote tunes with titles having to do with his own family, such as "Long Life to Stepmothers" and "Niel Gow's Fiddle" (ex. 84):[29]

Ex. 84   NIEL GOW'S FIDDLE

Nathaniel's life and work have never been as well known, except in his own lifetime, as his father's. His own compositions have become under-rated, possibly because of his father's stronger image, possibly because they are relatively inaccessible (some lacking his name the first time they were printed, as many of his father's did) and because they are scattered through so many collections, never having been published together like, say, the music of Marshall. Beyond that, had Nathaniel not been in Edinburgh to see all the Gow publications into print, it is probable that much of the music his father composed and collected, and which is contained in them, would have died with him. Finally, the immense amount of Scottish music he published over the years, twenty collections at a modest count (including those by "Niel Gow and Sons") and much sheet music, must put today's fiddlers ever in his debt.

Nathaniel's Final Years
The aim of the Gow publications generally was stated in the preface to the *Second Repository* in 1802:

> The original Scotch Strathspeys, Reels and Jigs of which this Collection consists, are brought forward with a view to serve as a Standard of those National Tunes and Dances, for we cannot avoid mentioning, that in every part of Scotland where we have occasionally been, and from every observation we were able to make [we] have not once met with two Professional Musicians who play the Same notes of any Tune. This being the case, the Standard now proposed, will, we hope, appear abundantly apparent; and that a conformity in playing those tunes, may with great propriety be adopted.

Nathaniel did succeed partially in his aim; at least, he standardized the titles of many popular pieces. No doubt the popularity of the Gow collections would have to some extent regularized the notes of the music, as well.

But in financial terms, in the long run, he was unsuccessful. His business of Gow and Shepherd, the ambitious music shop, failed in 1814, two years after his partner's death. Nathaniel went on to form a number of unfruitful collaborations with others, including his son Niel, which came to little.

Then too, Edinburgh tastes were beginning to drift away from the Scottish music which had brought him his early triumphs. Novelties like costume balls began to make inroads: "There will be no highland music or dancing, in order that the large room may solely be appropriate for the display of characters."[30] The quadrilles arrived from Paris; Purdie published "The First Set of the Favorite French Quadrilles as performed by Mr Gow and his Band", but Gow never took to them enough to compose any.

"Reels and strathspeys," wrote Dean Ramsay, "have become nearly quite obsolete."[31] Dalyell, earlier, in his *Musical Memoirs*, was more explicit:

> Many of the tunes most effectively enlivening the dance thirty or forty years ago, and then in the highest vogue, have been gradually falling into oblivion. The sterility of the orchestra being remarkably conspicuous in 1829, a list of twelve former favourites sent to the leader proved almost totally unknown.[32]

This had been building up gradually; for Nathaniel the final blow came in 1828, when all his property was confiscated for debts. There is no reason to doubt the words of Joseph M'Gregor, since he was the accountant brought in to handle his affairs, that he "was at one time worth upwards of £20,000", derived from "his balls, teaching, and playing."[33]

His public did not forget him; let their plea on his behalf be the final word on his career, which ended in 1831 after a long and debilitating illness:

> We are glad to direct the attention of our readers and the public to poor old Gow. . . . It may not be improper to mention, that since his last ball, his property has been sequestered and delivered over to his creditors. Of the proceeds of that ball, he received but little, as, to his infinite honour, he paid over the greatest proportion to liquidate his household debts, which otherwise would have ranked on his general estate. We hope it will be favourable to him that the meeting of the Caledonian Hunt . . . may ensure a large attendance. . . . Gow's claims on the public are of no ordinary description, for although the memory of his own exertions for forty years in almost every scene of pleasure and amusement must gradually fade away, yet the melodies he had composed are destined for more enduring remembrance, and will impart joy to the heart, and lightness to the heels, long after he has ceased to require the kindness of his friends, or to hear and feel the praise of his admirers.[34]

CHAPTER SEVEN

The Southern Lowlands, The Borders, and Burns

To Charles Sharpe, Esq. . . . . I am a fiddler and a poet; and you, I am told,
play an exquisite violin, and have a standard taste in belles lettres. The other
day, a brother catgut gave me a charming Scotch air of your composition. . . . I was pleased with the tune . . . and taking up the idea, I have spun
it into the three stanzas inclosed.[1]

Robert Burns, 1790

IT IS HEART-WARMING to think of Burns as a fiddler, but he was
never greatly accomplished. As his sister, Mrs Begg, admitted when
asked how proficient he was, "His playing was like his singing – 'rude
and rough; But crooning to a bodies's sel'/ does weel enough.'"[2]

That he loved the fiddle and its music is apparent from his drawing
extensively on fiddle repertoire to create his own songs, a justifiable
tribute to the appeal of so many melodies. Moreover, his wide
acquaintance with players and composers makes him an invaluable
link between the various musicians scattered throughout the south
and the southwest.

John Riddell

The first of these is John Riddell of Ayr (1718–95), the earliest-known
fiddler-composer to have issued his own works in Scotland. His
*Collection of Scots Reels or Country Dances and Minuets with two particular
Slow Tunes* may have appeared as early as 1766. The single extant copy
of the first edition claims that it was entered at Stationer's Hall, an
early and ineffective way of protecting the copyright of one's music,
and a useful fact for dating early publications. But Stationer's Hall
has no record of Riddell's collection, so its actual date is not yet
known. (Many publishers did not want to go to the trouble or expense
of going through the necessary paperwork, but still printed on the
music that it was registered, to deter those who otherwise would have
soon taken and printed the best tunes.)

It is difficult to imagine what prompted Riddell (or Riddle, as it is spelled in the first edition) to put his own works forward, unless he had been assured by his friends and patrons that his tunes were far superior to those being published by Stewart and Bremner. Bremner indeed might have inadvertently encouraged Riddell by publishing – unattributed, like everything in his collections – Riddell's "Merry Lads of Ayr" (ex. 85)[3] in 1757; he may have helped in other ways, too, since he is on Riddell's title page as selling his music in Edinburgh and London.

Ex. 85   MERRY LADS OF AIR

Some writers assert that Riddell was blind from birth. If so, he would have been precluded from being a dancing master, and may have concentrated his talents more practically on performing and composing, although the skills of whoever transcribed his music suggest that it was Riddell himself who wrote down – and could see – his own MS paper.

Burns, who used Riddell's "Finlayston House" as the music for his elegiac song "Fate gave the word – the arrow sped", is often incorrectly quoted as having called Riddell "that great bard-born genius of the family of Glencarnock". According to James C. Dick (*Songs of Robert Burns*) to whose research this chapter is indebted, John Riddell was really praised by Robert Riddel, who noted that comment on one of the blank interleaved pages of his copy of the *Scots Musical Museum*. Cromek, in his *Reliques*, extracted the compliment and said it had been made by Burns.

Robert Riddel (d. 1794)

Captain Robert Riddel (or Riddell) of Glenriddell, an amateur antiquary and musician whose family home was at Friar's Carse, was well-acquainted with Burns, who at one time had a farm at nearby Ellisland. Although Burns used three of Riddel's melodies for his songs, his compositions are of little merit compared with his useful *Collection of Scotch, Galwegian, and Border Tunes* (1794), which gives information on the melodies, "collected in various parts of Scotland and on the Borders; for the Selectors amusement, and chiefly wrote from Performers, who could not write or read Music".

One of these fiddlers was John Cowan, according to Riddel

a very noted performer on the Fiddle, at Newton Stewart in Galloway. He died (as I have been informed,) before the middle of the present Century, having obtained longevity in its plentitude. Old Peter Mac Naughtan Fiddler at Monniehive [Moniave] told me he was taught by John Cowan about the year 1725, and he was then an old man.

Riddel says one of Burns's favourites, "Rattlin Roarin Willie" (ex. 86),[4] (also in the Blaikie MS copy) was composed by Cowan:

Ex. 86 RATTLIN ROARIN WILLIE

followed by variations

John Bruce

Another of Riddel's informants was John Bruce, a "remarkable Reel Fiddler in Dumfries", who provided a set of a "Highland Tune" called "Shan dol Grigrugh". Although not published by Riddel, "Whistle

o'er the lave o't" has often been attributed to Bruce, Burns being the
first to make a (qualified) claim on Bruce's behalf:

> . . . the music said to be by a John Bruce, a celebrated violin player
> in Dumfries, about the beginning of this century. This I know:
> Bruce, who was an honest man, though a red-wud Highlandman,
> constantly claimed it; and by all the old musical people here, is
> believed to be the author of it. [5]

However, Burns's placing Bruce in Dumfries so early does not tie in
with another account by John Mayne. According to Mayne, Bruce
had been born in Braemar and as a Jacobite was imprisoned in
Edinburgh Castle after the '45, until his skill at fiddling helped free
him. Later "his celebrity as a player of Ball-music soon procured him
an invitation to lead the assemblies at Moffat, the Buxton of
Scotland", whence he finally settled in Dumfries. "Although an
admirable performer," Mayne admits, "he never was known as a
composer of music. The air in question was composed long before he
existed." [6]

It has been suggested that "Whistle o'er the lave o't" (ex. 87) [7] might
be in the Blaikie MS, which could help settle the question of its
authorship, but I have been unable to find it in the Wighton copy. Its
first printed appearance was in 1757, either in Bremner's *Reels* or
Oswald's *Caledonian Pocket Companion*.

Ex. 87   WHISTLE O'ER THE LAVE O'T

John McGill

In the interleaved copy of the *Scots Musical Museum* the tune "Johnny
McGill", used by Burns for "Tibbie Dunbar", is "said to be the

composition of John McGill, Fiddler, in Girvan" (Ayrshire). Else-where Riddel described him as the town piper, while Mayne wrote of his being remembered as "an excellent violincello player" and assistant to John Riddell.

What is certain is that McGill was a dancing master in Girvan in 1752, when he wrote down instructions for his pupils for a hornpipe, a jig, minuets, and the following reels and country dances:

Reels	*Country Dances*
Toluch Gorum	Up and war them a' Willy
Cameronian's March	Because he was a Bonny Lad
Doun youn Banks	Old Age and Young
Miss Frazer's	My Wife's a Wanton wee Thing
Miss MacDonald's	Rattling Roaring Willy
Queensbury House	The Cadgers of the Canongate
Your welcome to the Town again	Ephey M'Nab
A Mile to Ride	The Cornal or Backel
The Corporal	The Lads of Dunse
Lochel's	Jock of the Green[8]
Jock Hume's	
Miss Murray's	
Short Apron	
Lady Rothesse's new	
Miss Clark	
Mrs Murray	

It is impossible to know if "Johnny McGill" (ex. 88)[9] is hidden under a different title in this MS, for there are no music examples given, only the dance instructions. At least the list gives a picture of the teaching repertoire of McGill, whose name became attached to this lively jig, here in a setting from a Gow collection:

Ex. 88   JOHNNY MCGILL

Glasgow

It should have been natural for any nearby composer or collector to turn to Glasgow for publication rather than to far-off Edinburgh. But few music books were produced there, and Glasgow contributed little to the development of fiddle music in the eighteenth century, perhaps because it was far behind the capital economically and socially.

Louis de France, who had taught at the music schools in Edinburgh at the end of the seventeenth century, was also employed briefly by Glasgow, which appointed a dancing master in 1705. By the time "Jupiter" Carlyle was at university there in the 1740s the musical scene had hardly changed:

> There never was but one concert during the two winters I was at Glasgow, and that was given by Walter Scott, Esq., of Harden, who was himself an eminent performer on the violin, and his band of assistants consisted of two dancing-school fiddlers and the town-waits.[10]

Although there was some dancing, it was not until the 1770s that music publishing began to grow, with James Aird, Joshua Campbell, Archibald MacGoun (or MacGowan) and his son Alex, Alexander Givan and John MacFadyen all bringing out various collections. Aird took sizeable amounts of music from Gow, Marshall and others, as did Campbell, whose second collection, "a number of which are of his own composition", published by Aird, included unattributed compositions of McIntosh, Gow, and Marshall's famous "Miss Admiral Gordon", renamed by Campbell after the city's motto, as "Glasgow Flourish".

At the turn of the nineteenth century James Campbell (a relative of Joshua's?) published a collection of *Marches, Quadrilles, Strathspeys and Reels*, while others like the band-leader William Cunningham and dancing master Mr McIndoe brought out various musical offerings.

But the impact of these men – publishers, collectors and performers alike – on style and repertoire was minimal.

John French (1753-1803)[11]
John French, originally from Cumnock, was one composer who turned to Edinburgh for his publisher, no doubt with an eye to both better quality than Glasgow could provide and increased circulation. There is little information about French, although he may have been related to a William French, some of whose variations appeared in Robert Riddel's collection. Burns either knew John French, or knew of him, for in 1793 he tried (via the town provost) to get copies of French's sets of "The auld yowe jumpt o'er the tether", "Nine nights awa', welcome hame my dearie" and "A' the nights o' the year, the chapman drinks nae water".[12]

French's own compositions, in *Strathspey Reels &c*, were dedicated to Mrs Boswell of Auchinleck, wife of James Boswell, Dr Johnson's amanuensis, and were published in 1803 by Gow and Shepherd "for behoof of Mr French's widow and children", although it is likely that French himself instigated the publication before his death. Two of his tunes deserve resuscitation: "Mrs Boswell of Auchinleck's Reel" (ex. 89)[13] and "Mr James Boswell's Jig" (ex. 90),[14] despite its seeming like a stretched-out version of "Jenny come tie my cravat", found in Playford's *Apollo's Banquet* in the seventeenth century:

Ex. 89 MRS BOSWELL OF AUCHINLECK'S REEL

Ex. 90   MR JAMES BOSWELL'S JIG

Another of French's tunes is "Major Logan's Frollick, a strath-spey", but the first part is too similar to the second half of "Mrs Macleod's Reel" (too well-known to repeat here) to have any great interest. However, the title suggests that French was acquainted with the Major, to whom Burns wrote his "Epistle to Major W. Logan" beginning:

> Hail, thairm–inspirin' rattlin' Willie!   /fiddle-string
> . . .
>
> Hale be your heart! Hale be your fiddle!
> Lang may your elbuck jink and diddle . . .[15]   /elbow

The Major, who lived near Ayr, was himself a fiddler; several of his pieces appear in Gow collections, and at least one set in Simon Fraser's collection (1816).

John Anderson (1727–1808)
Despite his love of and knowledge of fiddle music, Burns seems to have been a most reluctant dancer, although he did have a little fling, as

it were, when he was seventeen: "To give my manners a brush", he wrote later, "I went to a country dancing school. My father had an unaccountable antipathy against these meetings; and my going was, what to this moment I repent, in opposition to his wishes."[16] Burns does not mention the name of his Ayrshire teacher. John French might have been one possibility; another could have been John Anderson, presumed to have worked in nearby Renfrewshire, since he dedicated his first collection (published in Edinburgh in 1789) to the gentlemen of the Greenock Musical Society.

Another edition of the same collection bears a Perth imprint; a John Anderson, unquestionably the same one, opened a music shop there in 1793, which issued it. Anderson, who published at least three collections, containing a few of his own pieces and many others taken from other works and re-titled, finally moved to Inverness. His gradual migration north, contrary to what so many other musicians did, suggests he may have originally come from the Highlands. Even if he did not teach Burns, it is possible that he served as the model for John Galt's caricature, in the *Annals of the Parish*, of one who had taught him "to walk minuets at Greenock":

> One Mr Macskipnish, of Highland parentage, who had been a valet-de-chambre with a major in the campaigns, and taken a prisoner with him by the French . . . took up a dancing-school in Irville, the which art he had learnt in the genteelest fashion . . . at the French court. Such a thing as a dancing-school had never, in the memory of man, been known in our country side; and there was such a sound about the steps and cotillions of Mr Macskipnish, that every lad and lass, that could spare time and siller, went to him, to the great neglect of their work. . . . He was, to be sure, a great curiosity, with long spindle legs, his breast shot out like a duck's and his head powdered and frizzled up like a tappit-hen.[17]

Anderson died in Inverness in 1808, at eighty-one, being described in his obituary as "the best composer of Scottish music since Oswald", an opinion not confirmed by posterity.

John Hall (c. 1788–1862)

John Hall taught dancing in Ayr, and added yet another collection to the repertoire in 1818, with his up-to-date *Strathspey Reels, Waltzes and Irish jigs* (but no fashionable quadrilles; he was a good businessman, and published them separately.) He is one of the few professional fiddlers and dancing masters whose MS books of music can still be studied to provide some idea of what he actually played, and his sources. (Another is John Anderson's, at the School of Scottish Studies, University of Edinburgh). Two of Hall's MS music books are in Glasgow, one in the Farmer collection at the University Library, the other at the Glasgow Museum and Art Gallery, Kelvinhall, along with Hall's kit (reg. No. 45–47f.)[18] (Illustration facing p. 93.)

He must have been a good, workmanlike musician. His music handwriting in the University MS is neat but not painstaking, an advantage when it came to noting down the more than three hundred pieces in this volume. He drew from many sources including, as well as many tunes by unknown composers, pieces by Niel, Nathaniel and John Gow, John Bowie, Finlay Dun, Alexander Givan, William Cunningham, William Marshall, and his own works. Many of these are set for two violins, the "Secondo" part often having double stops, with occasional bass parts scattered throughout the MS. Presumably this was the way Hall often played dance music, depending, of course, on the number of players available. One tune in this MS, "The Ready Penny" (ex. 91),[19] is justly credited to Niel Gow.

Ex. 91   THE READY PENNY

Some of Hall's pieces, as well as surviving in these MSS and in print, found their way into yet another MS "composed and arranged by John Fergusson, schoolmaster, Kirkpatrick", who died in 1829, aged eighty-seven. This, the McNaughton MS, in a private collection, contains music by, among others, Robert MacIntosh, Pate Baillie, the Gows, John Pringle, Daniel Dow and Simon Fraser. From that MS comes John Hall's "The Burns Club Reel" (ex. 92):[20]

Ex. 92   THE BURNS CLUB REEL

John was probably a member of the same family as Matthew Hall, for forty-five years a cellist for dances anywhere between Ayr and Glasgow, his venues often being Coilsfield House and Eglinton Castle, where Lord Eglinton occasionally joined in to play with the band. Matthew's life-long partner was James McLauchlan, "a highlander, who came to Ayrshire in a fencible regiment",[21] the fiddler addressed by Burns in "The Brigs of Ayr":

O had M'Lauchlan, thairm-inspiring Sage,   /fiddle-string
Been there to hear this heavenly band engage,
When thro' his dear Strathspeys they bore with Highland rage;
Or when they struck old Scotia's melting airs,

The lover's raptur'd joys or bleeding cares;
How would his Highland lug been nobler fir'd   /ear
And ev'n his matchless hand with finer touch inspir'd![22]

Alexander Givan (1752–1803)

Aside from the musicians already mentioned, there are two more men who published but seem to have been unknown to Burns. Both were from Kelso: Thomas Calvert, whose collection came out, to no great notice, about 1799, and Alexander Givan, who may have been the same Givan (or Given) who had a music shop in Glasgow before 1800.

Givan was well-liked in the area. "His talents as a musician", his obituary recorded, "have given animation to many a convivial party in the neighbouring districts. His execution upon the violin was considerable, and he was second to few persons as a strathspey player."[23] Aside from his evident martyrdom to the fiddle, he is in many collections as the composer of the jig "Teviot Brig", a bridge near Kelso. A less well-known composition is "Mr Douglas of Springwood Park's Strathspey" (ex. 92),[23] but, like others of his, worth being revived:

Ex. 93   MR DOUGLAS OF SPRINGWOOD PARK'S STRATHSPEY

Burns and Fiddle Music

The welcome mention of a "convivial party" brings to mind Burns's description of a scene which it is unlikely that the good Mr Givan would have ever witnessed, the goings-on in Burns's cantata "The Jolly Beggars", where the fiddler becomes smitten by the charms of a widowed Highland lady who had become reduced to purse-snatching to survive:

> A pigmy scraper wi' his fiddle,
> Wha us'd at trysts and fairs to driddle,   /dawdle
> Her strappin' limb and gaucy middle   /plump
>   (He reach'd nae higher,)
> Hae hol'd his heartie like a riddle,
>   and blawn't on fire.
>
> Wi' hand on hainch, and upward e'e,
> He croon'd his gamut, ane, twa, three,   /tuned up: EA, AD, DG
> Then, in a Arioso key,
>   The wee Apollo
> Set aff, wi' allegretto glee,
>   His giga solo.
>   . . .
>
> Tune – "Whistle o'er the lave o't"
>
>   . . .
>
> *Chorus:*
> I am a fiddler to my trade,
> And a' the tunes that e'er I play'd,
> The sweetest still to wife or maid,
>   Was whistle o'er the lave o't.
>
> At kirns and weddings we'se be there,
> And Oh! sae nicely's we will fare;
> We'll bouse about, till Daddie Care   /drink
>   Sings whistle o'er the lave o't.[24]

There is no doubt that, aside from his genius and humanity, Burns was as keen as anyone for a *céilidh* any time, anywhere, and, with it, alert enough to pick up any new or interesting tunes going the rounds, as shown by the numbers of tunes he collected from friends and acquaintances which were not recorded until published in Johnson's *Scots Musical Museum*.

He also drew on published works to find additional musical sources for his songs, his poems set to music. In putting new words to old melodies he followed the course set by Allan Ramsay, whom he admired, admitting his own leeway thus: "The songs marked Z in the Museum, I have given the world as old verses to their respective tunes; but, in fact, of a good many of them little more than the chorus is ancient, though there is no reason for telling everybody this piece of intelligence."[25]

His feelings about fiddle music and the other unsophisticated music he favoured reflect a reaction to the prejudice against it evident even in his day. Here he is writing to George Thomson, publisher of *The Select Melodies of Scotland* (settings of Scots songs by Burns and other poets to the totally unsuitable harmonization attempts of Pleyel, Beethoven, Kozeluch and Haydn):

> I am sensible that my taste in music must be inelegant and vulgar, because people of undisputed and cultivated taste can find no merit in many of my favourite tunes. – Still, because I am cheaply pleased, is that any reason why should I deny myself that pleasure?. – Many of our strathspeys, ancient and modern, give me most exquisite enjoyment, where you and other judges would probably be shewing signs of disgust. – For instance, I am just now making verses for Rothemurche's Rant, an air which puts me in raptures: and in fact, unless I be pleased with the tune, I never can make verses to it.[26]

The music of "Rothemurches Rant" (ex. 29) gives strains one and two. Burns used strains one and four for his song "Now Nature cleeds the flowery lea".

Many of the other airs Burns used for his songs, along with "Rothemurches Rant", came from printed collections of fiddle music such as Dow's *Ancient Scots Music*, Oswald's *Caledonian Pocket Companion*, Bremner's, Stewart's, McGlashan's, Cumming's and Gow's collections. A few of the tunes are: "Ha a' Chaillich", "The Lads of Leith", "The bonny wee thing", "My wife's a wanton wee thing (ex. 10), "The Miller's Wedding" (ex. 29), "The Dusty Miller" (ex. 6d), "Ballindalloch's Rant", "Stumpie", "Corn Rigs" (ex. 19),

"The Shoemaker's Daughter", and "The Sow's Tail to Geordie" (ex. 94).

The last title is a satirical song of ample invective against George I and his mistress Madame Kilmansegge, whom he raised to be Countess of Darlington. She was so large a personage that the English called her "the elephant"; the Scots' version, the sow, was rather more earthy. Certainly the Jacobite overtones of the original words would have pleased Burns's own style of patriotism. One of the mildest verses goes:

It's Geordie, he came up the town,
    Wi' a bunch o turnips on his crown;
"Aha!" qho she, "I'll pull them down,
    And turn my tail to Geordie."
Chorus: The sow's tail is till him yet,[27] etc.

The tune is an attractive and humorous one, set in a Gow collection as "The Sow's Tail" (ex. 94)[28] with symphony and variations by the

Ex. 94   THE SOW'S TAIL

enthusiastic amateur Mr Nisbet from Dirleton, east of Edinburgh. The symphony, the first four bars, and the last four bars feature in a set played today by Shetland fiddlers, who call the tune "The Soo's Lament for Tatties".

Not all the tunes Burns used were by unknown composers, like those mentioned above. In effect, he chose whatever melody took his fancy, although occasionally his editors' tastes forced on him music he did not care for, or ignored his preferences, substituting their own. Two examples of the latter are Isaac Cooper's "Miss Herries Forbes Farewell To Banff", and "The East Neuk of Fife" (early version ex. 25); although they have since become associated with two of his songs, Burns did not originally intend his words to be sung to either tune.

Burns's best-known song set to a fiddle tune by a known composer is "Of a' the airts the wind can blaw", written to fit Marshall's "Miss Admiral Gordon" (ex. 64). There are others too, amongst them "Niel Gow's Lament for Abercarney" (ex. 62) ("Where, braving angry winter's storms"), "Major Graham" [of Inchbrakie] (ex. 63) ("Ah, Chloris, since it may not be" and Burns's first choice for "My luve is like a red, red rose"), and a number by James Oswald: "The Stolen Kiss", "Thy love is lost to me", "The lovely lass of Inverness" and others.

Burns disagreed with several attributions of the music he used; for example, he did not support Niel Gow's authorship of "Loch Erroch Side" or his "Lament for the death of his brother", first published by Gow in 1788. Of the "Lament" Burns wrote: "This air is claimed by Niel Gow, who calls it his *Lament for his brother*. The first half-stanza of the song is old, the rest is mine."[29] Dick added the information that "elsewhere he instructed the editor of the *Museum* to leave out the name of the tune and call it a Gaelic air. Nothing more is known of the history of the song."

The identity of the composers of other fiddle tunes Burns used will probably always be uncertain, even though the melodies are associated with specific people. There is no proof that Patie Birnie wrote "The auld man's mare's dead", James Macpherson "Macpherson's Farewell", John McGill "Johnny McGill", or John Bruce "Whistle o'er the lave o't", all of which have already been discussed. But a final tune, "McLaunchlin's Scots Measure", could well have been written by John McLaughlan, a fiddler working around Edinburgh at the end of the seventeenth century, some of whose violin sets can be found arranged for lute in the Balcarres MS (*c.* 1700).

Sir Walter Scott criticized Burns for having expended so much of his poetic energy on making songs out of strathspeys and reels.[30] In the long run he has been proved correct, for only a few of Burns's songs, in Scots rather than English, are still sung to their Scottish fiddle tunes: "Comin' through the rye" ("The Miller's Wedding"); "MacPherson's Farewell"; "My luve, she's but a lassie yet" ("Miss Farquharson's Reel") and "Of a' the airts" ("Miss Admiral Gordon"), for instance. Musical and literary tastes change, of course, but it is the singers and their audiences, in each era, who finally decide what music appeals to them, and what will continue to be performed.

It has been much the same for the fiddle music of Burns's home county and the area around it. None of the fiddler-composers mentioned in this chapter has been known far beyond his own territory. Almost all the music they wrote was swamped by the greater productions, both in quality and quantity, of men like Marshall and the Gows. Professional provincial dancing masters and fiddlers like John Riddell, French and Hall should be considered as representing a far larger number of individuals who could be found all over Scotland. They made no great impact, but throughout their lives worked quietly and unobtrusively to play, teach, compose and, in general, contribute whatever they could to the continuation of Scottish dance music.

CHAPTER EIGHT

Into the Nineteenth Century

Captain Macdiarmid, a contemporary violinist of much repute, said of
Fraser, "I never heard anyone make the fiddle *speak Gaelic* so beautifully."[1]

THE BEGINNING OF the nineteenth century seemed to bode well for
Scottish fiddling. The Gow collections were still building up an
impressive number of collected and new tunes for the repertoire;
Marshall's 1822 collection would soon crown his musical achievements; John Hall was busy in Ayr; Archibald Duff had taken up where
Francis Peacock had left off in Aberdeen, not only teaching but
publishing, his subscribers' list showing what a surprising number of
men made some or all of their livings through music, and how many
of them were interested enough in fiddle music to buy it.

On paper it looks as if Scotland were overflowing with musicians
and, as a corollary, with music. While this may have been the case
superficially, there was little creativity left. Perhaps the spring had
dried up at its source, or had been diverted away from Scottish music
as the popularity of the fiddle and of dancing to Scottish tunes
dwindled.

Simon Fraser

In fact, no major figures, either as players or composers, emerge for
many years. Simon Fraser probably comes the closest, although his
work has come into its own only in this century as a source, not
only of dance music, but of many beautiful airs, some his own, others
from Gaelic sources, which have become welcome additions to the
concert repertoire.

He was born in 1773 at Ardachie, near Fort Augustus, in the Great
Glen, that natural fault which runs diagonally across the north of
Scotland from Inverness to Fort William. A one-time captain in the
army, he farmed at Knockie, near Errogy, Inverness-shire, where he
died in 1852. A fiddler himself, his real value lay in being the son and
grandson of musical gentlemen, and having the astuteness to publish
The Airs and Melodies peculiar to the Highlands of Scotland and the Isles

(1816)[2] based on his grandfather Fraser's and his father Captain John Fraser's work as collectors and singers of Gaelic and Jacobite melodies.

Grandfather Fraser was a cattle dealer throughout the far north, keeping company with the best-known men of the country, McKay of Bighouse and Alex Fraser of Culduthel, all three "anxious and interested . . . to obtain the music and words of their best songs".[3] So thorough were they in what they collected (preserved and added to by John) that Simon could admit of pieces included in *Airs and Melodies* that "it is well known I never left my own or my father's house to acquire them."[3]

This was not his debut in print, however. He was already sufficiently interested (and sufficiently well-off, one presumes) to have published his discreet *Thirty Highland Airs, Strathspeys &c* "by S. F★★★★r", in 1795. But he had run into difficulties on the way:

> The Publisher never intended these Tunes for the Press. But having some time ago given his first manuscript of them in order to get Basses made, neither the Basses or Manuscript have yet been returned; this gives him reason to suspect, that they were kept with a view to Publishing them, under a fictitious title, and with wrong names to the tunes. He was therefore advised to prevent that, by making a second manuscript of them for Publication . . .

It is likely, in the light of his comments, that the unscrupulous individual was James Aird of Glasgow, who published Fraser's "Miss Fleming of Moness" in 1794, a year before Fraser was able to do so himself.

Fraser and Alexander Campbell

Nor were circumstances easier for Fraser when he brought out *Airs and Melodies*, since he fell out with Alexander Campbell and several more influential people over the way he publicized it. Campbell was an Edinburgh-based organist and musician, music tutor to Sir Walter Scott (which must have been a long-suffering job, since Sir Walter had an unfailingly poor ear). Campbell too seems to have had his misfortunes, even from his first publication, sheet music which includes "Rev[d] Mr Patrick McDonald of Kilmore" (ex. 95),[4] used later as the melody for Tannahill's popular song "Gloomy winter's now awa'". But the Gows published the same melody, after

Campbell, as "Lord Balgonie's Favourite, an old Highland air", undermining his reputation (unless, of course, the Gows were right).

Ex. 95   REV^d MR PATRICK MACDONALD OF KILMORE

In 1816 Campbell issued the first volume of his *Albyn's Anthology,* consisting of music and Gaelic poetry, unfortunately just prior to Fraser's collection. Both men had sought the blessings of two Highland societies, the Scottish Society, with Sir John MacGregor Murray at its head, and the London Society, with James Hamilton as its secretary. Hamilton sent both books to be reviewed in London, and passed on the criticism – favourable to Fraser but not to Campbell – to Fraser, who had the comments published and circulated throughout Scotland. Fraser takes up the story, explaining what had happened in a letter to Hamilton:

> During my absence the zeal of many of my friends who were highly flattered by the critique of your musical connoisseurs insisted on several copies for their distant acquaintances – whereby I could not but allow them but throw off [print] about 100 to be communicated to none but confidential persons – along with the circular which conveys books from the city booksellers to their customers in the country.
>
> One of these, unluckily, Alex. Campbell has got hold of, and fumes like a madman with vexation – although every person of taste

here, equally condemns and contempts his production. I am, however, told he has got Sir John MacGregor Murray, with more zeal for his protégé than taste for the national melodies, to write you an angry letter on this subject, and condemning the imprudence of my thus publishing the critique, which absolutely never extended further than I have mentioned.[5]

Hamilton, to whom Fraser and Campbell were equally unknown, was furious at Fraser's advertisement, since it mentioned Campbell when he had specifically asked him not to:

. . . What can be stated in palliation of your conduct when in direct contradiction to the terms on which I granted you permission to publish a confidential communication you in serving your own purpose bring me before the world as the Enemy of a man I never saw. . . . I desire nothing more to do with you or your concerns, and shall moreover think it my duty to state the whole proceedings to those respected friends of mine who advocated your cause.[6]

Meanwhile, Campbell was writing to his supporter, Sir John MacGregor Murray, dramatizing his sufferings:

It is the decided opinion of . . . the publishers of *Albyn's Anthology* that the "circular" alluded to has greatly influenced the sale of that work – in so much that scarcely a copy of it has been sold during the last six weeks.
    Captain Fraser, I understand, has enlisted on his side the most of the musicians and teachers of music in this city [Edinburgh]. Mr Nath. Gow, the principal ball fiddler, is using his influence to bring into fashion his former pupil Captain Fraser's publication, and as correspondent Menzies [presumably the books' reviewer] is isolated in London by Mr [John] Gow (the brother of Nathaniel) in order to descry *Albyn's Anthology* and cry up Captain Fraser's Collection the result of these artifices may easily be anticipated – my labour lost – my publishers disappointed and disquieted will naturally decline having anything further to do with my labours. . .[7]

Campbell saved the opportunity to damn with faint praise until a postscript: "Captain Fraser was in commission in the Fraser Fencibles but never served in the line," thus simultaneously questioning his ability, honesty, honour and bravery.

But Murray had already been busy writing to Hamilton about the Fraser-Campbell affair:

> It is unlucky that [Fraser] having so confident an opinion of the superlative merit of his own collection of music, he did not remain contented with the enjoyment of that idea, and the prospect of pecuniary advantages promised by the result of his labours, and by his complacency towards himself.
>
> If as he says "everybody of taste in Edinburgh condemns *Albyn's Anthology*'s author", it does not appear to have been extremely necessary, nor extravagantly generous, to have sought to depress, even lower than contempt, the production of a fellow labourer; especially as the Captain had unluckily announced to the public "that a work of *Merit* proposed by Mr Campbell *occupied entirely a different ground!*"
>
> If so, there could be no collusion of interest, even if, in spite of the above profession Captain Fraser really held *Albyn's Anthology* beneath notice, it might be asked why he went so much out of his way to cry it down and to attach such strong symptoms of jealousy to his own conduct, which tho' perhaps merely intended to preserve the chastity of taste, will not, it may be believed, be ascribed by the public as motives so fiercely patriotic and scientific . . . concerning which I suspect bad taste is more general than Captain Fraser seems willing to admit, for *Albyn's Anthology* has already passed through two editions.[8]

In the long run neither Campbell nor Fraser seems to have suffered unduly, for both works went into several editions, and Campbell brought out a second volume in 1818. What was thought by some to be Fraser's better presentation (even Hamilton admitted Campbell's was "ill-set" and unprofessional) might well have been balanced by Campbell's business sense in giving the trade "the usual large commission" where Fraser offered no such inducement.

Fraser's "Prudery"

The political overtones of what he was publishing were not lost on Fraser – or rather, what he could have published, for he linked no words other than Gaelic titles (and these not always translated literally) to his tunes, in an attempt to steer clear of any accusations of propaganda-mongering. For much of the music originally expressed Jacobite sentiments, as he admits in his introduction:

> . . . Independent of how few of the British Public understand the Gaelic Language, many of the words attached to these airs are known to be objectionable in point of delicacy or loyalty, or frequently both; – indeed, numbers of them are unworthy of notice but for the melody, and an immense collection of the Jacobite Songs was publicly burnt by order of Government, soon after the 1746; – hence it would be unfair to obtrude them, were the Editor possessed of them; and to give them in a mutilated state would be unauthentic.[9]

This attitude, which Hamilton called "prudery", is understandable, the more so since according to Fraser his own family was loyal to the crown, despite his maternal grandfather Thomas Fraser being obliged to receive Prince Charles after Culloden, and then take to the hills. Simon's paternal grandfather was a member of the original Black Watch regiment; his father served in the British Army in the American War of Independence, and Simon was an army man too. When pressed by Hamilton to supply Jacobite lyrics, Fraser wrote:

> I could furnish abundance of interesting matter, but in an unknown language, whereby it could never attract a sale sufficient for indemnification – if translated into English with real justice and truth, it could not fail to give offence, from the strength of the language and energy of the sentiments. When the public mind could be easily fermented, as at present, by the application of a little yeast to it, along with the presence of [Bonar Meinstadt] a lineal descendent of the Stewart family, tho, by a marriage with a subject, and possessed of astonishing credentials, I am told. . . . We shall at present defer it . . .[10]

It is unfortunate that Fraser could not be persuaded, since Hamilton wrote: "My friend Col. Stewart [of Garth] informed me that Fraser possessed a greater number of the poetical effusions of the years 1688 to 1746 in favour of the house of Stewart, than any man he knew of."[11]

Fraser was more diffident about presenting Jacobite material than Hamilton, in far-off London, because he saw obvious danger in reminding Gaeldom of its unsuccessful attempt to reinstate the Stewarts. Not, of course, that all Gaels, Gaelic speakers, were Jacobites any more than all English speakers were Hanoverians, but it was a generalization which some thoughtlessly accepted.

But the safer aspects of the Highland Scot and his culture had been exploited and promoted for some time, as in piping competitions, which had been held since before 1781. By 1817, the same year as the Fraser-Campbell letters, an Edinburgh piping competition "of the Gathering of the Clans", advertised: "The overplus of the money drawn, after paying necessary expenses, to be applied in establishing a fund, for the support of those decayed Highlanders who have competed before the Public for a number of years."[12]

Even the Hanoverian nobility took up Scottish trappings; the Prince Regent first wore the kilt in 1789, the year after Prince Charles's death and, as King George IV, wore it on his 1822 excursion to Edinburgh, where he "offended all the southron Scots". Lady Saltoun stood up for him (in a sense) saying, "We should take it very kind of him; since his stay will be so short, the more we see of him the better."[13]

By the time Queen Victoria set up house at Balmoral, the teeth of the rampant lion had been well and truly drawn. "It is pleasant," she wrote in her *Leaves*, "to converse with the Highlanders, with whom one comes so often in contact in the Highlands."[14]

Towards the end of the century a Gaelic-English phrase-book appeared which, with unconscious humour, would have offered her Majesty a more spirited view of the Gael; the order is unchanged from the original:

An cluich thu 'phìob?	Can you play the pipes?
Thoir dhuinn port.	Give us a tune.
Theid sinn a dhannsadh	We will have a dance.
C'ainm 'tha ort, a chaileig?	What is your name, girl?
An danns thu na Tulaichean?	Can you dance the reel of Tulloch?
An danns thu leamsa?	Will you dance with me?
Thoir dhomh do làmh.	Give me your hand.
Thoir dhomh pòg.	Give me a kiss.
Am pòs thu mi?	Will you marry me?
Am bheil thu 'falbh?	Are you going?
C'uin thig thu rithisd?	When will you come again?[15]

Airs and Melodies

Captain Fraser could hardly have been expected to have guessed that his fears about the subversive aspects of Gaelic were groundless, or to

By Road and River
Country Side and Town
I wander ever
With my Fiddle brown.

Jimmy Dyer

Cumberland Bard.

Jimmy Dyer: A latter-day Birnie, he played in the Borders
across to Berwickshire in the late nineteenth century

A Highland Wedding: shotguns, horse races for the bride, music and *uisge beatha*; something for everyone

Mr Owen's Institution at New Lanark:
where entertainment was made educational

James Scott Skinner in his forties

Skinner: absolutely determined, indomitable

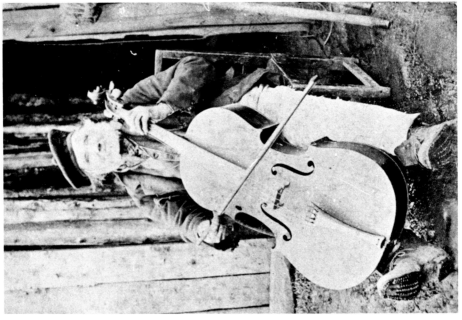

Right: Francie "Markis" Jameson: an old-style "bass" player from the Northeast, c. 1890

Far right: Captain Simon Fraser: combined the Gaelic with the modern

Right: Tom
Anderson and Aly
Bain: A humorous
look at Shetland's
best-known players

Far right: James F.
Dickie: A respected
player of the old
school, aged about
thirty

A century of fiddlers: (*l. to r.*) *standing*: Aly Bain, Alec Green (tin whistle), Mrs James Duncan (née Ivory Dickie), Veronica Burgess, James Duncan, George Webster (violin maker), Alastair J. Hardie; *sitting*: Bill Hardie, Mrs J. F. Dickie, J. F. Dickie, Tom Anderson have ever suspected how much the concept of Gaelic culture and tradition would have changed in so few years. Despite his stubbornness about releasing the lyrics, many tunes with obvious Jacobite associations can be found in *Airs and Melodies*, more than ten per cent of his total 232. (Fraser's Gaelic is inaccurate by modern standards, and his translations not literal. Modern equivalents can be found in the Notes and Postscripts p. 226.)

Some Jacobite-associated music in the Fraser collection

A' Bhean an taigh nach leig u steach am fear a tha air fogairt	Goodwife admit the wanderer
An crann tairadh or Chrois taire	The Fire Cross Song
An Cruineachadh iomlan ludhair	The General Gathering 1745
An Sealladh mo dheireadh do Thearlach	Prince Charles's last view of Scotland
Blar Leine	The Battle of Kinloch Lochy
Cuir a nall an eile' bheag is cur a nall an armacdh	Highland Dress and Armour
Do chinneadh bhi gun cheann	The Chieftain's Lament
Eiridh na Finnacha' Gaelach	The Rebel War Song
Gu mo maidh a thig an crun dhuit a Thearluich oig	Well may Charley wear the Crown
Gun duine aig a bhaile	None left at home but Wife and bairn
Ho ro gur comadh leam' h'uile ni a th'ann	I care for nothing now
Mac S'himi mor a basacha	Lord Lovat Beheaded
Morfhear Shimm'	Lord Lovat's Welcome
Mo Run geal og	A Lady to her Husband killed in Culloden
Nach bocdh a bhi fallach fodh chrag agus ghlean gach moch agus anmoch s aid as ar deidh	The Rebels in their Hiding Places
Nach truadh mo chas	Hard is my fate
N' Comun Rioghail Gaelach	The Highland Society of Scotland
N' cuala sibh mar thachair dhuin	Culloden Day
Och is ochan mo Charamh mar dheirich do Thearlach	Waes me for Charley
Oh Grain air no Briogasan	Deil tak the Breeks
Oh se mo run an t'oigfhear	The Rover [Prince Charles]

Prionsa Tearlach	Prince Charles
Se' n' Riogh a' tha aguin is fear linn	Wha'll be King but Charley
Tein aighair air gach beann dhiubh	The Bonefire
Tha Tairm ann sa Ghleann	The sound of War from the Glen
Tha tighn' fodham eiridh	The rising of the year 1715
Thuair MacShimi n'oighreachd	Lovat's Restoration
Tighearna Chulodair	Lord President Forbes

Four of these titles concern the Fraser of Lovat family, the chief of which was known also by his Gaelic patronymic MacShimi. Two in strathspey style are "The Bonefire" (ex. 96)[16] having to do with the celebrations and festivities which attended General Fraser's election to Parliament, which happened even before his estates (forfeited in 1745) were returned to him, the basis of "Lovat's Restoration"(ex. 97).[17]

Ex. 96   THE BON[E]FIRE

Ex. 97   LOVAT'S RESTORATION

Naturally there are tunes written for and about the Prince, the optimism of "Wha'll be King but Charley" contrasting with the unhappiness of "Hard is my fate" (ex. 98).[18] According to Fraser, the incident which suggested the latter music took place at his maternal grandfather Thomas Fraser's house, where the Prince spent the night after the battle of Culloden. Adjoining the Prince's room was one in which several small girls, including Simon's mother, were whispering. The murmurs so worried and distressed the Prince, who would have been in a highly excited state, that he threw open the door expecting to reveal the presence of men who had betrayed him. When he saw who were there, he said "Hard is my fate, when the innocent prattle of children should annoy me so much."[19]

Ex. 98 HARD IS MY FATE

There are quite a few modern touches in this piece, and it would not be surprising if it were an unacknowledged composition by Fraser himself, writing music associated with the past in the same way that Burns and Hogg wrote poems and songs with historic connections and, by not acknowledging them as theirs, left the reader to think what he would. Fraser makes no mention in his appendix of any source for this melody (as he does for many others), saying only "This delightful melody has been attached to a supposed soliloquy of Prince Charles . . ."[20]

Another air Fraser probably wrote is "Goodwife admit the wanderer", a brief piece of programme music describing the Prince and his companions knocking at a door hoping to find shelter after Culloden, but uncertain whether the people of the cottage are on his side. As Fraser describes it, "the air, at first, represents him as scarcely whispering his request, in broken sentences; but, on finding they were likely to be well received, he acquires more confidence, and the second part seems to picture a composure, however temporary, at their success." Again, no source for this tune is given, only that it "has an interesting incident attached to it".[21]

There are eighteen tunes Fraser admits writing, or which are clearly his from his notes. One is "Niel Gow's Style" (ex. 99),[22] an example of imitation being the sincerest form of flattery:

Ex. 99   NIEL GOW'S STYLE

"The Wedding Ring" (ex. 100)[23] is one of four which Fraser said he remodelled; whatever it was like before he improved it, it has been turned into a lively reel:

Ex. 100   THE WEDDING RING

Dance and song

Of the other tunes which have no sources given, it is likely Fraser wrote the medleys "North Hunt Medley" and "The Rendezvous", "The north side of the Grampians" and "Johnny Groats", "Glenmorriston" and "The Cross of Inverness". In many other tunes Fraser's background information is scanty, as when he writes of "Tyndrum": "The Editor has associated this melody with an event which involved all his connections in the deepest affliction, the death of James Fraser, Esq., . . . near Tyndrum."[24] Without admitting in so many words that he wrote the melody, Fraser's oblique reference to himself makes it almost positively one of his. There are so many other examples of this type that as many as fifty of the pieces need further investigation of background and style on the assumption that Fraser probably wrote them.

His Musical Style

Much of the music Fraser included came to him, he said, through his family. With the attitude of mind common to so many involved in traditional music, he believed these versions were the most authentic and accurate. As a consequence, he felt justified in disparaging both Campbell's anthology and Patrick McDonald's *Collection of Highland Vocal Airs* (1784), his two main rivals, different from his though they were.

Moreover, Fraser saw himself contributing a "restoration of simplicity of taste"[25] to the presentation of Scottish melodies, taking a snipe, in passing, at the "perverted taste" of variations in earlier works by McGibbon and Oswald. But Fraser's sets did not look simple to the antiquary Stenhouse, who criticized several of Fraser's versions in *Illustrations of the Lyric Poetry and Music of Scotland*:

> In Captain Fraser's Gaelic Airs, lately published, a set of this tune ["An Gilleadh dubh"] appears in two strains, loaded with *trills, crescendos, diminuendos, cadences ad libitum,* and other modern Italian graces. This gentleman professes, however, to give the airs in their ancient and native purity, but *ex uno disce omnes!*[26]

Stenhouse is quite correct about the decorations and dynamics; what he called a "*cadence*" is known today as a cadenza. Another of Fraser's sets which Stenhouse censured was "Morag", used by Burns for "Oh wat is ye wha lo'es me" and "Young Highland Rover". Stenhouse complained that Fraser used grace notes, ritardandos and sharp sevenths in place of the perfect fifths found in the "original and unsophisticated melody"[27] as printed in Johnson's *Scots Musical Museum.*

An example of Fraser's treatment of a song from a traditional source is "Tha mi tinn leis a Ghoal", "The Languor of Love" (ex. 101),[28] taken from his father's singing, but probably decorated and presented just as the son would have played it on the fiddle:

Ex. 101   THE LANGUOR OF LOVE

A more straightforward set, largely because it is a reel, is "Clach na Cudain", "The Cross of Inverness" (ex. 102),[29] possibly Fraser's own composition. The *clach* of the Gaelic title is, according to Fraser, the foundation stone of the town, that is, the market cross, where all the business – and the gossip – was carried on:

Ex. 102   THE CROSS OF INVERNESS

The Periphery

Fraser had published his first compositions at twenty-three, William Marshall at thirty-two; but as the nineteenth century lengthened, the older men, who had seen the flood of fiddle music which had been produced when they were young, took over, having determined to add their own contributions some day when they had composed and gathered enough music. Most of these were men from the provinces who supported themselves in other occupations than those of full-time dancing master or musician. William Christie (*c.* 1778–1849) of Cuminestown in Aberdeenshire was a postman, a dancing master and a collector who saved many melodies (including songs, published later by his son Dean William Christie) as well as a composer in his own right of tunes such as "Mr Gillan's Strathspey", found in many collections, and "John Cumine Esq. of Auchrey's Strathspey" (ex. 103)[30]:

Ex. 103   JOHN CUMINE ESQ. OF AUCHREY'S STRATHSPEY

Pate Baillie (1774–1841), who lived in Loanhead, Midlothian, brought out his compositions in 1825. He was a mason, although his nick-name was supposedly "the fiddling tinker". When Baillie was ten or eleven years old, "Lady Helenora Hume's Reel" was published in Gow's first collection. Baillie later printed it as his own strathspey; those who believed he had composed it as a boy said that Niel Gow had taken it down from Pate's playing. His name has been kept alive by "Pate Baillie's jig". Whether he composed it or not is not known; he never published it.

Forfar produced a musical family with the Allans, David, James and Archibald. All were well known as players and dancing masters, David was a composer, and Archibald (who died in 1831 at the age of thirty-seven) is best known for a tune he is unlikely to have written, "The Dean Brig of Edinburgh".[31] Compilers at least from the time of Skinner have written that Allan originally published this as "Miss Gray of Carse"; however, the tunes have nothing in common.

At the same time that fewer new compositions were being put forward, old collections such as Stewart's and Bremner's were becoming increasingly rare. James Davie, an Aberdonian, filled this gap, presenting the first part of *The Caledonian Repository*, a compilation mostly from old works, in 1829.

The two Lowe brothers, Joseph and Robert, originally dancing masters around Montrose and Brechin, did much the same thing in the 1840s, collecting and reprinting the music so it would be available to a wider audience. The brothers and their father, John,[32] wrote several tunes, but their teaching, which spread at widest from Inverness through the Northeast and down to Edinburgh, where Joseph finally settled, was probably more important in its influence.

Interestingly enough, Lowe's collections, on what authority it is not known, attributed a number of otherwise unclaimed airs in Fraser's collection to Fraser himself: "Inverary Castle", "Urquhart Castle", "Darling Annie", "The Scolding wives of Abertarff", "North of the Grampians" and "The Highlands of Banffshire", none of which Fraser said had come to him through his family connections, but all of which he could have written. Fraser was still alive when the Lowe volumes were produced; perhaps, nearer the source, the Lowes had better information than is available at present about Fraser's actual compositions.

Aside from melodies in Fraser's collection, which has not yet been exhausted, it is unlikely that much great new music will be discovered in publications from the first half of the nineteenth century, although some few tunes would reward the diligent seeker.

The decrease in new compositions had various causes, the most obvious being a surfeit of exisiting melodies and a decline in Scottish

dancing as quadrilles, lancers and other new styles became fashionable. The rationale for dancing had begun to change subtly at some
levels, more importance being given to its educational function and
its use as a method of instilling discipline and deportment through
exercise, less to the sheer pleasure of the dance and the music and its
social uses. Dancing had even gained a place in the established
schedule for the young workers at Robert Owen's famous mill at New
Lanark:

> April, 1821 . . . It is difficult to convey an adequate idea of these
> juvenile performers. Suffice it to say, that their dancing would not
> have disgraced an Edinburgh ballroom, and that their style of
> quadrilles could hardly be excelled, even by dancers in the "Champs
> Elysees" at Paris.[33]

Not all those involved saw it in the same light. One young girl from
Owen's institution who applied for work to better her situation said
"that there had been a number of new regulations introduced. That
they had got a number of dancing masters, a fiddler, a band of music,
that there were drills and exercises, and that they were dancing
together till they were more fatigued than if they were working."[34]

In other parts of Scotland the evangelical movement reappeared (as
it has from time to time ever since), an attempt by the church to
encourage conversions and thus suppress vices such as music and
drink. The behaviour of one Argyllshire fiddler after conversion
altered so drastically that the local people thought, since he had
stopped playing completely, that he had taken his fiddle and broken it
into pieces. "But," he said, "that was not true." He had simply given
up "when his eyes were opened".[35] Many fiddles were destroyed,
though, enough on one occasion to provide a bonfire – under the
watchful eye of the revivalist minister.

The general decline of fiddle music throughout Scotland seems to
have continued through the 1840s and the potato famine (not just
confined to Ireland), but it began to rise again with the cult of
Balmorality, unwittingly devised by Queen Victoria and Prince
Albert. By mid-century the musical centre of gravity had, perhaps
with the influence of the visiting royalty, swung round from its earlier
orientation on Speyside and Perthshire, thence to Edinburgh, and was
slowly and very surely coming to rest in Aberdeenshire and the
Northeast.

CHAPTER NINE

James Scott Skinner

(1843–1927)

Talent does what it can; genius does what it must. [1]

J. S. Skinner

BUILDING ON ALL that had gone before was the last great fiddler-composer, James Scott Skinner, whose long and varied career presents a virtual history of the development of the Scottish fiddler from untutored player to concert performer.

Like so many other fiddlers, Skinner came from a musical family. His father had been a gardener at Banchory-Ternan, on Deeside, until the bursting of a gun during wedding festivities (firing shots in celebration was commonplace) took several fingers off his left hand. He then turned to his other talent, music, teaching himself to play with the violin held in the right hand, using a loop on the damaged left to hold up the bow.

In this way he managed to support his family as a dancing master. The eldest son, Alexander (Sandy), was born in 1833; James appeared ten years later, just before the potato famine struck the countryside, born, as he said, "wi' mair feet than stockings".[2] His father died soon after, leaving Sandy to give his brother the rudiments of fiddle playing by rote, when he was about six years old. James then learnt how to vamp on the cello, "'the bass fiddle' . . . transported from place to place in a green baize bag."[3] When he became proficient enough he joined Sandy and Peter Milne playing at dances in the district to supplement the family income, receiving the princely sum of five shillings a month, regardless of the number of dances at which he played.

Dances in the Country, c. 1850

Skinner left his own account of what the entertainments were like in his childhood in a series of articles he wrote for the *People's Journal* in 1923:

The barns in which the dancing took place had earthen floors and were not always quite level. Planks laid on sacks of corn turned on their sides formed the sitting accommodation. Tallow dips mounted on wooden brackets on the walls supplied the lighting, candles not being introduced until about ten years [later].

The preliminary arrangements were made in the neighbouring farmhouse by a Committee . . . who generally saw that a gallon of whisky was included in the refreshments. The . . . dancers divided themselves according to sex . . . the males sitting on one side of the barn and the females on the other . . . but once they were all on the floor they were not decorous, let alone sanctimonious.

Stewards went round at a suitable interval (generally when the "cratur" had made the dancing gallants amiable) and took up a "lawin" (collection) to defray the expenses. Men were expected to contribute not less than sixpence, the hauflins threepence, the "fair sex" getting in free.

After several hours dancing, refreshments were served . . . about midnight. These consisted of ginger wine for the ladies and whisky "toddy" for the men. Bread and cheese were carried round and served out from a riddle, which was made presentable by a wide white cloth.

The musicians at the far end of the barn extemporized a platform out of the fanner. The orchestra generally consisted of small fiddle, bass fiddle (cello) for vamping, and an octavo flute.

. . . About four o'clock in the morning the ball broke up, and many of the lady dancers had to trudge home a distance of from eight to ten miles, and of course, their chiels would have to perform double the distance at least. . . .

I often wonder how I, a boy of eight or nine years, survived the physical strain and the loss of sleep which my duties with the band occasioned. It was nothing unusual for Peter and me to trudge eight or ten weary miles on a slushy wet night in order to fulfil a barn engagement. . . . There were times even when I slept over the bass fiddle at the dances, and kept up the vamp subconsciously.[4]

Peter Milne (1824–1908)

Milne was a great influence on the young Skinner for, aside from shepherding him around the countryside, he gave him his first lessons in playing strathspeys. Milne was, in Skinner's opinion, "one of the grandest strathspey players that ever graced Scotland. . . . He was a genius and a great preserver of the finest of the old Scottish melodies, and a leader of the progressives among Strathspey exponents."[5]

He was born in Tarland, north of Aboyne, on Deeside, and although it is not known where he learnt his own unique playing style, he was equally at home with classical music, leading the orchestras later at the Gaiety and Prince's Theatres in Edinburgh, and M'Gork's Theatre in Leith. According to Skinner, Milne had the misfortune to become an opium addict, which gradually made it increasingly difficult for him to make a living. Finally he was reduced to busking (along with a blind harmonium player) on the ferries which travelled between Queensferry and Burntisland for whatever pennies the travellers might donate. When the Forth Bridge was built even that source of income ended, and he returned to Aberdeen, where he died at the age of eighty-four, having been an invalid for ten years.

Milne was a composer, too, Middleton of Keith having published his *Selection of Strathspeys, Reels* in 1870, which ran into five editions selling more than 15,000 copies. One fine strathspey seems to have been written in collaboration with Skinner (so Skinner credits it in his *Miller o' Hirn Collection*), "The Shakins o' the Pocky" (ex. 104):[6]

Ex. 104   THE SHAKINS O' THE POCKY

Dr Mark's Little Men

It was not long before the young Skinner was removed from Milne's influence and sent to Aberdeen to attend school. But Aberdeen was only a stepping-stone to a much wider world, for in 1855 the city was visited by "Dr Mark's Little Men", "the most famous juvenile musical combination of its time",[7] a group of boys who gave concerts throughout Britain (the laws against child labour not being what they are today, to say the least), directed by Dr Mark.

Sandy Skinner saw an opportunity there for his brother, who duly auditioned for the group and was accepted, entering a six-year apprenticeship with them at the age of twelve. An entry in Dr Mark's prospectus of 1860 describes the group:

GREAT MUSICAL TREAT AND NOVELTY

★   ★   ★

DR. MARK AND HIS PUPILS

Forming a complete Juvenile Orchestra, composed of
little English Boys

FROM FIVE TO FIFTEEN YEARS OF AGE

Who have been taught gratuitously by Dr. Mark in order to illustrate an entirely new and highly successful method of Musical Education, their performance being characterized by the unanimous voice of the Press and Public testimonials as the most pleasing, instructive, interesting, and highly approved MUSICAL ENTERTAINMENT ever introduced to the public.[8]

Under "Names of Pupils" is "Master James Skinner, from Aberdeen, Highlands, 11 years of age", a cellist. In 1860 Skinner was at least sixteen, but no doubt it suited Dr Mark to have his protégées appear younger than they were to gain sympathy from their audiences. Skinner was not tall (even as an adult he was only about five feet three inches) and, like the rest of the Little Men, was no doubt chosen for height as much as ability.

In fact, Dr Mark was well-meaning and well-respected. He fed, clothed and educated the children (often orphans from musical families) in return for their playing at various concerts throughout Britain; Skinner claimed to have visited about six hundred towns and villages before he was sixteen, with the group.

When not on the road, they were based in Manchester, and took lessons at the Royal College of Music, recently formed by Sir Charles Hallé. It was there that Skinner received his musical education, primarily from Charles Rougier, a French violinist with the Hallé Orchestra, who had studied at the Paris Conservatoire. Rougier soon discovered that Skinner had never learnt to read music and, having dealt with that, he taught him theory and technique so well that Skinner acknowledged Rougier as responsible for all his later successes.

After playing with the "Little Men" before Queen Victoria in 1858 – but nevertheless being reduced to busking in the streets of Bristol during one tour because the Doctor's finances were so reduced – Skinner absconded from the band three months before the end of his apprenticeship and, homesick, returned to Aberdeen.

Dancing Master
Once released from Dr Mark, Skinner had to decide what he wanted to do with his life and how he would make his living. Fortunately Peter Milne came to his rescue, introducing him to "Professor" (as dancing masters were sometimes called) William Scott of Stoneywood, near Dyce, who became his next mentor:

> For two nights a week for nearly a year I trudged out and in the four miles between Stoneywood and my home in order to put me in the way of earning my livelihood as a dancing teacher. The "Professor" taught me the quadrilles, polkas, &c. . . . When I had become proficient I sallied forth as a full-blown teacher, carrying my operations away up into the Strathdon region. I gathered a number of classes for which I acted both as dancing instructor and fiddler.[9]

Skinner felt so indebted to Scott for his teaching that he took his last name as his own middle one, becoming James Scott Skinner. In 1862 Skinner won first prizes for dancing in competitions in Belfast and Dublin. The following year, since as a dancing master he was automatically barred from competing as a dancer, he entered the violin competition at Inverness:

> Mr Lowe, dancing master, had the band of the Northern Meeting playing to his children's assembly in the afternoon, and lent his best

players for the violin competition; but in spite of all, I came out first in playing Marshall's "Marquis of Huntly's Farewell". . . . I then played "Auld Robin Gray", and finally conducted the other players . . . in the strathspey and reel "Clach na Cuddin".[10]

This was all good publicity, and Skinner was soon invited to teach the tenantry on the Queen's estate at Balmoral, where he had more than one hundred pupils. John Brown, the Queen's right-hand man, seems to have been on Skinner's side, at least during one large ball Skinner attended:

I remember him shoving me right up to where sat Her Majesty in company with the then Duchess of Atholl.
"Noo, Skinner," he said in quite a loud voice when opposite the Queen (he didn't seem to care whether she heard or not!) "ye're in the richt quarter noo! Shak' yer fit, man! Shak' yer fit!"[11]

(The Queen's official fiddler when she was in residence was Willie Blair, from nearby Crathie, supposed to have been a pupil of Peter Hardie's. After Blair's death in 1884 the Queen arranged to have some of his compositions published, including his best-known strathspey, "The Queen's Fiddler Salutes Mr Troup", written for Alexander Troup, himself a fiddler and dancing master in Ballater.)

Skinner gradually widened the area in which he taught dancing, travelling a circuit which included Inverness, Nairn, Elgin, Forres, Dingwall, Tain, Invergordon and Wick, assisted by his wife and adopted daughter and, after his first wife's death, by his brother Sandy's widow, Mme de Lenglée. To cover such a wide area Skinner would have had to stay in different hotels or boarding houses for three or four weeks at a time, sometimes perhaps using them as a centre from which he could go to other towns nearby, teaching classes afternoons and evenings, then returning to his temporary base.

The sheer number of dances he had to impart to his students shows that this career made more demands on the dancing-master than just getting from place to place. This programme of dances was exhibited at one of Skinner's fancy dress balls in Forres about 1880:

German Schottische and Hungarian Polka; Long Live the Queen, with flags; Reel, Marquis of Huntly's Farewell; the French Quadrille *Polo*; The National Dances – Scotch Steps, Sword Dance, The

Graces, Highland Fling, Cane Hornpipe, Scotch Medley, Jack Tar, Mazurka, Valse, Gorlitza; Quadrille and Scotch steps; Indian Rod Exercises, Valse Country Dance, and Galop, Reel of Tulloch &c.[12]

It is unlikely that he could have taught all these dances to a full complement of young people within the usual twelve lessons; no doubt the more accomplished dancers would have been taught the more difficult dances and helped out afterwards by teaching the younger students the basic steps.

Newspaper reports of Skinner's public dancing displays make it clear that the dancing was not necessarily the most important aspect of Skinner's teaching: "The Indian rod exercise deserves to be mentioned, not only on account of the precision and taste shown by the pupils in its manipulation, but also on account of its value as a means of expanding the chest and improving the figures of the young people."[13] In a Peterhead account what the public expected of a dancing master is quite clear:

The manner in which the scholars acquitted themselves proved Mr and Mrs Skinner's efficiency as teachers of dancing, calisthenics and deportment. . . . Not the least important part of the business of a teacher of dancing is to improve the deportment, and to teach the pupils to keep good order. In both these particulars Mr and Mrs Skinner's scholars gave signs of careful training.[14]

One of Skinner's methods of training his pupils is probably as old as teaching itself. This account came from David Grant, a lad of seventeen when he went to Skinner:

Scott Skinner was rather hasty-tempered, and . . . did not hesitate to rap an erring pupil on the head with his fiddle bow. He was completely democratic in this – the guinea pupils were just as likely to receive a rap as the seven and sixpenny pupils.[15]

The Scottish Violinist
It is no wonder that by 1880, the time of that ball in Forres, Skinner had already begun to try to extend his professional horizons. Aside from playing for his juvenile and senior dancing assemblies (which allowed him to choose and lead the band and perform Scottish solos featuring his own compositions), he embarked on a tour of the

Northeast in March 1879, his venues including Banff, Inverness, Huntly, Elgin, Tain, Forres, Rothes, Nairn, Dingwall and Peterhead. The concert programme for the last is typical; he was supported by Hugh Dunlop, flute (a popular virtuoso instrument at the time) and accompanied by a Mrs Allan:

Part I

1.	Overture – "Figaro"	Mozart
2.	Violin solo – "O' a' the airts"	Marshall
3.	Flute solo – "Du! Du!"	T. Boehm
4.	Scotch Selection – "Auld Robin Gray", "Mrs Scott Skinner", Strathspey "Miller o' Hirn", and "Auld Wheel"	Scott Skinner
5.	Violin Solo – Seventh Air in E major	De Bériot
6.	Duet – "Deh! Conte", from Norma	Bellini
7.	Violin Solo – "Air Varié", Op. 10,	P. Rode
8.	Rondo – "Pizzicato"	Paganini

Part II

1.	Overture – "Rob Roy"	Skinner
2.	Flute Solo – Fantasia from "Faust"	E. D. Jong
3.	Violin Solo – First Concerto, Op. 12	De Bériot
4.	Scotch Selection – "The Marquis of Huntly's Farewell" Strathspey, "The Marquis of Tullibardine" Reel, &c., &c.	
5.	Flute Solo – "There's Nae Luck"	Richardson
6.	Violin Solo – "Carnival de Venice"	Paganini
7.	Flute Solo – "Rule Britannia"	Drouet
8.	Violin Solo – "Keel Row"	C. Rougier

Finale – "God Save the Queen"[16]

Skinner's ability to perform pieces by De Bériot and Paganini certainly came from his early training, which he appreciated and encouraged others to follow:

To become a good player the services of a firm and strict master [are] indispensible. Kreutzer, Rode, Baillot . . . Spohr, Papini are all very fine. . . . A good violin, a good bow . . . plenty of energy and eight hours a day. . . . The writer remembers with gratitude . . . the solid lessons he received from Rougier in Manchester.[17]

It is touching that twenty years after he left "The Little Men" he chose as his final solo "The Keel Row" in an arrangement by his old teacher, M. Rougier.

In 1893 Skinner accompanied the famous piper and dancer Willie McLennan on a tour to the United States and Canada. But McLennan died there, and the tour was a disaster. Nevertheless, the experience seems to have given Skinner visions of a greater future:

> When I returned from America I made up my mind on two points. Firstly, I decided to have done with dancing. As a solo violinist I meant to stand or fall. Secondly, I decided to make the kilt my platform dress . . .
>
> With the exception of myself, there was no Scottish violinist of any eminence at this time. MacKenzie Murdoch, of whom I hold the highest opinion, was still but a stripling, and the field was held by English fiddlers of the calibre of William Henley and Johannes Wolf, so I felt the time had arrived for me to make a bold bid for national laurels. Success happily crowned my endeavours, and, with its realization, I bitterly resented the many years I had wasted as a country dancing master.[18]

Although Skinner equated himself with two of the best classical players of his era, he made his name playing not great concertos, but the music of his own country. In pursuit of his new career he organized his own concerts as well as joining various concert parties (made up, say, of himself, a pianist, an elocutionist, a singer and so on) touring the country. The high point of these activities was probably his appearance with "The Caledonian Four" at the opening of the London Palladium, in 1911, at the behest of Sir Harry Lauder:

> The triumph of the evening . . . was left to Mr Scott Skinner, who treated the audience to a brilliant display on the violin. The appreciation of the audience reached its climax when the veteran danced a step or two to his own strathspeys and reels. The whole turn, which concluded with "Auld Lang Syne", was received with the utmost cordiality.[19]

The heather-and-haggis skit in which Skinner also performed at the Palladium would draw no praise today, but the visit gave him the opportunity to see that even in London he was the greatest Scottish violinist, "The Strathspey King".

From that time on he seems to have worked out a settled routine for most of the concerts he played in, which gave him, as a rule, two long sets to play, one in each half, of his own and others' compositions, under an overall romantic title. In 1921, for example, two of his sets[20] were "Warblings from the Hills" and "Spey's Furies". In the first were "MacRimmon's Weird", "The Braes o' Auchtertyre", "The Queen's Welcome to Invercauld", "Balmoral Highlanders", "Laird o' Drumblair", "Gladstone's Reel", "Our Highland Queen", "Kirrie Kebbuck" and "Spey in Spate". In the second, "Hector MacDonald's Lament", "Cameronian Highlanders", "Gay Gordons", "Forbes Morrison", "The Bungalow", "Bovaglie's Plaid", "Marquis of Huntly's Farewell", "De'il Among the Tailors" and "Speed the Plough", although he changed occasional tunes in each from time to time.

It is difficult today to know just how Skinner sounded when he played, even though he was the first Scottish fiddler to be recorded, and some of his old discs have been resuscitated and put on to long-playing records. But the old recording techniques were crude, and there are many alterations in speed and pitch even in the same brief cylinder or disc. About all that can be said is that he seems to have had excellent intonation and fine bow control, along with a very good left-hand technique. If the apparent recorded speed is anything to go by (the length of recordings was severely limited), he played very fast – faster than is usual today – but, as he termed it himself, "with fire and force".[21]

Scottish music occupied the whole of Skinner's life; perhaps because of this he found it extremely difficult actually to stop performing, although there were probably financial considerations as well. In his eighty-first year he played at least thirty-six concerts, including a Burns supper in London and at the Royal Albert Hall. But time and fashion were no longer on his side, and the tour must have been a great blow to his pride:

Mr J. F. Dickie, New Deer . . . *Private.* I lost £200 on my South tour, but don't publish that as there were greater losses at Culloden.
So lay this scrap in yer kist and no lats giet to daws to pick at.
So courage and humour to the end.

> The Strathspey King
> Bon Accord 17 Jan. 1924[22]

In 1926 Skinner was unwisely persuaded to return to the United States to play in a fiddle competition; after not appearing due to a disagreement about the choice of music, and with the accompanist, he returned to Scotland much weakened, where he died the following year, with little to show for his long lifetime's service to Scottish music.

His Compositions

Skinner came into his own as the best-known Scottish fiddler by taking to the concert platform and playing Scottish music for the audience to listen to rather than staying in village halls and playing much the same music for dancing. This was not entirely new: fiddlers had always played slow airs and laments; Nathaniel Gow played slow airs and strathspeys at various assemblies; Marshall developed the slow strathspey as a solo piece ("slow when not danced"), which Skinner took and expanded into "solo strathspeys", while adding "solo" or "concert" reels and "pastorals". All these gave him the opportunity to demonstrate his playing at its best and most effective.

He began composing early; his first composition, "A Highland Polka", published when he was seventeen, was followed the next year by "The Ettrick Vale Quadrilles", which went into four editions. In 1865 his *12 New Strathspeys and Reels* came out, and in 1868 *30 New Strathspeys and Reels*, both incorporated into his first major work, the *Miller o' Hirn Collection* in 1881.

In this last collection Skinner made the first serious attempt to demonstrate and regularize bowings, especially of strathspeys. He introduced what he called "the straight slur" (♩ ♩), "performed by lifting the bow smartly off the strings, between the notes, both notes being taken in one up or down bow as the case may be. The short note is taken with the end of the bow." (His teacher Peter Milne had earlier used a figure like two short slurs ⌣⌣ , to indicate the same stroke, but carried it no further.)

"The arrow", another device ⤙——— , indicated "the first note is taken down and the other three all up, taking care to re-emphasize the third note". This had the effect of stressing the second or fourth beat, adding distinct rhythmic interest. Another symbol was "the loop" ⌣ℓ⌣ , "used only at the termination of a strain, the bow being dragged along, generally in a down bow." He also added: "In playing strathspeys, the D's, A's and E's should be played in unison [using the open string, and fourth finger on the lower string] then the effect will be greater." (He added elsewhere that these should be "resorted to in passages requiring great fire and force".)[23]

"The Miller o' Hirn" strathspey (ex. 105),[24] named after his friend James Johnston, the miller at Hirn, near Banchory, shows all these devices. (The editorial additions translate his bowings and their effect on the music into conventional notation. Double-dotting has only been included where it is likely to arise from the bow being lifted during the straight slur, but in practice more of the rhythms would have become double-dotted, as can be seen in Skinner's later sets of this and other tunes.)

Ex. 105   THE MILLER O' HIRN

But Skinner did not pursue this notation systematically in subsequent publications, where substantial differences of bowings are obvious. Still, these changes reflect his own attitude and the spontaneity of his behaviour. As he wrote of printed music, a rule that he followed, "The tune in the book is simply a skeleton. You must catch the character by contagion."[25]

His compositions, too, display an uneven quality, not surprisingly, though, since he wrote over six hundred tunes. At best they still sparkle and shine; at worst they are banal, whether wallowing in Victorian sentimentality or imitating snippets of inconsequential music-hall fare. Some of his dullest efforts are his songs, to which local Northeast poets like William Martin, "Gramin" (G. G. Ingram) and others set words; it is clear that Skinner wrote them with singers rather than fiddlers in mind. One or two are still played as slow airs, "The Flower o' the Quern" and "The Cradle Song" (ex. 106),[26] extremely popular when he was alive.

Ex. 106 THE CRADLE SONG

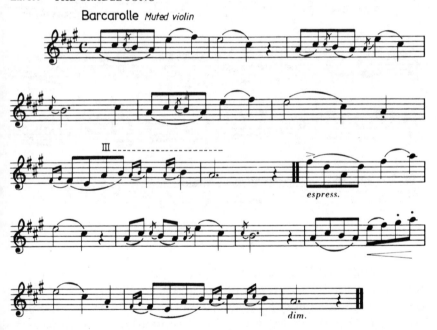

"The Bonny Lass o' Bon-Accord" (ex. 107)[27] (an affectionate name for the city of Aberdeen) is the piece probably best known to the general public. "Its inspirer", wrote Skinner, "was a young girl named Wilhelmina Bell . . . [whose] father used to play bass fiddle for my father." She was a splendid dancer, but was having to work as a servant, for her father had been ruined by taking on a friend's debts. "'Never mind, my lassie,' said I, cheerfully . . . 'I'll ma' a tune that'll maybe keep ye in min' when we're baith deid.'"[28]

Ex. 107   THE BONNY LASS O' BON-ACCORD

"The Bonny Lass", here from Skinner's *Logie Collection* (1888) is followed there by two strains of variations, to which he later added one in the tonic minor, following the practice of the many fiddlers who had, since the eighteenth century, written sets with variations. He wrote seven variations to "The Reel of Tulloch", five to "The East Neuk of Fife" (early version ex. 25), and more to other popular tunes. A simple though effective variation (ex. 108)[29] is one to Nathaniel Gow's "Largo's Fairy Dance" (ex. 83); Skinner's set and variations are in D, while Gow's melody was originally in C.

Ex. 108   VARIATION TO LARGO'S FAIRY DANCE

Skinner's more ambitious fiddle compositions contain technical difficulties which would have been awkward if not impossible for fiddlers without his background. Skinner knew this and, taking great pride in his classical training, felt this put him above the famous fiddlers of the past and above his own contemporaries:

> Captain Simon Fraser . . . Niel Gow . . . Marshall, Reid Rob [MacIntosh], Duncan MacIntyre, Archie Menzies, Peter Milne, Drumnagarrow (John Strachan), Geordie Donald, James Young, Alexander Skinner, Charles Hardie. All these men did good work, but would have soared even higher had they received a good sound training in manual equipment . . .[30]

His most technically demanding piece for the left hand is "The President". It is too long to be printed here in full, but variation II (ex. 109)[31] gives some idea of the type of music Skinner could write and play.

There is no doubt that some of Skinner's abilities both as a player and composer came from his tuition and study; by his own admission he was unable even to read music when he began working with Rougier. The influence of this training, which would have

Ex. 109   THE PRESIDENT, VARIATION II

unquestionably included arpeggios and chromatic studies, is notice-
able in many of his other compositions such as the hornpipe "The
Mathematician" (ex. 110):[32]

Ex. 110   THE MATHEMATICIAN

People and Places

Like many composers of fiddle music before him, Skinner named his tunes after people he knew and places where he had been. "The Mathematician" was a Dr Clark, Cairo, for instance, while the reel "Sandy Grant" was named for Alexander Grant, inventor of the rondello, a round fiddle, and conductor of the Highland Strathspey and Reel Society. Another reel, "The Baker", was written to George Gordon; "The Fallen Chief", a dirge to the dancer and piper Willie MacLennan who had died in Canada during Skinner's tour with him; "Jamie Hardie" is a reel to the Edinburgh violin maker, while the "Laird of Thrums" was to Alex MacPherson of Kirriemuir.

"The Laird o' Drumblair" (ex. 111)[33] and "The Iron Man" were both composed for his "friend and benefactor" William McHardy of Drumblair, who gave Skinner the use of a rent-free cottage. Skinner described his inspiration for the former:

> Suddenly [one night] a tune, "pat" and complete, flashed into my head in his honour. I jumped out of bed [looking for music

Ex. 111   THE LAIRD O' DRUMBLAIR

manuscript paper] . . . but a search produced nothing better than a piece of soap paper, and on this I promptly dashed off "The Laird o' Drumblair". And the tune was dispatched as it had been written.[34]

Travelling so much throughout Scotland, Skinner naturally wrote tunes to places where he had been as well as to his own native district: "Inverurie", "The Burn of Forgue", "Glencoe", "Ballochmyle Burn", "Bonnie Banchory", "Mar Castle", "Tulloch Castle", "The Brig o' Potarch", "The Brig o' Feugh", "The Weeping Birches of Kilmorack", "Balmoral Castle" and the reel "Mains of Gartly" (ex. 112):[35]

Ex. 112   MAINS OF GARTLY

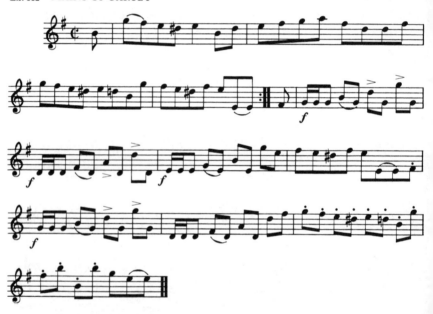

Skinner was, as an understandable product of his era, a sentimentalist; his personal feelings about the music reached even to describing the emotional content of various keys:

C – bold and piercing	A – the fiddle key
A min. – sad and plaintive	F min. – exquisitely harrowing
G – plenty of body	E – brilliant but lacking in body
E min. – sterile, thin	B flat – velvet, very rich and fine
D – splendid body	E flat and C min. – weird, fascinating
B min. – rather sad	and beautifully sad[36]

The descriptions are strikingly reminiscent of comments at a wine-tasting, although it would seem from his compositions that Skinner preferred to celebrate the wine of his country in tunes such as "Talisker", "There's naething like the Talisker", "Gibson's Whisky", "Glengrant", "Johnny Walker" and his famous strathspey "The Glenlivet" (ex. 113):[37]

Ex. 113 THE GLENLIVET

Skinner did not only compose songs and fiddle tunes; he was quite proud, in fact, to have written many pipe tunes, which appear in his own collections and in a bagpipe collection published by David Glen in Edinburgh. "The Duke of Fife's Welcome to Deeside", for instance, is still popular for both fiddle and pipes, although the pipe set differs from the fiddle set due to its limited range and added grace notes.

His hundreds of tunes may have brought him fame, but probably little financial success, as it seems he often had to pay for his works to be published:

The Miller o' Hirn Collection . . . *I paid* Hume and MacDonald Edinburgh about £195 for 2000. Probably 200 copies are now (1915) with Bayley and Ferguson and when sold acknowledged each year. . . . I have had to see the solicitors about getting the money due me from Middleton's estate, but he had many creditors.[38]

"The newspapers are grand upon the Logie Collection. We have yet to pay 150 half guineas . . ." "The Scottish Violinist – belongs to Bayley and Ferguson . . ." "The Beauties of the Ballroom – My own but Hirn, Glenlivet and Bonny Banchory. Published by Middleton – afterwards by Bayley and Ferguson on Royalty system." "Monikie series – I published these six 1/- sheets and paid them (B & F) so *plates are mine.*"[39]

Aside from his *12 New* and *30 New Strathspeys and Reels* (1865 and 1868), Skinner produced the *Miller o' Hirn Collection* (1881), the *Elgin Collection* (1884), the *Logie Collection* (1888), *The Beauties of the Ballroom* (n.d.), *A Guide to Bowing* (c. 1900), *The Scottish Violinist* (1900) and *The Harp and Claymore* (1904). In addition he published much miscellaneous sheet music: lancers, solos, airs with variations, overtures such as "Rob Roy" (a pastiche of Scottish tunes) and several sheet music series, among them "The Bon-Accord Series", "Scott Skinner's Famous Airs", "The Monikie Series" and, in 1922, "The Cairngorm Series".

Considering the large amount of music he produced, this chapter can, of necessity, give only a glimpse of his melodies. Fortunately *The Scottish Violinist* is still in print, *The Harp and Claymore* has recently been reprinted, and others of his tunes not included there can be found in James Hunter's *Fiddle Music of Scotland* (1979), in Alastair J. Hardie's *Caledonian Companion* (1981) and in most Scottish libraries.

Skinner's Influence on Fiddlers
For the totally untrained player, the "country sort", Skinner had little time. To these, in both defence and attack, he wrote a poem which his niece, Mrs Ethel Key (his accompanist for his last recordings in 1922), remembers as beginning:

Hail, champions of the barnyard,
List' to a poor, untutored bard,
Whose muse has often, loft in barn,
Danced to thy dire but unexpressive charm.
Woe sic a dark and lonely spot,
Where men of genius ne'er resort,

And tear the very strings asunder,
'Mongst midnight owls and beasts of plunder.[40]

Nevertheless, perhaps because he felt so strongly about Scottish fiddle music, Skinner did help and encourage many fiddlers over the years. He suggested what to play and how to play it, often – understandably – mentioning his own compositions.

To James F. Dickie, who was renowned for his interpretations of slow strathspeys and for composing variations, Skinner wrote, of the last piece he published, "Johnnie Walker" (1924), "Here's my latest and be careful with the slurring as therein lies the character."[41] He was more detailed – though romantic – to Dickie about his "pibroch" "Dargai":

The pibroch is a sad and dowie strain – pianiste holds on drones – give the feature or large notes due prominence as *large* branches and make the small grace notes like leaves fluttering in the wind – playing them as if they were almost absent. And ever repeating the one desolate thought that fills the heart.[42]

Bill Duguid, an Aberdeen fiddler, received advice about Skinner's tune "The Rockin' Step": "Play four times through with *great force*. This will be the leading strathspey in my future collection, 50% of which are ready. . . . Learn this tune as I want to associate it with the Reel o' Tulloch and Highland Fling."[43] Elsewhere he gave Duguid some suggestions on interpreting several of his other pieces:

Wallace: Very slow and majestic
Ossian: Elegie, delicate and refined and mute.
Bruce: War March
MacPherson: Desperately[44]

Then Skinner added a very personal note: "*Don't drink*, or you will be lost – 'The man that thinks more highly of himself than his art, is a lost man.'" A number of years later, Skinner was still worried about Duguid: "People are drinking others' healths until their own become affected – Ah! Willie beware . . . I like ye well man."[45] But Bill Duguid paid scant attention, and died in an inexplicable accident in 1905.

Another fiddler of whom Skinner thought highly was Charlie

Hardie (1849–1893), pupil of his father William Hardie and probably of his grandfather Peter Hardie (see Chapter Five and Notes and Postscripts). In the *Elgin Collection* Skinner praised him: "The composer considers that Mr Charles Hardie, Aberdeen, is the best exponent of his compositions living." Elsewhere, in John M. Henderson's *The Flowers of Scottish Melody*, Skinner is quoted as having said that Hardie "excelled in slow airs, light reels and hornpipes, particularly The Banks."[46]

Many other musicians came under Skinner's influence, among them John M. Webster of Strichan, who had been a pupil of Peter Milne's; Charles Sutherland, a "great friend and admirer" who copied Skinner's "fiery style",[47] and, especially, John Murdoch Henderson. Henderson, who met Skinner when Henderson was a young man and Skinner in his seventies, preserved and recorded much of his unpublished music and went on to pursue a lifelong interest in all aspects of fiddle music.

These are only a handful of the people who knew Skinner personally. Hundreds more would have taken the occasional lesson from him or played in competitions he adjudicated; thousands more would have heard him in concerts over the years; even more may have been reached by his gramophone recordings, which were circulated from Canada to Hong Kong. All these people would have heard fiddle music becoming freed from the restrictions imposed on it by the requirements of the dance, and its potential being expanded by Skinner's style and technical ability. He was the first fiddler to have a truly wide public, and his influence on the development of Scottish fiddle music cannot be underestimated.

Today, however, his compositions, which he justifiably regarded as the pinnacle of all his achievements, have, as he predicted, consolidated his reputation and kept his memory alive:

> The great work of my life has been composing music for the people of Scotland. I have not composed symphonies for a full orchestra, nor set to music a play or poem . . . to be produced . . . before musical dilettanti and played or sung once or twice a year . . . I am bold enough to hope that many of my airs will live, circulate among, and permeate the life of the people . . .
>
> Some of you may ask if my reputation rests on two airs ["The Bonny Lass" and "The Cradle Song"], and I would reply – By no means, but even if it did, I maintain it is a highly creditable performance to have written one song or composed one melody that is destined to live . . .

The music that reaches and lives in the hearts of the people is the music that they whistle or sing at their daily toil or in their hours of recreation, that the mother croons o'er the cradle and that accompanies her children, a joyous companion, through life. Music thus entering into the hearts of the people proves by this test its real worth.[48]

CHAPTER TEN

Changes

No publishing now, at any rate; no demand.
Everybody busy killing every living thing.[1]
James Scott Skinner, 1916

THIS BOOK HAS, until now, dealt mainly with the men who collected
or who wrote fiddle tunes which were published. However, the
present century has seen little important new publishing, and if this
chapter were to consider only that, its material would be slight. For
today's best-known fiddlers have made their most important contributions not in composition or publication, but in performing,
teaching and collecting. Although the work these men have done
would justify an entire book, something, even if inadequate and a
departure from the preceding pages, should be said about the
changes in the role of the fiddler and the attitudes towards the music
which have taken place this century.

It may be thought that the most significant outside force acting on
fiddling came from the two world wars, which severed the musical
continuity of centuries. Certainly many fiddlers never played during
the war years, and others were tragically killed, never to have the
opportunity to contribute or pass on their music to their children. But
wars and other upheavals which drastically changed the social
make-up of Scotland have always been with us, in some guise: the
colonization, the '45, clearances, famine, migration to the cities,
emigration to other countries. Music has still continued.

Despite the cultural disruptions of the present century, it is likely
that technology has, in the long run, produced more alterations to
fiddling habits. First came records, the cylinders on which Skinner
was the first fiddler to record, then the flat, fragile 78s (until after the
Second World War a record's maximum length was four minutes),
45s, LPs and lastly, cassettes, all of which in the last hundred years
have provided more, better music to wider audiences than even
Skinner could have dreamt.

Radio created new popular musical personalities. Television

followed, giving some small scope for fiddlers, but most televised Scottish music today is played by Scottish country dance bands, where the sound of the fiddle is often lost, overwhelmed by accordions, and sometimes piano, bass and drums as well, a far cry from the music of Niel and Donald Gow, fiddle and cello.

New Presentation

The innovations of recording and radio did not have to create entirely new audiences which were prepared to listen, rather than dance. The groundwork had long been laid; the many laments, slow strathspeys ("slow when not danced") from Marshall, and both forms from the Gows and Simon Fraser, were obviously designed just for listening. Concerts where Scottish fiddle music was performed were not unknown, and by the mid-nineteenth century James Allan (1800–77) of Forfar was a featured player in some of the extravaganzas organized by the impresario Jullien.

It was another technological advance which dominated the last century, the upright cottage piano. Fifty years on, more people all over the world owned pianos than any other instrument. For the fiddler, the piano was a breakthrough; it gave him new dynamic, harmonic and psychological support which helped him make the final step on to the concert platform.

If there were few fiddlers in that Victorian creation the music-hall, its rural equivalent, the concert party, more than made up for it. Skinner, and many, many others, performed in these touring groups; indeed, the major part of his playing was probably done in that type of situation; it is most unusual, even today, for any fiddler to give an entire evening's programme of Scottish fiddle music on his own.

The idea was to give the local community some good, general, and varied entertainment. A typical example is a concert party in Buchan just after the turn of the twentieth century. There were two fiddlers, James F. Dickie from New Deer, and George I. Taylor, who played left-handed. Jim's brother John Dickie played tin whistle, Bill Crichton trumpet; James Duncan was the almost obligatory elocutionist, offering comic relief or dramatic monologues, and the whole group was held together by the pianist, Miss Maria Carr, a fine blind musician from Aberdeen.

Strathspey and Reel Societies

Even as Skinner was publishing his first major collection, the *Miller*

O' Hirn, in 1881, yet another way of presenting fiddle music to the public had been thought of. In that year James Stewart Robertson (who in 1884 brought out *The Athole Collection*) became the president of the Edinburgh Strathspey and Reel Society, the first of many.

Interest in fiddle music then seemed to be in decline; as Robertson said in the Society's minutes,[2] it was "very desirable that this class of music should not be allowed to fall back as undoubtedly it was doing for the past few years". The outcome was the formation of the Society, for "upholding and developing the taste for our old national highland strathspey and reel music on the fiddle."

The idea spread gradually; amongst others, the Highland Strathspey and Reel Society was started in 1903 by Sandy "Battan" Grant, who led it for almost forty years. Alex Sim re-formed the Aberdeen group in 1928, while the Elgin Society, now led by Bill Brown, begun in 1937, grew out of the "Dominies' concert party" which performed around Morayshire in the late 1920s.

Strathspey and Reel Societies today focus definitely on the fiddle and its music, but on a grand scale. Large numbers of fiddlers, sometimes in the hundreds, gather on stage to play; the music is often arranged for first and second violins, violas, cellos and piano, like a Scottish – in all senses of the word – string orchestra. As in any orchestra, there is little room for individual interpretation, but these groups draw vast audiences for their concert appearances.

The Accordion
A simple accordion was invented on the continent in the 1820s, and began to make inroads into popular music; it had a new, different sound and, like the melodeon, invented soon after in England, it was easy to play. By the 1850s it had already been taught in Aberdeen for twenty years; by the time the radio became commonplace the accordion had supplanted the fiddle as the preferred instrument for dance music.

There are several practical reasons for this change: it takes only one person to play for dancing, since the modern button key or piano accordions have both treble and bass; unlike the piano, the accordion is portable, and needs less frequent tuning; it is louder than the unamplified fiddle and, like the piano, melody and harmony can be played by one person. The accordion gradually went on to acquire numerous stops which, like those on the organ, radically alter the sounds produced, giving more variations in timbre, and special effects.

Peter and Daniel Wyper were early recording artists on the melodeon, Will Starr and Bill Powrie on the accordion, but the most famous name is Jimmy Shand, who began his long and impressive recording and broadcasting career in the 1930s.

Fiddlers did not vanish, of course, Angus Fitchet being Shand's player for many years. The player with accordionist Bobby MacLeod was Alex "Pibroch" MacKenzie, and some fiddlers, such as Adam Rennie and Ian Powrie, had their own bands, although they used the "box", as the accordion is familiarly called, too.

Many of the accordionists and their fiddlers published collections of their own tunes, but few seem to have passed into the average fiddler's repertoire, although commercial dance bands naturally still play them. One of the few recent accordionists and pianists whose compositions are in general playing circulation was a Shetlander, the late Ronnie Cooper (d. 1982), with such tunes as "Miss Susan Cooper", "Da Tushkar", "Mickie Ainsworth" and "The Headlands".

Although the accordion has the tendency to overwhelm the fiddle (some modern accordions, incorporating electronic rhythm and bass, even more than most), balance has been helped by the growing use of microphones, which can solve problems of dynamic inequality.

One area where both instruments get along well together are at Accordion and Fiddle Clubs (of which there are now 55) begun in Scotland in the 1970s. These groups usually meet once or twice a month, holding informal concerts which generally feature a soloist or group from outside the area, the remainder of the programme being supplied by local talent. The clubs are especially important as a source of experience for young players, who gain valuable stage presence and have the opportunity to see excellent musicians at work.

Records and Radio
From the very beginning, the impact of records was enormous. Tom Anderson, the Shetland fiddler, of whom more later, recalled his reactions to the impact of Skinner records:

> I was smitten with the gramophone bug in early age, so that I played a lot of Scottish [as opposed to Shetland] music when I was in my teens, played all Skinner tunes. . . . He was the great idol, because he was the man who could rip it out. . . . In Shetland when the strathspey came in, nobody knew anything about it in the country districts, it was a strange type of rhythm. But the gramophones were invariably playing at a higher speed [than the original

performance] and it became a reel, and they adapted it to their own dances. So you get tunes such as "Lady Mary Ramsay" being re-christened under a Shetland name, and played as a reel.[3]

Skinner, of course, was playing as a soloist, with piano accompaniment, as others did later, for instance, MacKenzie Murdoch, Hiram Hosie, and Florence MacBride, and, more recently, the late Hector MacAndrew, Willie Hunter, Bill Hardie, Arthur Scott Robertson, the late Ron Aim, Angus Cameron and Ron Gonnella. Of the last group, almost all have also been recorded playing with Scottish country dance bands which, with their distinctive sound, dominate dance music today.

The Royal Scottish Country Dance Society

The bands' continuing popularity is certainly due in part to the work of the R.S.C.D.S. (which became "Royal" in 1951). This organization was founded in 1923 by Miss Jean Milligan and Mrs Ysabel Stewart of Fasnacloich to collect, preserve and encourage the dances which they feared were vanishing from the countryside. Dancing schools were still teaching step-dancing and country dancing, but the majority of the teacher's time was taken up with the two-step, fox-trot, tango, and other modern, and jazz-related, favourites. To counter this invasion, Miss Milligan and her helpers consulted old sources, among them the Holmain MS and Peacock's *Sketches*, and went into the rural areas to recover old dance directions from those of earlier generations who could still remember them.

The Society enterprisingly published collections, and instructed all who wanted to learn the old – and sometimes reconstructed – dances, attempting to set up standards of performance not only of the steps but of the music. Their current aim of having the music played in strict tempo has clearly influenced the ways in which Scottish dance music is now played:

It is well known that R.S.C.D.S. dancers expect their music to be maintained throughout each set of tunes without the slightest boost or cut in tempo, almost, many others believe, to the threshold of obsession, but there is no doubt the policy reaps rewards for a band which aims to create and keep a strict beat.[4]

In its early days, though, the Society was much less demanding:

"The music should not be played too fast. Strathspey time should be the pace of a horse trotting – Ex.: Road to Isles – and Reel time the pace of a horse cantering – Ex.: Bonnie Dundee."[5] Few musicians today would be much the wiser for that.

Influences of Records on Players

The most obvious influence of recorded music is on repertoire. In Shetland, new Scottish strathspeys were absorbed and turned into Shetland-style reels; in Scotland, tunes which had not been heard before could be learnt by repeatedly listening to them, a process much closer to that of the direct personal contact which has always been a part of tune transmissions. As early as the 1930s William Cameron of "The Cameron Men" (three brothers who lived and worked in Angus), a pupil of "Dancie" Reid, recorded a medley of tunes "that was taken directly from a Skinner record".[6]

A more subtle but perhaps longer-lasting effect of recordings is on style. All the individual eccentricities of playing any piece, rhythmic and tonal alterations, speed, intonation, decorations and, for someone with a quick mind and an extensive playing background, bowings, could be found on a record, a concrete and repeatable example for any who wanted to follow it.

These mechanical aural sources could be said to have taken the place, to some extent, of the many hundreds of printed collections which had flourished earlier. Certainly, being able to hear the music played would have had an overwhelming impact on fiddlers accustomed to learning from other players, and on those who managed to make musical sense out of the bare notes in the printed books.

Some of the information culled from these sources may have been acquired consciously, but there is no overestimating the unconscious level at which music can be absorbed. In the present era, for example, the fiddler Angus Grant's recorded set of "Niel Gow's Lament for the death of his second wife" may have been influenced by "a recording of Hector MacAndrew, some of whose mannerisms can still be recognized in the rubato and ornamentation";[7] sometimes the inner musical ear is at work, and no fiddler is ever unaffected by it.

William C. Honeyman (1845–1919)

It is generally thought today that there are three main styles of fiddle playing: Northeast, West Highland and Shetland. A hundred years ago, however, the picture was quite different:

Coming by rail one day from Aberdeen . . . I chanced to speak to an Aberdeen player, who spoke with the most crushing contempt of the "Forfarshire style" and the "Perthshire style", but further along the line a Forfarshire player entered the carriage, and in talking to him I gently enquired which style he considered the best . . . he promptly answered, "Oh the Forfarshire style, of course." As an impartial onlooker, I must confess that I have never been able to discover any difference in the three styles; the difference has been entirely in the players . . .

The writer here is William C. Honeyman, fiddler, teacher, author and novelist, in *The Strathspey, Reel and Hornpipe Tutor* (1898), based largely on material in his book, *The Violin: How to Master it*, published some twenty years earlier. The purpose of the former was threefold: to provide the first printed tutor; "to preserve the style"; and to compile a standard collection for players of all grades and for Strathspey and Reel societies, with music clearly marked so they could all perform with the same bowing, a reasonable response to that growing movement.

Honeyman's choices of reels and strathspeys are generally uncomplicated sets, arranged in groups of four, alternating strathspeys and reels, all completely bowed. There are a half dozen interesting slow strathspeys, and some study of Honeyman's background, and the sources for his sets and bowings, would be worthwhile. He discusses the driven bow, and attempts nobly to explain one particular effect of some strathspey playing, where, because of the bowing, the accents in the music no longer fall on the beats as in the printed versions, but are advanced. Despite his instructions and admonitions, he is finally forced to admit that "no two strathspey players play the same tune exactly alike – each one scraping away according to his own sweet will." That, of course, is the result of the last of his "points requiring special study – 1st, freedom of bowing; 2nd, intonation; and 3rd, spirit and expression."

Although Honeyman's name is scarcely mentioned these days, he must have had some success in his own time; certainly he adjudicated at fiddling competitions, and players such as James F. Dickie used his *Tutor* as a guide at the turn of the century. So highly was his name regarded by some that after "The Cameron Men" of Kirriemuir were recorded by Beltona in 1934, their music was re-released under a new title: "Honeyman's Fiddlers".

John Murdoch Henderson (1902–72)

Perhaps influenced by the work of early collectors like his New Deer neighbour Gavin Grieg, and the very individual style of local fiddlers such as Dickie, George I. Taylor and others, Henderson, an Aberdeen-based mathematics teacher, set out to record on paper the ways in which his contemporaries played, and what they played, valuable work which is only part of his contribution.

Although basically unable to play, having broken both wrists when young, Henderson had an almost obsessive interest in the origins of fiddle tunes and their various sets. As a young man he met the elderly Skinner; he later edited and published in *The Scottish Music Maker* (1957) many of Skinner's melodies which may otherwise have been lost. It is possible that in some cases his editing and "collaboration" with Skinner may have been heavy-handed, but it was still a useful service.

More important in the long term is *The Flowers of Scottish Melody* (1935), in which he succinctly lists and shows examples of various styles of bowing strathspeys: hacking, cross-cut sawing, cross-bowing, swinging bow, snap-bowing, back-bowing, up-driven bow, down-driven bow, and fore-phrasing, which Honeyman had diligently tried to explain. Henderson recommends three books of fiddle music for study: Skinner's *Scottish Violinist*, Honeyman's *Tutor*, and Kohler's *Violin Repository* (1881–5). The last, edited by Honeyman, included many old standards as well as some new pieces by aspiring fiddlers; the London-born W. B. Laybourne, for instance, contributed sixteen hornpipes.

It was from players, though, that Henderson took some of the meticulously bowed sets he included. One was "after A. F. Skinner", Scott's brother; one came from G. I. Taylor, the left-handed player in the Buchan concert party; another from Joseph Lowe, the Marykirk dancing master; one was Charlie Hardie's, son of William Hardie of Methlick; one of Scott Skinner's was a transcription, indeed, from a Regal gramophone record, and two came from J. F. Dickie, of whom Henderson wrote, "he is my friend and sole inspiration in traditional fiddle music."

James Fowlie Dickie was born at Cartlehaugh, Old Deer, Aberdeenshire, in 1886. Skinner had a strong influence on him, not only through his concert appearances and adjudications, but through one of his pupils, Bill Duguid, mentioned earlier, who gave Dickie lessons for a year or so. James Duncan, Dickie's son-in-law and a fiddler himself, describes Dickie's individual style as a versatile one "in his interesting use of chording, in his variations to the theme, and in his distinctive strathspey bowing style.'"[8] It is a much more rarefied type of performance than is common, especially in the slow strathspeys, with rubato and accellerando and greatly altered dynamics all within the same bar, a miniaturization process, where the maximum musical content is expressed in the smallest space, in the shortest length of time. Dickie was never recorded professionally, although some of his playing has been issued, saved from amateur 1950s tapes.

Certainly Henderson was absolutely dedicated to pursuing and noting down bowing from players throughout the Northeast; stories abound of his following them around, getting them to repeat their sets over and over until he had their bowings as they played them. Nor was he in awe of his sources; deviations from what he considered to be right were promptly dealt with: "What do you mean by playing that? Skinner never played it that way, man! Accent the C sharp, accent the C sharp!"[9] (of the "Braes of Auchtertyre").

Henderson composed, as well, forty of his pieces appearing in *The Flowers of Scottish Melody*. One of these, "James F. Dickie's Delight" (ex. 114),[10] he wrote for Dickie, "a player of great taste and polish":

Ex. 114   JAMES F. DICKIE'S DELIGHT

Unfortunately, Henderson did not get the general appreciation that was due him during his lifetime, perhaps because he was a perfectionist; if he was critical of fiddlers who played the old stand-bys, he was even more so about the interpretation of his own works, and anyone playing them ran the risk of incurring Henderson's displeasure. But his absolute devotion to the music, his scholarly curiosity about the sources, in which he was the natural successor to John Glen, and his single-mindedness, saved many tunes and interpretations which otherwise would have been lost, and gave later students of fiddle music high standards indeed at which to aim.

The Fiddle Music of Scotland

It is a long wait, over forty years, for the next book which attempts to deal with fiddle style at all. Compiled by James Hunter, now Head of Television, BBC Scotland, *The Fiddle Music of Scotland* (1979) contains a tidy 365 tunes. It explains, as Henderson had, some of the basic bowing techniques, and gives some background information to the music.

Some of the sets in Hunter's collection have come directly from fiddlers well-known this decade: Arthur Scott Robertson of Shetland, winner of the National Fiddle Competition organized by the BBC in 1969; Angus Cameron, relative of "The Cameron Men" and winner of the Golden Fiddle Award, sponsored by the *Daily Mail*, in 1977; Douglas Lawrence, winner of the National Fiddle Championship, sponsored by Lothian Regional Council in 1977, and Bill Hardie, an adjudicator at the last mentioned, and a player regarded highly for many years.

The majority of the sets, however, are Hunter's own choices, combining existing bowing with his own. Since he is not primarily a fiddler (although neither was Henderson), this book is more useful for the good cross-section of fiddle tunes that it contains than for its stylistic accuracy.

The Caledonian Companion

Hunter wrote, with some reason, that where and when to use the various bowing techniques "can only be learnt from direct contact with a good exponent". In 1981, however, Alastair J. Hardie's *Caledonian Companion* appeared, a book which for the first time has tried to deal with the problems of technique and bowing style – and methods of solving them. Hardie (b. 1946) comes with good credentials, for he is the son of Bill Hardie (see below) and a trained musician, having studied at the Royal Scottish Academy of Music and Southampton University; he also teaches, plays, and adjudicates Scottish fiddle music.

Although the thoroughness of the bowing given to each piece naturally owes a debt to Bill Hardie and to the example of Henderson, whom Alastair knew, this tutor goes into the greatest detail thus far about explaining precisely how to play each stroke, warning the player in advance of tendencies which will need to be corrected: sloppy rhythm, hack-bowing, and the like.

The tunes are set out generally in order of increasing difficulty, ranging from "The White Cockade" to "The President". Italianate bowings, scordatura tuning, multiple stopping, position changing – all are dealt with to the player's advantage.

Included also are eighteen sets "as played by" representative fiddlers from the three accepted styles. The sets are not perfect transcriptions (as can be heard by comparing them with an accompanying cassette) but they reflect the playing much more accurately than is usual; having the cassette as a back-up to the tutor produces an opportunity to learn only surpassed by the player in the flesh.

Accurate transcriptions are still very much the property of musicologists, for example, those at the School of Scottish Studies, University of Edinburgh, and interested groups such as the English Folk Song and Dance Society, whose member Patrick Shuldham Shaw recorded and transcribed Shetland music during 1947–51. But in the context of this book, the introduction of additional drones, inadvertent or otherwise, variations from normal pitch, or rests where the bow is lifted off the string as the result of certain bow strokes, for example, would no doubt have interfered with the teaching process.

The Stylists: William J. Hardie

The man who collaborated with Alastair Hardie on the bowings for his book is his father, Bill Hardie. Bill was born in Aberdeen in 1916, and learnt his first Scottish tunes from his grandfather William Hardie Jnr, said to be the grandson of Peter Hardie, possibly a pupil of Niel

Gow's. Like most of the best-known fiddlers today, Bill has a classical background, too, having studied with Theodore Crozier and A. Milne Smith in Aberdeen.

Although he knew Henderson well, Bill was more influenced by the playing of Skinner and Dickie, in whose music he would have found inspiration for his own sensitive and intensely personal style. For Bill "the music reflects the country. Scotland has mountains and fields, seacliffs and lochs. It is a rugged country; the sun, the clouds and the seasons are always passing over it, so it is always changing. The music should be the same, with colour and character, light and shade."[11]

In common with other fiddlers who have turned increasingly to concert work, Bill played with dance bands during his early career before branching out through winning competitions. He has broadcast from the age of sixteen, recorded, taught and adjudicated, and was for a time the conductor of the Aberdeen Strathspey and Reel Society.

His most lasting contributions are probably his playing and his work as a teacher, continued through his son's book, which incorporates so many of Bill's bowing techniques and so much of his knowledge and understanding of Northeast playing, thus keeping alive and passing on the musical language of generations.

Hector MacAndrew (1903–80)
Another Northeast player is the late Hector MacAndrew, born in Fyvie, Aberdeenshire. He too came from a musical family, his father being a piper and fiddler, his grandfather supposedly a pupil of Niel Gow's. He also studied formally, often saying that he had played in the Reid Orchestra at the University of Edinburgh in his youth.

Before he concentrated on concert work, dance bands were his means of expression, sometimes at Balmoral Castle. As he grew older he taught occasionally, having amongst his pupils Florence Burns, second prize-winner at the 1969 competition, and Douglas Lawrence, mentioned above. His most famous if shortest-lived pupil was Yehudi Menuhin, in the BBC television programme *Mr Menuhin's Welcome to Blair* (1972).

Hector's own playing on his Andrea Guarnerius violin was very smooth, well-phrased and musically polished, with excellent intonation and a rich tone. Although he composed about eighty tunes, none has yet been published, and they are little known. However, Hector will long be remembered for his poised and assured performances, and his deeply musical interpretations of fiddle music.

Tom Anderson

Tom Anderson is widely known and respected for his work as a fiddler, collector, composer and teacher. Born in Eshaness, on the west coast of Mainland, Shetland, in 1910, he began playing as a child, learning from his grandfather, and by the age of sixteen was travelling around the islands beginning to collect fiddle tunes.

In 1949 he started to use a wire recorder, and since then has collected hundreds more tunes, particularly from the older fiddlers, which might otherwise have vanished. The majority are not available publicly, although they are being catalogued, and some may be published shortly; a few have been published in *Da Merrie Dancers* (1970) and *Haand me doon da fiddle* (1979).

Tom saw, early on, that fiddle music in Shetland was starting to suffer from the effects of records, radio and television, where Scottish – rather than Shetland – players and music were featured, and began to devote himself increasingly to encouraging the music and style of his own islands, much influenced by Scandinavia (Shetland was owned by Norway until pledged to Scotland as part of a dowry settlement in 1468; the Norwegians never paid the debt, and Scotland annexed the islands in 1612).

A fine fiddler, Tom was involved in the early years of the fiddle group formed by the Shetland Folk Society in 1945, later becoming its leader. In 1960 another fiddle band was formed for a "Hamefarin", to welcome back expatriate Shetlanders; today this group is known as "The Forty Fiddlers". Playing Shetland music and led after Tom's retirement in 1980 by his protégé Trevor Hunter, the group flourishes, travelling throughout Britain to perform the music Tom helped save.

Tom is a prolific composer in his own right, having written around 500 tunes. As only a handful have as yet been in print, here are two characteristic pieces published for the first time, the slow air "Maas" (ex. 115)[12] and the reel "Bluemel Soond" (ex. 116).[13]

As a teacher Tom has taught the Shetland style of playing to many aspiring fiddlers over the years, from Aly Bain, fiddler with the folk group "The Boys of the Lough" (folk groups and folk clubs, along with the work of the Traditional Music and Song Association of Scotland, with its festivals and competitions, are other areas where

Ex. 115   MAAS

Slow

Ex. 116   BLUEMEL SOOND

Scottish fiddlers are finding new outlets) to the hundreds who have passed through his classes in Shetland, where he has worked as a traditional fiddle instructor, and at Stirling University where he is principal tutor to the "Heritage of Scotland" Summer School. He received the MBE for services to Shetland music in 1977.

Angus Grant

Angus, born in 1931 in Fort Augustus, Inverness-shire, represents what is called today the Highland, or West Highland style. Coming from a family of Gaelic singers, pipers and fiddlers (many left-handed, like himself) he seems to have transferred certain elements from the pipes to the fiddle: decorations in the pipe style, in effect (the fiddle can only approximate the pipe graces); intonation, often using a flat seventh, lower than concert pitch; and some of the repertoire, pipe marches, reels and retreat airs, for instance.

His is the regional style most closely related to the Gaelic culture and, naturally enough, he has often competed in the Mod, the Gaelic equivalent of the Eisteddfod, which he has won four times; for several years he shared the honours at the festivals with another Highland player, Farquhar MacRae, who now seldom performs. Angus has recorded, broadcast, performed here and abroad, and is appreciated for his unusually spirited and pipe-influenced interpretations, as different from the styles of Shetland and the Northeast as they are from each other.

Into the Future

The players mentioned above represent the three distinctive fiddling styles which most people would argue are the most influential at the present time. Although each musician has in his background a family tradition of music which he is continuing, the real storehouse of style remains in each individual. It is in the way he plays, his sets, his repertoire, which consciously or not he has drawn from many possible sources; his family, friends, other fiddlers, records, radio, television, and printed collections.

There seems to have always been some general geographical orientation to style and composition, as if they corresponded musically to regional accents in speech. Honeyman spoke of Forfar, Aberdeen and Perthshire styles; today one hears about Northeast, Shetland and Highland. Tomorrow it may well be the Borders, Dumfries-shire and Argyll.

But the special ingredient which has made these styles of playing important enough to be commented upon has been the individuals who played the music in their own ways and, moreover, have been strong enough in character and musicality to have stood out above the rest.

As with most aspects of the human condition, everyone would like to be right most of the time, if not all the time; there will always be people who think their ways of playing are the only correct ones, and their interpretations the only traditional ones (and so they are, to them). This is an advantage, in the long term, since it encourages, even demands, that those players who believe in their versions will continue to uphold them, having in their minds a certain combination of sounds, rhythms, bow strokes and decorations which are "right" to them.

Thankfully, it is almost – if not entirely – impossible to copy another person's playing slavishly. Nor, indeed, is it usual for most fiddlers even to be able to repeat exactly what they have just played; unless the music is being played rigidly and automatically, in intellectually or spiritually sterile conditions, spontaneity is always present.

Of course, different demands are made on fiddlers depending where and what they are playing, and with whom: with a dance band, a huge Strathspey and Reel group, at an Accordion and Fiddle club, in a folk group, or as a soloist in a competition, concert or *céilidh*. In no two are the performance demands the same, no more than a player will still play the same tune in the same way twenty years from today.

Thus music is always changing, even if the differences are imperceptible to those in the midst of them. What will never change about Scottish fiddling, though, is its essentially amateur nature. No one, not even Niel Gow, has ever made his entire lifetime's living out of only playing Scottish fiddle music. All the men and women who have contributed to the creation of the fiddle as an instrument as evocative of Scotland as the pipes, have done so in the old sense of the word amateur; they gave what they could because they loved it; it was, and is, an essential and natural part of their lives.

NOTES AND POSTSCRIPTS

CHAPTER ONE: *The Beginnings*

1. Holland, Stanza 59.
2. Dauney.
3. *Ibid.* Although recorded in 1503, Bennet may be the same person as "Benat", orthography being what it was, paid for some unspecified work in 1491.
4. *Ibid.* Accounts for 1530.
5. *Ibid.* Further study of the records may show that fiddlers were still employed, although violers had become more popular.
6. Farmer. Spelling modernized M.A.A.
7. *Ibid.*
8. Scott, *Minstrelsy.* Claiming to paraphrase Ritson, the antiquary, author of *Scottish Songs*, 1794. An optimistic description of pre-Reformation music, and dancing, comes from *The Complaynt of Scotland* [1549]. Eight instruments played by shepherds for dancing, in an ideal world, include "ane fiddil", the bagpipe, and a "trump" (jew's or jaw's trump): "It was ane celestial recreation to behold their licht lopene, gambolding, stendling backward and forward, dancing basse dances, pavans, galliards, turdions braulis and brangles, buffons, with many other licht dances, the whilk are ower prolix to be rehearsit."
9. Knox, I.
10. *Ibid.* Spelling modernized M.A.A.
11. Brantôme, II.
12. Chambers, *Dom. Ann*, I. Quoting *Booke of the Universall Kirk of Scotland*, Edinburgh, 1839–40, 3 vols.
13. Quoted in Ritson, I. Some accounts of the trial call her Agnes Sampson, and mention no tune names.
14. Dauney. Quoting *Abstract Records of Justiciary*, Advocates Library, Edinburgh.
15. "Kilt thy coat, Maggie", mus. ex. 1: *Ibid.* This work contains a transcription by George Farquhar Graham of some of the music from the Skene MS, now at the National Library of Scotland (henceforth abbreviated NLS). This MS, in seven small volumes or sections, was made *c.* 1620 by Sir John Skene of Hallyards, Midlothian, for the mandora, a small, mandoline-type lute. The date of the MS has been disputed, although Scottish music historians now agree it was made

during the first half of the seventeenth century, Kenneth Elliott suggesting *c.* 1620, Francis Collinson *c.* 1615–30. The few harmony notes have been omitted from the music example.

16. Chambers, *Dom. Ann.* I.

17. "Who learned you to dance and a towdle", mus. ex. 2: Dauney. The few harmony notes omitted. In Dauney another eight bars follow this section.

18. Chambers, *Songs.*

19. "Pitt on your shirt on Monday", mus. ex. 3: Dauney. Transposed from F to D, crotchets changed to quavers; in original, sixteen bars of variations follow. A similar title, "Put on your smock a Monday", is mentioned in Thomas Heywood's play *A Woman Killed with Kindness,* performed in London in 1603, but it is impossible to know if this is the same tune.

20. 2nd, 1666; 3rd, 1682.

21. "Ouir the Dek, Davie", mus. ex. 4: Rowallan MS (lute, *c.* 1620).

Original lacks key signature ("Harp Sharp"), time signature, and has irregular bar lines. The two sections given here are not adjacent in original. Lower B♭, B. 13 is A in original, probably in error.

22. "Put up thy dagor Jennie", mus. ex. 5: Blaikie MS (?) 1692. From a MS copy headed "The following tunes are copied out of a copy of the Blackie [sic] Manuscript dated 1692 in the possession of James Davie Aberdeen, in the tablature of the Skene MS. . . ." Copy by A. J. Wighton, Dundee.

Irregular bar lines. No time or key signature given in original, no rhythms. First original full bar erroneously one space too high. It should be:

B. 6: 5th and 6th notes presumed crotchets; 6th divided into two quavers for text. B. 8: first two notes originally slurred. B. 11: slur added; last two quavers originally one crotchet. B. 12: 1st note divided into quavers, slur added. Double bar added B. 8. The few harmony notes omitted. "Put up thy dagger, Jamie" was set by Giles Farnaby in the Fitzwilliam Virginal Book, *c.* 1620.

23. Chappell, II. This law was passed in 1656–7, during Cromwell's Third Parliament.

24. Aubrey.

25. Kidson, "Playford".

26. Pepys.

27. "A Scotish Jigg", mus. ex. 6a: J. Playford, *Ap. Banq.*, 1690. Time signature added; transposed from F to C, from 6/4 into 6/8. First six bars only; twelve more follow.

28. "A Scotish Jigg", mus. ex. 6b: mus. ex. 6a; B. 2–6 transposed down to the next line or space.

29. "Binny's Jigg", mus. ex. 6c: Blaikie MS copy.

"Harp Sharp"; bar lines regularized; repeat dots added final bar; B. 7 first note changed from A to C; B. 13 first note changed from D to C.

30. "Dusty Miller", mus. ex. 6d: *Dances, Marches*, 1730. Transcribed from G to C, 3/2 to 6/8 for comparison.

31. Chambers, *Dom. Ann.*, II.

32. D. Johnson, *M and S*. Following list of towns with sang-scules from Dauney.

33. Patrick.

34. "Lessones for ye violin", MS from Newbattle Abbey, Midlothian, *c.* 1680; NLS MS. 5778.

35. D. Johnson, *M and S*.

36. Chambers, *Dom. Ann.* II.

37. "The deal stick the Minster", mus. ex. 7: H. Playford. Time signature added; double bar B. 4 moved back one quaver.

38. Chambers, *Dom. Ann.* II. Quoting *Historical notices of Scottish Affairs*, from the MSS of Sir John Lauder of Fountainhall, Edinburgh, 1848, 2 vols.

39. "Madam Mc.Keenys Scotch-Measure", mus. ex. 8: H. Playford. Repeat dots added B. 8, 9, and at the end of the first time bar.

40. "The comers of Largo Areell", mus. ex. 9: *Ibid.* Time signature added, notation changed from 9/4 to 9/8.

41. "Bride next", mus. ex. 10: *Ibid.* Time signature added; C♮s originally notated C♭.

CHAPTER TWO: *The Eighteenth Century, I*

1. Kirk. He visited Scotland in 1677.

2. Tytler. Saint Cecilia, although the patron saint of music, neither played nor sang. A martyred Roman matron, she first gained a reputation as a musician from an error in translation of the original text, amplified by the works of artists who then portrayed her with musical instruments.

3. *Ibid.* Around this time, in 1707, the earliest known violin maker, Ralph Agutter, came to work in the capital.

4. Allan Ramsay, *Works.* All following quotations about Patie are from Ramsay's poem or his footnotes to it.

5. "The auld man's mare's dead", mus. ex. 11: J. Johnson, *SMM*, vol. 5, [1796].

6. Dunbar. Letter from Miss Anne Stuart. It has been suggested that public assemblies had been attempted in 1710, but this seems to be undocumented. See both Maitland's and Arnot's respective histories of Edinburgh.

7. "A Letter from a Gentleman".

8. *Biog. Pres.*

9. Allan Ramsay, "Elegy on John Cowper" (1714).

10. "Stool of Repentance", mus. ex. 12: first section, Gow *First.* Double bar and repeat dots added at beginning. B. 8 first two notes originally semi-quaver, dotted quaver. All decorations omitted; transposed from A to E. Second section: Dixon MS.

Transposed from G to E; time signature added. 6/4 changed to 6/8. Followed by several strains of simple variations. That what is now the first section was added later is made more likely since the same tune as Dixon's appears as "The Border Reel" (first section) in Young's Duke of Perth MS dated the same year, 1734.

11. Allan Ramsay, *Works,* I.

12. Burt, I. Written between 1724–6.

13. EAMB, I.

14. "John Anderson my jo", mus. ex. 13: Agnes Hume MS. Time signature added; double bar with repeat sign inserted B. 8.

15. Carruthers.

16. "Green Slievs and pudding pys", mus. ex. 14: Margaret Sinkler MS. Time signature added; changed from 6/4 to 6/8. Repeat dots added. Original gives only one flat in key signature, so naturals have been added to Es to correspond. The date of registration comes from Chappell, I.

17. Lawrence. Lawrence also refers to another Young MS, "A Collection of Scots airs with variations for 2 violoncellos. By David Young, Writing-Master in Aberdeen, 1753". This was seen in Exeter earlier this century by a Dr J. F. K. Johnstone; nothing more is known about it.

18. Copies of the MS are at Glasgow University Library and the NLS.

19. "Tullochgorum", mus. ex. 15: Young, D of P MS. The title means "blue hill" in Gaelic.

20. "A Collection of the newest Countrey Dances Perform'd in Scotland." Bodleian Library, Oxford, MS. Don.d. 54.

21. 3 vols., NLS MSS 2084–5. Vol. I was lost *c.* 1800. (See Laing, Introduction to J. Johnson's *SMM*.) For a study of eighteenth century fiddle variations see David Johnson, *Scottish Fiddle Music in the 18th Century*, Edinburgh, 1983.

22. "Hilland [Highland] Tune", mus. ex. 16, John Young.

23. "Athol Brays", mus. ex. 17: *Dances, Marches*.

24. Edinburgh, 4 vols. 1723 on.

25. "Jenny Beguil'd the Webster", mus. ex. 18: Thomson, II. Double bar added.

26. "Jenny Dang the Weaver", mus. ex. 19: MacDonald.

27. Patrick.

28. "Corn Riggs is Bonny", mus. ex. 20: Craig. (See Glen, *Early Scottish Melodies*, Edinburgh, 1900, and D. Johnson, *SFM*, for possible datings of this work as 1725 and 1727.) The decorations given by Craig as two diagonal lines over a note have been transcribed as trills.

29. Kidson, "Oswald".

30. *A Collection of Musick by several hands*, both vocal and instrumental. Most of which never before printed, and now published for the use of Orpheus's Clubs by James Oswald, Dancing Master in Edinburgh [*c.* 1740]. Oswald advertised an earlier work, a collection of minuets, from Dunfermline in 1734, but no copy is known.

31. "The low lands of Holand", mus. ex. 21: Oswald, *Coll. of Cur.* B. 3 and 11, bt. 3, rhythm regularized.

32. Melville.

33. See Laing, Introduction to Johnson's *SMM* for evidence that the melodies ascribed to Rizzio in Oswald's *Coll. of Cur.* are actually by Oswald. However, Oswald claimed none of them as his own in *CPC*, where they later appeared.

34. Allan Ramsay, "Epistle to Oswald".

35. Kidson, "Oswald".

36. Burney's being of Scottish descent is mentioned in Charles Burney, *Music, Men and Manners in France and Italy, 1770*, ed. H. Edmund Poole, published by The Folio Society for its members, London, 1969.

37. "The Bottom of the Punch Bowl", mus. ex. 22: Oswald, *Second Coll. of Cur.*

38. "Scr. Mus", III. Letter from Franklin to Lord Kames. Franklin was Colonial envoy to Great Britain between 1757–75.

39. "a new Strathspey reel", mus. ex. 23: Oswald, *CPC*, III, [*c.* 1745]. Second section: anacrusis originally a semiquaver; final note originally a crotchet. The dating of the many various volumes and editions of the *CPC* is as yet incomplete and uncertain. Dates given here are from *British Union Catalogue of Early Music* or NLS.

40. "Strath spray's Rant", mus. ex. 24: Walsh.

41. "My Love's bonny when She Smiles on me", mus. ex. 25: Oswald, *Cur Coll*. Trills have been substituted for the decoration marked + at B. 4 bt. 4, B. 6 bt. 1, B. 7 bt. 3.

42. Liverpool, [*c.* 1760].

43. "She griped at the greatest on't", mus. ex. 26: Oswald, *CPC*. IV, [1750]. Followed by four 8-bar strains of variations. No bass line given.

44. Included in the first volume of Oswald's *Airs for the Four Seasons*, London [1755]. Licence dated 1747.

45. "The Last Dance", mus. ex. 27: *Queen Mab*.

CHAPTER THREE: *The Eighteenth Century, II*

1. Forbes.
2. Topham.
3. "This is not my ain house", mus. ex. 28: Aird.
4. Allan Ramsay, *Works*, I. First published 1716.
5. Cockburn [1713–95]. The ball took place before 1771, when she moved to Edinburgh's New Town.
6. EAMB.
7. Goldsmith.
8. EAMB.
9. Chappell, II. Song published 1734.
10. EAMB.
11. Chambers, *Traditions*.
12. Glen, I.
13. "Rothemurches Rant", mus. ex. 29: Bremner, *Reels*.
14. "The Miller's Wedding", mus. ex. 30: *Ibid*. First section: B.s 1, 2 and 4, ties added to lower notes; B. 2 bt. 1, rhythm corrected. Followed by 2 4-bar and 1 9-bar strains of variations, all repeated.
15. mus. ex. 31: The first two bars of "The Miller's Wedding", mus. ex. 30, as it sounds when played.
16. "McIntosh's Lament", mus. ex. 32: Oswald, *CPC* Vol. 10. All trills sharpened. First section: B. 2, top notes changed from C♯A to EC♯. B. 5 bt. 2, G changed to A; B. 10 bt. 3 changed from C♯A to EC♯. Second section: B. 5, dots added; B. 8 bt. 1 originally G; B. 10 bt. 3 C♯A changed to EC♯. These changed chords could not be played as written.

17. "The Hen's March", mus. ex. 33: Bremner, *Airs*, 1761. Second section: B. 6, vln. 1, semiquaver changed from G to D to continue imitation. B. 8 bt. 3, 4, vln. 2, lowered a third.

18. "The Hen's March or Farmyard", mus. ex. 34: *Fortunatus*.

19. "Bernard's Well", mus. ex. 35: Stewart, Vol. 4, 1762. This work was issued in 9 books of 8 pages each, beginning in 1761. Stewart published "Bernard's Well" later with the title "Shamboe Breeks".

20. *Guide*, I.

21. "The Braes of Tully met", mus. ex. 36: Stewart, Vol. 8, date uncertain. Final repeat dots added.

22. "Braes of Auchtertyre", mus. ex. 37: *Ibid.* Vol. 6, 1762. This tune was said by the antiquarian William Stenhouse (*Illustrations*) to have been written by James Crockat, who, about 1723, took the old tune "Lennox love to Blantyre", and turned it into a reel called "How can I keep my maidenhead". Although collectors since that time have accepted this claim (presumably because Stenhouse stated he had the music "in the handwriting of James Crockat"), "Lennox Love" and the "Braes of Auchtertyre" are not similar. Moreover, no trace of the MS, the missing link, is known, the only reference coming from Stenhouse.
    Another MS Stenhouse quoted from extensively was the Mrs Crockat [James's mother] MS, dated 1709. Using this MS, he tried to show certain tunes were definitely Scottish, not English, as Chappel, *op. cit.* believed, since they were in that MS prior to English publication. Unfortunately, the MS has since disappeared; consequently there remain doubts about both its authenticity and its existence. George Farquhar Graham (*Songs*) said it was at that time in the possession of another musical antiquarian, Charles Kirkpatrick Sharpe.

23. "Invercalld's Reel, A strathspey", mus. ex. 38: Stewart, Vol. 7. First section: B. 3, bts. 3 and 4, B. 5 bt. 3, semiquaver flags added; B. 4 rest added to correct repeat length. Second section: B. 6 bt. 4, semiquavers changed to quavers; B. 11, bts. 3 and 4, semiquaver flags added.

24. Dalyell.

25. Emmerson.

26. Somerville.

27. Gallini. First published in 1765.

28. "The Marquis of Huntlys Highland Fling. A strathspey", mus. ex. 39: Gow, *Part Second*. "By the late Mr Geo: Jenkins".

29. "Miss Coxe's Strathspey", mus. ex. 40: Gow, *Fifth*, "By Mr McIntyre".

30. Geminiani.

31. Farmer. Also in *The Musicians' Journal*, Oct. 1931.

32. EMSMB, III.

33. "Sir John Stewart of Grantully's Reel, a strathspey", mus. ex. 41: Dow, *Thirty-seven*. "Composed by Daniel Dow". This is the first collection to

use the word "strathspey" in the title, if the date of [*c.* 1776] is correct. Sharps added to trills; repeat dots removed first bar second section. This piece should have had another sharp in the key signature to make it F♯ minor; presumably Dow didn't bother with the G♯ because there were no Gs in his pentatonic melody, except in the trills, where the ear would have automatically supplied the sharps. Dow also published his own *Twenty Minuets and Sixteen Reels or Country Dances* [*c.* 1775].

34. "Sir Arch^d Grant of Monemusk's Reel", mus. ex. 42: *Ibid.*

35. Gow, *Comp. Rep.*

36. "The Black girl is not Cheerfull", "*Cha n eil fonn aira n ighean duibh*", mus. ex. 43: Dow, *Ancient.* Repeat dots removed from B. 1 second section.

37. "The Isla Reel", mus. ex. 44: McGlashan. Final bar changed from crotchet, two quavers, to dotted crotchet, to end the piece cleanly. Followed by two more 8-bar sections. The other version, "The Braes of Glenorchy", appears in his first collection [1780], the same year as the similar "The Mason Laddie" was published by Robert Ross in *A Choice Collection of Scots Reels or Country Dances*, Edinburgh.

38. EMSMB, III. In 1777 the Society, having financial difficulties, discussed various possible dismissals: "Robert M'Intosh is a good hand but the band may want [i.e. do without] him". In 1779 "they received a letter from Mr McIntosh complaining of the smallness of his salary – They are sensible of his merits, but cannot afford him more than £10. p[e]r annum". (By comparison, Schetky, the composer and cellist, was receiving £50 yearly, a decrease of £30 since 1777, when he'd been "neglecting his practise by which means he had fallen off greatly of late".)

39. "By Robert MacIntosh of Inver".

40. "Lady Charlotte Campbell's New Strathspey", mus. ex. 45: "Composed by Robert MacIntosh", sheet music, n.d.

41. "Lady Charlotte Campbell's Reel", mus. ex. 46: *Ibid.*

42. "Miss Jessie Scales Hornpipe", mus. ex. 47: Abraham MacIntosh. He later moved to Newcastle-on-Tyne.

43. Topham.

CHAPTER FOUR: *The Northeast*

1. J. Johnson's *SMM*, II, no. 114. The ballad was previously printed in *Ancient and Modern Scottish Songs*, ed. David Herd, Edinburgh, 1776, 2 vols. I. There is no mention in Herd of Macpherson as a fiddler.
   Burns wrote of the song: "'Mcpherson's Farewel' is mine, excepting the chorus, and one stanza".
   The word rant, when used in a title, is almost always associated with the name of an individual or a group of men, as in "Inverey's Rant" or "The Cameronian's Rant". Although the word comes from Old Dutch, there

may be some overlapping meanings with the Gaelic, where *rann* means verse, and *ran* a melancholy cry. "Spring", as used in Burns's chorus and elsewhere, is another word for tune, found as early as 1500 in the poems of Henryson and Dunbar.

2. "Process against Egyptians".

3. *c.* 1705. NLS.

4. "McFarsance's Tesment", mus. ex. 48: Sinkler MS. Key and time signatures added; dots added to crotchets B. 4 and final bar.

5. Patrick.

6. I have modernized his Gaelic translations.

7. Peacock.

8. Glen, I. From an advertisement.

9. "Glen Morisone's Reell", mus. ex. 49: Cumming. "By Angus Cumming at Grantown in Strathspey".

10. "Lethen's Reell", mus. ex. 51: *Ibid.* Errors as in original.

11. "Bonnie Annie", mus. ex. 50; Dow, *Thirty-seven*. First two bars.

12. "The Bishop", mus. ex. 52: Cumming. B. 3 fourth note originally a quaver. Last note first section changed to a quaver.

13. Marshall letters, 11. The information about Marshall in these papers is said to have been supplied by Marshall's son, Colonel Marshall, and Archibald Young of Banff. Some of this material, under the supervision of the last Duke of Gordon, was used by Joseph M'Gregor for his biography of Marshall published with Marshall's posthumous collection in 1845.

14. Marshall did play for his friends and associates at Gordon Castle. The Duchess's newly-arrived hairdresser-valet, Matthias D'Amour, danced a hornpipe "while the butler was playing the violin by himself" (George Gordon, *The Last Dukes of Gordon and their Consorts*, Aberdeen, n.d.).

15. Marshall letters, 11.

16. Poem, "Tullochgorum", blank in original MS. Written by Rev. James Skinner (1721–1807). Many published scources, including Glen.

17. "Marquis of Huntly's Reel, A strathspey", mus. ex. 53; Marshall, 1781, I.

18. "The Marquis of Huntly's Farewell", mus. ex. 54: *Ibid.* II.

19. "William Marshall, violinist".

20. "Chapel Keithack", mus. ex. 55: Marshall, 1822. Natural added under turn. The first two notes B. 4 could be slurred, as in the second section.

21. Information on Father Gordon: Alex Grant.

22. Marshall letters, 1. Letter of 20 April 1822. Marshall mentions sending 30 copies of his collection to the Marchioness and her family; although she had ordered all 30, she told him to send only two, so he could have had the profit on the other 28 by re-selling them.

23. Glen, I.
24. *Ibid.*
25. *Ibid.*
26. "Mr Hoy, Gordon Castle", mus. ex. 56: Marshall, 1822. Naturals added under turns. Dots removed from top Cs B. 14, B. 30. Hoy was the Duke of Gordon's librarian; Burns met him on his visit north, and corresponded with him.
27. "Miss Wharton Duff", mus. ex. 57: *Ibid.* Final note originally a quaver.
28. "Miss Burnet's Reel", mus. ex. 58: Marshall, 1781, I. Dot added to second quaver B. 1. First four bars only.
29. Marshall letters, 11.
30. *Ibid.*
31. *Ibid.*
32. "Craigellachie Bridge. A strathspey", mus. ex. 59: Marshall, 1822. Missing dots added B.s 13, 15. Rhythm regularized first bt. final B. Craigellachie in Gaelic means the hill of alarm, where beacons would be lit if danger threatened.
33. Marshall letters, 8.
34. Alex Grant.
35. *Ibid.*
36. *Aberdeen Press and General Advertiser*, April 1805.

CHAPTER FIVE: *Niel Gow*

1. Burns, *Works*, I.
2. Atholl, Bund. 1481. Typescript presumed to be by Lady Dorothea Ruggles-Brise (1866–1937), n.d. Also quoted in Elizabeth Stewart, *Dunkeld*, Perth, 1924.
3. Sainsbury. Amongst the letters is an A. L. S. Nathaniel Gow, 2/1/1824, giving his father's biography as "Extract from the Scots Magazine . . . in January 1809, wrote by the Revd Principal Baird of the College, Edinburgh". Other writers on Gow have followed M'Gregor in ascribing the magazine piece to Dr McKnight, a subscriber to Gow's first collection, although no name is signed to the article. Whether Baird or McKnight was the author, the article can be taken with greater trust since Nathaniel was willing to sign his name to the information in it.
4. Atholl, Bund. 1587. "Diary of Mary, daughter of Lord John Murray son of John 1st Duke of Atholl by his second marriage". (Probably a copy, not autograph.) Wed. Sept. 1, 1779. Mary was almost sixteen when she heard Niel.
5. Glen, II.
6. Rogers.

7. "A brief . . . account".

8. Hardie.

9. "A brief . . . account".

10. "Athole House", mus. ex. 60: Dow, *Edinburgh Magazine*. Gloss of Gow rhythms, Gow, *Part First*. Gow added intervening notes B. 4 second section, D[E]F, E[F]G.

11. Honeyman, *Violin*.

12. Garnett, II.

13. "Niel Gow's Lament for the Death of his Second Wife", mus. ex. 61: Gow, *Fifth*.

14. *Guide*, II.

15. Elizabeth Grant. Her book gives a date of 1804 for her meeting with Niel.

16. "A brief . . . account".

17. Murdoch. This is received information, Murdoch getting the story from "Alexander Robertson . . . a native of Dunkeld", who heard it from "Peter Murray, who long outlived the poet and the fiddler, and who played bass fiddle on the memorable occasion." Certainly there is a Murray, Patrick, as a subscriber to Gow's *Second*, and a "Mr P Murray, Invar", to his *Third*. Another Inver resident wrote (Atholl, Bund. 1480): "Patrick Murray . . . I can remember him well; he continued to practice on the bass to the very last". This supports Murdoch's account.

18. "Niel Gow's Lamentation for Abercarney [Abercairney]", mus. ex. 62: Gow, *First*. Time signature altered from ₵ to C because the instruction is "Slow".

19. Garnett, II.

20. Glen, II.

21. "Major Graham" ["of Inchbrakie" added later], mus. ex. 63: Gow, *First*.

22. "Miss Admiral Gordon's Reel. A Strathspey", mus. ex. 64: Marshall, 1781, I. In the 1822 as "Miss Admiral Gordon's Strathspey, or Of a' the airts the wind can blaw". I have used the earlier set since any correspondences between the two tunes would have come from it. In the later version Marshall corrected the error arising from the first quaver by making the last note in the first section a quaver.

23. "Lady Georgina Gordon's Strathspey", mus. ex. 65: Marshall, 1822. First two bars.

24. "Loch Erroch Side", mus. ex. 66: Gow *Second*. It is the largest loch in Perthshire.

25. "I'm o'er young to marry yet", mus. ex. 67: Bremner, *Reels*, Part 4, 1758.

26. "The Marquis of Huntlys Snuff Mill. or the Royal Gift", mus. ex. 68; Gow, *Fourth*. "By Niel Gow".

27. "Miss Dallas's Reel", mus. ex. 69: Marshall, 1781, II. Transposed from G to F to facilitate comparison.

28. "Miss Stewart of Grandtully's Strathspey", mus. ex. 71: Gow, *First*.

29. "Strathearn. A Strathspey", mus. ex. 71: Gow, *Fifth*.

30. "Farewell to Whisky", mus. ex. 72: *Ibid*. Whisky making had been banned due to poor harvests. It is followed in Gow by "Whisky Welcome Back Again".

31. Drummond. The words fit Niel's tune if the first bar is subdivided into two quavers.

32. "Athole Brose or Niel Gow's Favourite Strathspey", mus. ex. 73: Gow, *Third*. Probably by Abraham MacIntosh. First published as "Buckingham House". See Glen.

33. Southey.

34. M'Gregor.

35. Glen, II.

36. Atholl, Bund. 49. Letter from W. E. Hill & Sons to Lord James Murray, 19 Dec. 1921. Pencil note on the letter says "Violin said to have belonged to Niel Gow – bought from [?] Donald Perth". The fiddle now at Blair Castle is labelled "Niel Gow, 1784".

37. Glen, II.

38. *Ibid*.

39. *Ibid*.

40. Rogers.

41. Finlay Dun and the date 1815–16 for the importation of quadrilles are taken from Elizabeth Grant. However, it was Barclay Dun, his father, who in 1818 published "Translation of Eight Quadrilles", so Grant may have been in error.

42. Dryerre.

43. M'Gregor.

44. *Ibid*.

45. *Ibid*.

46. William Marshall, *Historic Scenes*. "The Tay", by David Millar.

47. Garnett, II.

48. Atholl, Bund. 1466. Notes by Lady Dorothea Ruggles-Brise.

49. "The Craig of Barn's. A Strathspey", mus. ex. 74: Gow, *Second Repos*. First Bt. B. 4 rhythm regularized. Last note first section originally a quaver. Found elsewhere as "Craig-y-barns".

50. William C. Honeyman, *Scottish Violin Makers*, Dundee, 3rd ed., n.d. The Hardie family tree is difficult to work out, since the Dowally records vanished at the beginning of the nineteenth century, presumably to help locals avoid conscription in the Napoleonic wars. There seems to be no

proof of Peter's relationship with Matthew as yet, although Peter certainly made instruments. Peter's son is said to have been William Hardie (1787–1884). (Matthew was established in Edinburgh at least as early as 1784, when the Edinburgh Musical Society paid him for some repairs.)

51. "Peter Hardie's Lament for Sir M. Dick", mus. ex. 75: Hardie MS. Time signature added. First two notes originally quavers. Second section B. 10 2nd note changed from C to B.

CHAPTER SIX: *Nathaniel Gow*

1. Scott, *Ronan's*.
2. EMSMB.
3. Sainsbury; "A brief . . . account".
4. Glen, II.
5. Guide, I.
6. "Scr. Mus.", III. 3 March 1821.
7. *Ibid*. March, 1822. I have found little information on just how the music was played at the Assemblies. However, Honeyman (*Strathspey Players*) wrote: "Strathspeys and reels were played in two parts only, all the violins joining in the melody and all the violoncellos in the bass, just as they do to this day in the Edinburgh Assembly".
8. James Hogg, quoted in Graham.
9. "The Memory of Joys that are past", mus. ex. 76: Gow, *Sixth*. "By Mr John MacDonald of Dundee". Slur added B. 3 bt. 4.
10. "The Earl of Dalhousie's Welcome from the Pyrenees", mus. ex. 77: Nath. Gow, S.M., 1814.
11. Duke of Atholl.
12. Wilson.
13. M'Gregor.
14. *Ibid*.
15. *Ibid*.
16. *Ibid*.
17. *Ibid*.
18. *Ibid*.
19. *Ibid*.
20. Dean Ramsay.
21. M'Gregor.
22. "Giga", mus. ex. 78: *CPC*, Bk. III. Gow gloss, *Second*. Trill in B. 3, bt. 1 is common to both.
23. Glen, II.

24. "The Millar of Drone. A strathspey", mus. ex. 79: Gow, *Second Repos.* "By Nath: Gow". Second section: slurs added B. 3 and B. 5 to match B. 1.

25. "Lady Elizabeth Lindsay's Strathspey", mus. ex. 80: Gow, *Beauties.* "By Nath Gow".

26. "Mr Barnard's Reel", mus. ex. 81: Gow, *Fifth.* "By Nath Gow".

27. "Coilsfield House", mus. ex. 82: *Ibid.* "By Nath. Gow".

28. "Largo's Fairy Dance. A Reel", mus. ex. 83: *Ibid.* "By Nath. Gow".

29. "Niel Gow's fiddle, A Strathspey", mus. ex. 84: Gow, *Fourth.* "By Nath. Gow".

30. *Edinburgh Advertiser*, Tues. Mar. 15, 1814.

31. Dean Ramsay.

32. Dalyell.

33. M'Gregor.

34. "Scr. Mus.", III. 25 Feb. 1828. "Ball on behoof of Gow and Family".

CHAPTER SEVEN: *The Southern Lowlands, The Borders, and Burns*

1. Burns, *Works*, II. Burns added: "Whenever I feel inclined to rest myself on my way, I take my seat under a hedge, laying my poetic wallet on the one side, and my fiddle on the other. . . ."

2. Graham. A letter from Captain Charles Gray to Graham, Jan. 1847, quoting Mrs Begg.
   Burns knew his musical limitations: (from his commonplace book, begun April, 1783) "Twas at the same time I set about composing an air in the old Scotch style. I am not musical scholar enough to prick [write] down my tune properly, so it can never see the light, and perhaps 'tis no great matter". According to Gray's interview with Mrs Begg, Burns could read and write music, but couldn't play fiddle well enough for the music to be danced to.

3. "Merry Lads of Air", mus. ex. 85: Gow, *Comp Rep.* I prefer the Gow set to Riddell's. B. 9 bt. 1, a turn could be added, to match B. 5.

4. "Rattlin Roarin Willie", mus. ex. 86: Riddel. Naturals added to Cs.

5. Burns, *Letters.*

6. Mayne. There are two men named John Bruce listed as prisoners of the '45; neither was imprisoned in Edinburgh Castle. (One was from Brechin, the other from Aberdeen.)

7. "Whistle o'er the lave o't", mus. ex. 87: Bremner, *Reels*, 1757. Followed by 2 4-bar sections.

8. "Dancing".

9. "Johnny McGill. Jig", mus. ex. 88: Gow, *Comp. Rep.* This set is less decorated than that in the *First Repos*. The tune was published earlier in

Campbell's *Reels* (1778). It is reminiscent of many others, and, according to Jeremy Barlow, is a variant of "Greensleeves".

10. Carlyle.

11. Warwick.

12. Burns, *Letters*.

13. "Mrs Boswell of Auchinleck's Reel", mus. ex. 89: French.

14. "Mr James Boswell's Jig", mus. ex. 90: *Ibid*. The modern key signature would be D, 2 sharps, with accidentals for the C naturals.

15. Burns, *Works*, I.

16. *Ibid*.

17. Galt. "Walk minuets", notes to same, originally by Galt in *Literary Life*, vol. 1.

18. Glasgow Museums and Art Galleries, reg, no, 45–47f. Labelled James Aird at his Shop, the corner of Gibson's Wynd, New Street.

19. "The Ready Penny", mus. ex. 91: Hall MS. "The Ready Penny", "by Niel Gow", was first published in *Beauties*, Edinburgh, 1819.
Naturals added to low Fs.
This title probably refers to "penny weddings", popular in Scotland for centuries. To pay the fiddler, a penny was collected from each person at the bridal dance. The fiddler would have needed a great deal of stamina, and would have been prepared to play as loudly as possible. A comment attributed to Niel Gow concerns the playing of Giornovichi, a contemporary violinist said by some to rank near Paganini: "It's vera pretty, but it wadna tell at a penny wedding". (Honeyman, *Strathspey Players*.)

20. "The Burns Club Reel", mus. ex. 92: McNaughton MS.

21. *Ballads*.

22. Burns, *Works*, I.

23. "Mr Douglas of Springwood Park's strathspey", mus. ex. 93: Givan. Despite Givan's apparent death in 1803, it is rather odd that this music was not published until seven or eight years later; it may be that the obituary ("Scr. Mus.", III) does not refer to the same man.

24. Burns, *Works*, I.

25. *Ibid*., II.

26. Burns. *Letters*. Letter to Thomson, Sept. 1794. (Thomson was also the editor of *A Select Collection of original Scottish Airs*, 6 vols., 1793–on.)

27. Hogg, I.

28. "The Sow's Tail", mus. ex. 94: Gow, *Second*. The last four bars originally had rests where I have inserted ♩ s.
The instruction under the tune reads: "N.B. The time of the rests the bow of the violin to be drawn behind the bridge in imitation of a sow". "The Sow's Tail" is said to have been played in Dalmellington in 1720 at a wedding. The participants were charged with "dancing and singing on a fast-day morning". (*Ballads*.)

29. Dick.

30. Sir Walter Scott on Burns's song output, *Quarterly Review*, no. 1, quoted in Burns, *Works*, I: "Notwithstanding the spirit of many of his lyrics, and the exquisite sweetness and simplicity of others, we cannot but deeply regret that so much of his time and talent was frittered away in compiling and composing for musical collections. . . . Even the genius of Burns could not support him in the monotonous task of writing love verses, on heaving bosoms and sparkling eyes, and twisting them into such rhythmical forms as might suit the capricious evolutions of Scotch reels and strathspeys."

CHAPTER EIGHT: *Into the Nineteenth Century*

1. Henderson, *FSM*.

2. In April 1817 a new edition of Fraser's works was advertised which would be in 4 vols., basically the same music which appeared in 1816, but "with appropriate verses [newly written, in English or Scots], symphonies and accompaniments". This work never appeared, although the 1816 work in a new edition (more than thirty settings altered, and some titles changed) was published in Inverness in 1874, reprinted in 1884. Vol. 1 of part two was prepared by Angus Fraser, "a natural son of the late Captain Fraser – He died a few years ago and the work proceeded no further". (Reply from Mr J. Noble, publisher, Inverness, to an enquiry by A. J. Wighton, Dundee, 10 Oct, 1877. Written on Fraser 1816 Coll. copy, Wighton Coll., Dundee Public Library.)

3. Fraser.

4. "The Rev^d Mr Patrick McDonald of Kilmore", mus. ex. 95: Campbell, S.M. Only known copy Wighton Coll., Dundee Public Library. Final quaver first section changed to crotchet, for repeat. First and second time bars added, rhythm regularized B. 2 and 4.

5. Atholl, Bund. 1524. 27 Feb. 1817. These letters appear to be copies of the originals, kept for reference.

6. *Ibid.* 4 Mar. 1817.

7. *Ibid.* 15 Mar. 1817.

8. *Ibid.* 12 Mar. 1817.

9. Fraser.

10. Atholl, Bund. 1524. 27 Feb. 1817.

11. *Ibid.* 4 Mar. 1817.

12. "Scr. Mus.", III. When the Disarming Act was in force (1747–1782) the bagpipes were considered as weapons, and banned. However, drovers, because of the dangerous nature of their work, were exempt, and thus could play the pipes legally and publicly. The first Highland Society piping competition was held during the Falkirk Tryst, the yearly cattle market, in 1781.

13. Elizabeth Grant. Quoting Lady Saltoun.

14. [Victoria R.]

15. MacKellar.

Modern Gaelic equivalents of Fraser's Jacobite titles,★ with translations:

A' bhean an taighe nach leig thu steach am fear a tha air fogairt	Goodwife will you not admit the wanderer
An crann tara or A' Chrois tara	The fiery cross
An cruineachadh iomlan ludhair	The general gathering 1745
An Sealladh mu dheireadh do Thearlach	The last sight of Charles
Blar Leine	Battle of the shirt
Cuir a nall am feile beag is cur a nall an armachd	Pass over the small kilt (filabeg) and hand across my armour
Do chinneadh bhi gun cheann	Your clan without their chief
Eiridh na Finneacha' Gaidhealach	The rising of the Highland clans
Gu mo maith a thig an crun dhuit a Thearlaich oig	Well may the crown sit on you, young Charles
Gun duine aig a' bhaile	Nobody at home
Ho ro gur comadh leam a h'uile ni a th'ann	I care for nothing now
MacShimidh mor a basachadh	Lord Lovat dying
Mor fhear Shim	Lord Lovat
Mo run geal og	My fair young love
Nach bochd a bhi falach fo chreag agus ghlean gach moch agus a sid as ar deidh	Woeful to have to hide in hill and glen with the coming of morning, with . . . in pursuit of us
Nach truadh mo chas	Hard is my fate
An Communn Rioghail Gaidhealach	The Highland Society of Scotland
An cuala sibh mar thachair dhuinn	Did you hear what happened to us
Och is ochan mo Charadh mar dh'eirich do Thearlach	I am distraught at (what) happened to Charles
O grain air na briogaisean	A curse on the breeks
O 'se mo run an t'oigfhear	He is my love, the young gallant
Prionnsa Tearlach	Prince Charles
Se' n righ a tha againn is fearr leinn	We have the King of our choice
Tein aighear air gach beann dhiubh	A bonfire on every mountain
Tha tairm anns a' ghleann	There is the sound of war in the glen
Tha tighn' fodham eiridh	I am moved to take up arms
Fhuair MacShimidh an oighreachd	Lord Lovat has got the estate (back)
Tighearna Chulodair	Lord President Forbes

★ From Fraser's text. Different spellings and translations appear in his index.

16. "The Bonefire", mus. ex. 96: Fraser.

17. "Lovat's Restoration", mus. ex. 97: *Ibid.*

18. "Hard is my fate", mus. ex. 98: *Ibid. Piano* at B. 13 should probably be at the end of B. 12.

19. *Ibid.*

20. *Ibid.*

21. *Ibid.*

22. "Niel Gow's Style", mus. ex. 99: *Ibid.* Repeat dots at double bar for second section probably error in original, which has the first section written out in full, then repeated.

23. "The Wedding Ring or Mrs Nicols Fancy", mus. ex. 100: *Ibid.*

24. *Ibid.*

25. *Ibid.*

26. Stenhouse.

27. *Ibid.*

28. "The Languor of Love", mus. ex. 101: Fraser.

29. "The Cross of Inverness", mus. ex. 102: *Ibid.*

30. "John Cumine Esq. of Auchrey's Strathspey", mus. ex. 103: Christie.

31. I have been unable to find a tune by Allan similar to "The Dean Brig". "Miss Gray of Carse", in S.M. (n.d.) "by David and Archibald Allan", bears no resemblance to it. Honeyman (*SRHT*) claimed "The Dean Brig" was composed by the Rev. Mr Tough, and "improved by Peter Milne".

32. John Lowe advertised himself as teacher to the Royal Family.

33. "Scr. Mus.", III.

34. "Evidence to the select committee on the State of Children employed in Manufactories", 1816.

35. MacRae.

CHAPTER NINE: *James Scott Skinner*

1. Skinner, *SV.*

2. *People's Journal*, 3 Feb. 1923.

3. *Ibid.*

4. *Ibid.*

5. *Ibid.*

6. "The Shakins o' the Pocky", mus. ex. 104: Skinner, *MH.*

7. *People's Journal*, 10 Feb. 1823.

8. *Slater's.* Dr Mark d. 1868.

9. *People's Journal*, 10 Feb. 1923.

10. *Ibid.*

11. *Ibid.*

12. Skinner, *MH.*

13. *Ibid.*

14. *Ibid.*

15. Flett.

16. Skinner, *MH.*

17. Skinner, *Guide*.

18. *People's Journal*, 10 Mar. 1923.

19. *Ibid.* Quoting "a Scottish evening newspaper".

20. Henderson papers, NLS ACC 7327 (i).

21. Skinner, *Guide*.

22. Dickie.

23. Skinner, *Guide*.

24. "The Miller o' Hirn", mus. ex. 105: Skinner, *MH*.

25. Skinner, *Guide*.

26. "The Cradle Song", mus. ex. 106: Skinner, *Logie*.

27. "The Bonny Lass o' Bon-Accord", mus. ex. 107: *Ibid.*

28. *People's Journal*, 21 April 1923.

29. Variation to "Largo's Fairy Dance", mus. ex. 108: Skinner, *HC*.

30. Skinner, *Guide*.

31. Variation II, "The President", mus. ex. 109: Skinner, *HC*. Flags added first time bar.

32. "The Mathematician", mus. ex. 110: *Ibid.*

33. "The Laird o' Drumblair", mus. ex. 111: Skinner, *HC*.

34. *People's Journal*, 14 April 1923.

35. "Mains of Gartly", mus. ex. 112: Skinner, *Logie*.

36. Skinner, *Guide*.

37. "The Glenlivet", mus. ex. 113: Skinner, *Elgin*. First and second time bar indications added.

38. Henderson papers, NLS ACC 7327.

39. *Ibid.*

40. Poem transcribed from a tape-recorded interview given by Skinner's niece, Mrs Ethel Key, to the late Arthur Argo in 1969.

41. Dickie.

42. *Ibid.*

43. *Ibid.*

44. *Ibid.*

45. *Ibid.*

46. Henderson, *FSM*. Also known as "Mrs Taff" and "Kinloch's Grand Hornpipe". This hornpipe is usually attributed to an as yet unknown composer "Parazotti", but it could possibly be a set of a piece which was danced to by one Mme Parisot, who retired from the London stage to marry in 1809.

47. *Ibid.*

48. *People's Journal*, 21 April 1923. Paragraph order altered.

CHAPTER TEN: *Changes*

1. Henderson papers, NLS ACC 7327.

2. "Edinburgh Strathspey and Reel Society Minute Book", property of the Society.

3. Tape-recorded interview with Tom Anderson, Lerwick, Shetland, July, 1977.

4. David Silver, sleeve note, "Reelin' n' Ramblin'", Glendaruel Scottish Dance Band, Lismore Recordings (1976), L1LP5046.

5. *The Scottish Country Dance Book*, Bk. 5, London, 1928.

6. Tony Engle and Tony Russell, sleeve note, "The Cameron Men", Topic Records, n.d. 12T321.

7. Alan Bruford, sleeve note, "Angus Grant – Highland Fiddle", Topic Records, 1978, 12T347.

8. James Duncan, sleeve note, cassette, "The Dickie Style", Ross Records, 1980, CWGR 004.

9. Tom Anderson interview above.

10. "James F. Dickie's Delight", mus. ex. 114: Henderson, *FSM*. Although Henderson did not indicate clearly which of the multiple stopped notes were to be played on the fiddle (this is set simultaneously for piano), the fingering given suggests most of the notes were to be attempted. Dots added to quavers section 2, B. 5 and 6, bt. 2 and 4.

11. Tape-recorded interview with Bill Hardie, Aberdeen, July, 1977.

12. "Maas", mus. ex. 115
    and

13. "Bluemel Soond", mus. ex. 116: Tom Anderson, MS in possession of the author. His notes read: "'Maas' is my description of the flight of the Fulmar petrel, called the Maaly in Shetland. Maas is a loose sort of name for all gull types of bird. The last bar is where the bird lands on its rock near the nest. 'Wheels down, Wings folded', says to me 'You can't do that'.
    "'Bluemel Soond' is the sea channel between the Islands of Unst and Yell in Shetland. It is never still, even on the finest day, as the tide can attain a speed of nine knots. This was composed at 5 a.m. on a beautiful morning looking across the soond from a cottage at the side of the sea where I was staying at the time."

PRINCIPAL REFERENCES CITED

PRINTED BOOKS AND OTHER WORKS

Atholl, John, Seventh Duke of, *Chronicles of the Atholl and Tullibardine Families*, Edinburgh, 1908, 5 vols.

Aubrey, John, *Brief Lives*, ed. Richard Barber, printed by the Folio Society for its members, London, 1975.

Biographia Presbyteriana, Lives of Alexander Peden, etc., Edinburgh, 1827, 2 vols.

"A brief biographical Account of Neil Gow", *Scots Magazine*, Jan. 1809.

Burns, Robert, *Letters*, ed. J. de Lancey Ferguson, Oxford, 1931, 2 vols.

— *The Works of Robert Burns*, Edinburgh, 1863, 2 vols.

Burt, Edward, *Letters from a gentleman in the north of Scotland*, London, 1754, 2 vols. Written between 1724–6.

Carlyle, Alexander, *The Autobiography of Dr Alexander Carlyle*, ed. John Hill Burton, Edinburgh, 1910.

Carruthers, A. T., "Some Old Scottish Dances", *Proceedings of the Society of Antiquaries of Scotland*, Vol. LIX, 9 Mar. 1925.

Chambers, Robert, *Domestic Annals of Scotland*, 2nd ed., Edinburgh, 1859, 3 vols.

— *The songs of Scotland prior to Burns*, Edinburgh, 1862.

— *Traditions of Edinburgh*, Edinburgh, 1868.

Chappell, William, *Popular Music of the Olden Time*, London, 1859, 2 vols.

Cockburn, Alison, *Letters and memoir of her own life by Mrs Alison Rutherford or Cockburn*, ed. T. Craig-Brown, Edinburgh, 1899.

Cromek, Robert H., *Reliques of Robert Burns*, London, 1808.

Dalyell, Sir J. Graham, *Musical Memoirs of Scotland*, Edinburgh, 1849.

"Dancing and Dancing Tunes", by "W.J.", *Scottish Notes and Queries*, 1 Sept. 1855.

Dauney, William, *Ancient Scotish Melodies from a manuscript of the Reign of King James VI*, Edinburgh, 1838. App. III: "Extracts from Documents preserved in the General Register House at Edinburgh."

Dick, James C., *The Songs of Robert Burns*, London, 1903.

Drummond, P. R., *Perthshire in Bygone Days*, London, 1879.

Dryerre, Henry, *Blairgowrie and Strathmore Worthies*, Paisley, 1903.

Dunbar, Capt. E. Dunbar, *Social Life in Former Days, chiefly in the Province of Moray*, Edinburgh, 1865.

Emmerson, George S., *A Social History of Scottish Dance*, Montreal, 1972.

Farmer, Henry G., *A History of Music in Scotland*, London, 1947.

Flett, J. F. and T. M., and Rhodes, F., *Traditional Dancing in Scotland*, London, 1964.

Forbes, Robert, *The Lyon in Mourning*, Edinburgh, 1895, 3 vols.

Fraser, Capt. Simon, *Airs and Melodies peculiar to the Highlands and Isles of Scotland*, Edinburgh and London, 1816. Introduction and notes.

Gallini, Sir John, *Treatise on the art of Dancing*, London, 1772.

Galt, John, *Annals of the Parish*, London, n.d.

Garnett, Dr Thomas, *Observations on a Tour through the Highlands of Scotland*, London, 2nd ed. 1811, 2 vols.

Geminiani, Francesco, *The Art of Playing the Violin*, London, 1751.

Glen, John, *Glen Collection of Scottish Dance Music*, Edinburgh, 2 vols., 1891, –5. Biographical notes.

Goldsmith, Oliver, *The Collected Letters of Oliver Goldsmith*, ed. Katherine Balderston, Cambridge, 1928.

Graham, George Farquhar, *The Songs of Scotland*, Edinburgh, 1849, 3 vols. Notes.

Grant, Dr Alexander, "Strathspey – Banff Composers", *Transactions of the Banffshire Field Club*, 14 Dec. 1921.

Grant, Elizabeth, *Memoirs of a Highland Lady*, London, 1911.

— *Guide through Scotland*, Edinburgh, 1818, 2 vols.

Hardie, Alastair J., *The Caledonian Companion*, London, 1981.

Hogg, James, *Jacobite Reliques*, Edinburgh, 1819–21, 2 vols.

Holland, Richard, *The Buke of the Howlate*, ed. David Laing, Edinburgh, 1823.

Honeyman, William C., *Strathspey Players, Past and Present*, London, 1922.

— *The Strathspey, Reel, and Hornpipe Tutor*, 1898.

— *The Violin: How to Master it*, Edinburgh, n.d.

Hunter, James, *The Fiddle Music of Scotland*, Edinburgh, 1979. Introduction.

Johnson, David, *Music and Society in Lowland Scotland in the Eighteenth Century*, London, 1972.

Johnson, David, *Scottish Fiddle Music in the Eighteenth Century*, Edinburgh, 1893.

Johnson, James, *Scots Musical Museum*, Edinburgh, 6 vols. 1787–1803.

Kidson, Frank, "James Oswald, Dr Burney, and the Temple of Apollo", *The Musical Antiquary*, vol. I, Oct. 1910.

— "John Playford, and 17th Century Music Publishing", *The Musical Quarterly*, vol. 4, New York. 1918.

Kirk, Thomas, *A Modern Account of Scotland by an English Gentleman*, London, 1679.

Knox, John, *History of the Reformation*, from MSS ed. David Laing, Edinburgh, 1848, 4 vols.

Lawrence, Robert M., "Music of the Northeast", reprint from *Banff Journal*, Aug. 15, 22, 29, 1933.

"A Letter from a Gentleman in the Country to his Friend in the City; with an Answer there to, concerning the New Edinburgh Assembly", anonymous printed pamphlet, 1723. NLS Hall. 149c. 1723.

M'Gregor, Joseph, "Memoir of Niel Gow", "Memoir of Nathaniel Gow", *A Collection of Airs, Reels and Strathspeys, being the post-humous compositions of the late Niel Gow, Junior*, Edinburgh [1837].

MacKellar, Mrs Mary, *The Tourist's Handbook of Gaelic and English Phrases*, Edinburgh [1879].

MacRae, Rev. Alex, *Revivals in the Highlands in the 19th Century*, Stirling, n.d.

Marshall, William, D.D., *Historic Scenes in Perthshire*, Edinburgh, 1881.

Mayne, John, *The Siller Gun*, London, 1838. Notes.

Melville, Sir James, *Sir James Melville's Memoirs*, ed. D. Laing, Edinburgh, 1827.

Murdoch, Alexander G., *The Fiddle in Scotland*, London, 1888.

Patrick, Millar, *Four Centuries of Scottish Psalmody*, London, 1949.

Peacock, Francis, *Sketches Relative to the History and Theory but more especially the Practice of dancing as a necessary accomplishment for the youth of both sexes*, London, 1805.

Pepys, Samuel, *The Diary of Samuel Pepys*, ed. Richard, Lord Braybrooke, London, 1889, 6 vols.

"Process against the Egyptians at Banff", *Miscellany of the Spalding Club*, Aberdeen, 1846, Vol. 3

Ramsay, Allan, "Elegy on John Cowper, Kirk-treasurer's Man, anno 1714". NLS Cwn. 1117.

— "Epistle to James Oswald', *Scots Magazine*, Oct. 1741.

— *The Works of Allan Ramsay*, Edinburgh, 1852, 2 vols.

Ramsay, Edward B., Dean of Edinburgh, *Reminiscences of Scottish Life and Character*, 6th ed. Edinburgh, 1860.

Ritson, Joseph, *Scottish Songs*, London, 1794, 2 vols.

Rogers, Charles, *Life and songs of the Baroness Nairne*, London, 1869.

Scott, Sir Walter, *Minstrelsy of the Scottish Border*, London, 1931.

— *St. Ronan's Well*, Waverley Novels, Vol. XXXIV, Edinburgh, 1832.

Skinner, J. Scott, *A Guide to Bowing*, London and Glasgow, [c. 1900].

— *The Scottish Violinist*, Glasgow, [1900].

Slater's Manchester Directory, 1861.

Somerville, Martha, *Personal Recollections of Mary Somerville*, London, 1873.

Southey, Robert, *Journal of a Tour in Scotland in 1819*, London, 1929.

Stenhouse, William, *Illustrations of the Lyric Poetry and Music of Scotland*, Edinburgh, 1838.

[Topham, Edward], *Letters from Edinburgh written in the years 1774 and 1775*, London, 1776.

Tytler, William, "On the Fashionable Amusements and Entertainments in Edinburgh in the last Century", *Archeologica Scotia*, Vol. I, 1792.

[Victoria R], *Leaves from the Journal of our Life in the Highlands*, ed. Arthur Helps, London, 1868.

Warwick, John, *History of Old Cumnock*, Paisley, 1899.

"William Marshall, violinist and composer, 1748–1833", "by A. T. McR", *Scottish Notes and Queries*, Vol. II, no. 9 (Third Series), Sept. 1924.

Wilson, Thomas, *A Companion to the Ballroom*, London, 1816.

PRINTED MUSIC

Aird, James, *A Selection of Scotch, English, Irish and Foreign Airs*, James Aird, Glasgow, 6 vols, 1782–1803, II. [1782].

Bremner, Robert, *Airs and Marches*, Edinburgh, 1756–61, [1761].

— *A Collection of Scots Reels or Country Dances*, London, [c. 1765].

Campbell, Alexander, "The Rev^d Mr Patrick McDonald of Kilmore", S.M., n.d. "Sold by Stewart and Co., Edinburgh". Only known copy in Wighton Coll., Dundee Public Library.

Christie, William, *A Collection of Strathspeys, Reels, Hornpipes, Waltzes*, Edinburgh, [1820].

"A Collection of Scots Dances, Marches, and other airs", London, 1730. Lacks t.p. Wighton Coll. Dundee Public Library, G. 53676. Only known copy.

Craig, Adam, *A Collection of the Choicest Scots Tunes*, Edinburgh, [1730].

Cumming, Angus, *A Collection of Strathspeys or old Highland Reels*, Edinburgh, 1780.

Dances, Marches: See: "A Collection of Scots . . ."

Dauney, William, *Ancient Scotish Melodies from a Manuscript of the Reign of King James VI*, Edinburgh, 1838. Music examples.

Dow, Daniel, "Athole House", *Edinburgh Magazine and Review*, 1773.

— *A Collection of Ancient Scots Music*, Edinburgh, [1778]. "By Daniel Dow".

— *Thirty-Seven New Reels and Strathspeys*, Edinburgh, [c. 1776].

Fortunatus, published for James Oswald, London, [1753].

Fraser, Simon, *Airs and Melodies peculiar to the Highlands of Scotland and the Isles*, Edinburgh, 1816.

French, John, *A Collection of New Strathspey Reels*, Edinburgh, [1803].

Givan, Alexander, "Mr Douglas of Springwood Park's strathspey", S.M., pub. Gow and Shepherd, Edinburgh, [1811–12].

Gow, Nathaniel, "The Earl of Dalhousie's Welcome from the Pyrenees", S.M., printed and sold by Robert Purdie, Edinburgh, 1814.

Gow, Niel, *A Collection of Strathspey Reels*, Edinburgh, 1784. "Niel Gow at Dunkeld".

— *First*: See: *A Collection . . .*

— *A Fourth Collection of Strathspey* Reels, Edinburgh, [1800].

— *A Second Collection of Strathspey Reels*, Edinburgh, [1788].

— *A Third Collection of Strathspey Reels*, Edinburgh, [1792].

Gow, Niel, and Sons, *The Beauties of Niel Gow*, Edinburgh, 1819.

— *A Complete Repository*, Edinburgh, [W.M. 1799].

— *A Fifth Collection of Strathspey Reels*, Edinburgh, [1809].

— *Part First of the Complete Repository*, Edinburgh, 1799.

— *Part Second of the Complete Repository*, Edinburgh, [1802].

— *A Sixth Collection of Strathspey Reels*, Edinburgh, 1822.

Henderson, John Murdoch, *The Flowers of Scottish Melody*, Glasgow, 1935.

Johnson, James: See: *Printed Books*. Musical examples.

MacDonald, Keith Norman, *The Skye Collection*, Edinburgh, 1897.

McGlashan, Alexander, *A Collection of Reels*, Edinburgh, 1786. "Consisting chiefly of Strathspeys, Athole Reels".

MacIntosh, Robert, "Lady Charlotte Campbell's New Strathspey", S.M., n.d. Printed and sold by John Hamilton, 24 North Bridge St., Edinburgh.

— "Lady Charlotte Campbell's Reel", same S.M. as above.

Marshall, William, *A Collection of Strathspey Reels*, Edinburgh, 1781. Parts 1 and 2.

— *Marshall's Scottish Airs, Melodies, Strathspeys, Reels,* Edinburgh, 1822.

Oswald, James, *The Caledonian Pocket Companion*, London, [1743] on, Twelve books. There are many varied editions of this work. Dates in the text come from B.U.C.E.M. or NLS.

— *A Collection of Curious Scots Tunes*, London [c. 1742].

— *A Curious Collection of Scots Tunes*, (Bk. 1), Edinburgh, [c. 1740].

— *A Second Collection of Curious Scots Tunes*, London [1742].

Playford, Henry, *A Collection of Original Scotch-Tunes, (Full of the Highland Humours)*, London, 1700.

Playford, John, *Apollo's Banquet for the Treble Violin*, London, 6th ed., 1690.

Queen Mab, published by James Oswald, "Composed by the Society of the Temple of Apollo", London, 1752.

Riddel, or Riddell, Robert, *A Collection of Scotch, Galwegian, and Border Tunes*, Edinburgh, [1794].

Robertson, James Stewart, *The Athole Collection of the Dance Music of Scotland*, Edinburgh, 1884.

Skinner, James Scott, *Elgin Collection of Scotch Music*, Elgin, 1884.

— *The Harp and Claymore*, . . . 1904.

— *Logie Collection of Original Music*, Keith, 1888.

— *Miller o' Hirn Collection of Scotch Music*, Elgin, 1881.

Stewart, Neil, *A Collection of the Newest and Best Reels and Country Dances*, Edinburgh, 9 vols. from [1761].

Thomson, William, *Orpheus Caledonius*, London, 1733, 2 vols.

Walsh, J., *Caledonian Country Dances*, London, Bk. III, [c. 1740].

Young, John, *A Collection of Original Scotch Tunes for the violin*. The whole pleasant and comicall being full of Highland humour. [London, c. 1720.]

MANUSCRIPTS

Anderson, Tom, Music MSS, Autograph, in the possession of the author.

Atholl Muniments, Duke of Atholl, Blair Castle, Blair Atholl, Perthshire. (0234) Bundles: 49, 1466, 1481, 1524, 1587.

Blaikie MS, from a MS copy headed "The following tunes are copied out of a copy of the Blackie [*sic*] Manuscript dated 1692 in the possession of James Davie Aberdeen, in the tablature of the Skene MS . . ." Copy A. J. Wighton, Dundee Public Library, 10455 H.

Dickie Letters, Property of Mr J. F. Dickie; held by Mr James Duncan, Cuminestown, nr. Turriff, Aberdeenshire.

Dixon, William, Music MS, 1734, Atholl Collection, Sandeman Library, Perth, N. 27.

Duke of Perth MS, "A Collection of Countrey Dances written for the use of his Grace the Duke of Perth by Dav. Young, 1734". Property of the Grimsthorpe and Drummond Trust; Drummond Castle, nr. Crieff, home of the Earl of Ancaster. Copies at G.U.L. and NLS.

Edinburgh Assembly Minute Books, No. 1, Edinburgh Public Library, Y/ML/28/A.

Edinburgh Musical Society Minute Books, Edinburgh Public Library, 4 vols., 1728–98. W/Y/ML/28/MS.

Edinburgh Strathspey and Reel Society Minute Books; Property of the Society.

Hall, John, Music MS, Glasgow University Library, Bi.22-y.18.

Hardie, Peter, Music MS, Atholl Collection, Sandeman Library, Perth, N.23.

Holmain MS: See: Carruthers (Printed Books).

Hume, Agnes, MS, 1704, NLS Adv. MS.5.2.17.

McNaughton MS, c. 1825. In a private collection.

Marshall, William, Letters; NLS ACC 7035/1, 8, 11.

Rowallan MS (lute, *c.* 1620); made by William Mure of Rowallan; EUL MS. La. III, 487.

Sainsbury Letters, Letters of eminent musicians who had been asked to contribute to his *Dictionary of Musicians*, 1827. GUL R.d.89.

"Scrapbook of Musical Activities"; a collection of advertisements and articles from newspapers, magazines, etc. 3 vols, Edinburgh Public Library, W/ML/46.

Sinkler, Margaret, MS, 1710, NLS MS. 3296.

Willsher, Harry M., Music in Scotland during three centuries. Unpublished St. Andrew's D. Litt. thesis, 1945. St. Andrew's University Library.

MUSIC EXAMPLES

(Glosses above music examples are mine)

GENERAL INDEX

(Notes and Postscripts are italicized)

INDEX OF TUNES

Titles from Fraser's Jacobite list (161–2, *226*) and Marshall's renamed tunes (82–4) are not included.

Only one version of each title is given here, regardless of variations in the text.

Music examples are shown in bold type, Notes and Postscripts in italics.